ADVANCES IN TAXATION

Volume 2 • 1989

ADVANCES IN TAXATION

A Research Annual

Editor: SALLY M. JONES
Department of Accounting
University of Texas at Austin

VOLUME 2 • 1989

 JAI PRESS INC.

Greenwich, Connecticut   *London, England*

CONTENTS

LIST OF CONTRIBUTORS

Urton Anderson	Graduate School of Business University of Texas at Austin
Chee W. Chow	School of Accountancy San Diego State University
William A. Duncan	Arthur Young and Company Reston, Virginia
Charles R. Enis	College of Business Administration Pennsylvania State University
Marshall A. Geiger	College of Business Administration Unversity of Maine
Herbert G. Hunt, III	School of Business Administration University of Vermont
Betty R. Jackson	College of Business and Administration University of Colorado at Boulder
Pauline R. Jaouen	College of Business Administration University of Northern Colorado
Stewart S. Karlinsky	School of Business San Jose State University
David W. LaRue	McIntire School of Commerce University of Virginia
Garry Marchant	Graduate School of Business University of Texas at Austin
Valerie C. Milliron	College of Business Administration Pennsylvania State University

P.M.J. Reckers   School of Accountancy
                             Arizona State University

William A. Raabe   School of Business Administration
                             University of Wisconsin-Milwaukee

William R. Reichenstein   College of Business Administration
                             University of North Texas

John Robinson   Graduate School of Business
                             University of Texas at Austin

Debra L. Sanders   College of Business and Economics
                             Washington State University

Michael S. Schadewald   Graduate School of Business
                             University of Texas at Austin

W. Ron Singleton   College of Business and Economics
                             Western Washington University

Michael D. Shields   School of Accountancy
                             San Diego State University

Kevin T. Stevens   School of Accountancy
                             De Paul University

Richard B. Toolson   College of Business and Economics
                             Washington State University

Paul R. Watkins   School of Accountancy
                             University of Southern California

Gerald E. Whittenburg   School of Accountancy
                             San Diego State University

Robert W. Wyndelts   School of Accountancy
                             Arizona State University

AIT STATEMENT OF PURPOSE

Advances in Taxation (AIT) is a journal for the publication of academic tax research. We publish articles of interest to a wide range of tax academicians and, therefore, research in all possible subject areas will be considered. Such areas may include the current Federal individual income tax system, and possible alternatives to the system such as a comprehensive base, flat-rate income tax, a consumption base/cash flow tax, or a value-added tax. The Federal corporate income tax is another fruitful area for research, as are the Federal estate, gift and generation-skipping transfer taxes, the Federal employment taxes, and various Federal excise taxes. The Federal tax structure affects not only the domestic economy, but the international economy as well, and the subject of international taxation has become a research area in its own right. Finally, the area of state and local taxation offers opportunities for innovative and useful research.

Submitted research may employ methodologies ranging from empirical and behavioral to legal analysis. Articles must be readable, relevant, and reliable. To be readable, articles must be understandable and concise. To be relevant, articles must be directly related to problems inherent in systems of taxation. To be reliable, conclusions must follow logically from the evidence and arguments presented. For empirical reports, sound research design and execution are critical. For theoretical reports, reasonable assumptions and logical development are essential.

AIT welcomes all comments from readers.

Editor correspondence pertaining to manuscripts should be sent to:

Professor Sally M. Jones, *Editor*
Department of Accounting, CBA 4M.202
University of Texas at Austin
Austin, Texas 78712-1172
(512) 471-5215

EDITORIAL POLICY AND MANUSCRIPT FORM GUIDELINES

1. Manuscripts should be typewritten and double-spaced on 8½" x 11" white paper. Only one side of a page should be used. Margins should be set to facilitate editing and duplication except as noted:
    a. tables, figures and exhibits should appear on a separate page. Each should be numbered and have a title.
    b. literature citations should be presented by citing the author's name and the year of pubication in the body of the text, for example, [Schwartz, 1981]; [Reckers and Pany, 1980].
    c. textual footnotes should be used only for extensions, the inclusion of which in the text might disrupt its continuity. Footnotes should be numbered consecutively throughout the manuscript with superscript arabic numbers, and placed at the end of the text.

2. Manuscripts should include a cover page which indicates the author's name and affiliation.

3. Manuscripts should include on a separate lead page an abstract not exceeding 200 words. The author's name and affiliation should not appear on the abstract.

4. Topical headings and subheadings should be used. Main headings in the manuscript should be centered and typed in uppercase, secondary headings should be centered with initial capital letters, tertiary headings should be lefthand justified, italicized (underlined), with initial capital letters. (As a guide to usage and style, refer to William Strunk, Jr. and E.B. White, **The Elements of Style**.)

5. Manuscripts must include a list of references which contain only those works actually cited. The entries should be arranged in alphabetical order according to the surname of the first author. Samples of entries are as follows:

    Swenson, C.W., and M.L. Moore, "Use of Input-Output Analysis in Tax Research," *Advances in Taxation*, Vol. 1 (1987), pp. 49-84.

    Porcano, T.M., "The Perceived Effects of Tax Policy on Corporate Investment Intentions," *The Journal of the American Taxation Association* (Fall 1984), pp. 7-19.

6. In order to be assured of an anonymous review, authors should not identify themselves directly or indirectly. Reference to unpublished working papers and dissertations should be avoided. If necessary, authors may indicate that the reference is being withheld for the reasons cited above.

7. The author will be provided one complete volume of the **AIT** volume in which his or her manuscript appears and ten off-prints of the article.

8. Manuscripts currently under review by other publications should not be submitted. Complete reports of research presented at a national or regional conference of a professional association (e.g., AAA, AIDS, etc.) and "State of the Art" papers are acceptable.

9. Three copies of each manuscript should be submitted to the Editor at the University of Texas address. Copies of any and all research instruments should be included.

10. For additional information regarding the type of manuscripts that are desired, see **AIT Statement of Purpose.**

A COGNITIVE MODEL
OF TAX PROBLEM SOLVING

Garry Marchant, John R. Robinson, Urton Anderson,
and Michael S. Schadewald

ABSTRACT

The pragmatic theory of induction as developed by Holland et al. [1986] provides
the basis for a model of tax problem solving in which the basic cognitive processes
of legal reasoning are identified. The theory operates on the presumption that
people reason through the manipulation of selected goals and knowledge. The
model is a general model for tax reasoning in both the compliance and planning
settings. Four basic legal reasoning processes of (1) goal determination, (2) fact
and issue identification, (3) rule selection, and (4) analogy are explained in terms
of their basic cognitive mechanisms. Analogy, in particular, is hypothesized to
play a fundamental role in tax problem solving and in the development of tax
expertise. The model provides a comprehensive account of the cognitive processes
involved in tax problem solving in contrast to previous research which either
addresses only isolated psychological phenomenon or concentrates solely on
choice among outcomes.

Advances in Taxation, Volume 2, pages 1-20.
ISBN: 0-89232-783-9

Tax problem solving is a form of legal reasoning which has been extensively described in textbooks such as Sommerfeld and Streuling [1981] and Raabe, Whittenburg, and Bost [1987]. The methodology is normally presented as a procedure which begins when the tax practitioner is presented with a set of facts. Tax practitioners utilize their knowledge of the tax laws to identify the relevant tax issues and, if possible, draw conclusions about the proper resolution of these issues. Often, the practitioner's tax expertise is insufficient to identify or resolve the issues, and he or she must therefore search out and examine the tax authorities which describe and apply the tax laws.

While the textbook models provide a description of how to do tax research (what the relevant tax authorities are, how to locate them, and the like), there is little elaboration of the cognitive processes underlying the various judgments required. The purpose of this paper is to begin filling this void by presenting a descriptive model of the cognitive processes used by tax practitioners in problem solving. This model is intended to provide a reasonably complete answer to the question: How does a tax practitioner arrive at a professional judgment?

The model of tax problem solving presented is based on recent research in cognitive psychology as it is summarized in a pragmatic theory of inductive inference proposed by Holland, Holyoak, Nisbett, and Thagard [1986]. Our model consists of four basic processes: (1) goal identification and evaluation, (2) fact and issue identification, (3) rule selection and (4) analogy. Holland et al. posit that people reason through the manipulation of specific goals and selected knowledge. The key conceptual variable in their theory is the *mental model* which is a dynamic representation of the problem. The raw materials of mental models are rules which relate conditions and actions. The mechanisms for generating and manipulating these mental models, it is argued, form the basic reasoning skills used in the professional's tax judgments.

This model of tax problem solving provides a comprehensive account of the cognitive structures and processes involved in the judgments of tax professionals. As such, it provides a basis for future empirical and theoretical work which is intended to increase our understanding of these reasoning and judgment processes. This differs from most existing research regarding tax decision making. Previous studies have tended to either consider the effects of isolated psychological phenomenon [Chang, Nichols, and Schultz, 1987; Helleloid, 1988; Jackson and Jones, 1985] or, when based on a comprehensive model, have adopted the framework of "risky-choice," where problem definition is a given and the cognitive processes that underlie belief and preference determination are ignored [e.g., Anderson and McIntosh, 1988; Fellingham and Wolfson, 1985; Sanders and Wyndelts, 1989]. Although the "risky-choice" approach has much to offer in terms of simplicity and precision, it lacks sufficient detail to provide complete explanations of the intermediate cognitive reasoning processes and judgments which form the basis of

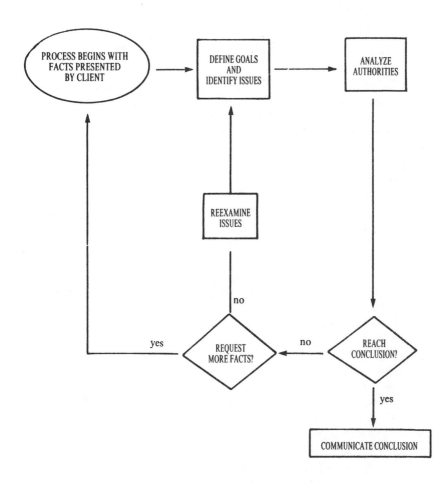

Figure 1.   A Model of Tax Research

professional expertise [Schoemaker, 1982; Waller and Jiambolvo, 1984]. Knowledge of these processes is necessary to understanding professional judgment, and that understanding is necessary for evaluation and, ultimately, prescription.

The remainder of the paper is organized into four sections. In the first section the four components of the tax problem solving model are presented. The second section develops the cognitive model and illustrates its application in both a compliance and a planning setting. The third section examines the role of analogy in the analysis of tax authorities. The paper concludes with a discussion of the model's contribution to understanding tax expertise and directions for further empirical research.

THE METHOD OF TAX RESEARCH

The legal task environment, particularly the tax domain, is rule based. Statutes are fixed by legislative enactment but their interpretation is an open question based on an understanding of the legal predicates used in the statutes. Thus, there are two types of tax authorities that may be brought to bear in legal reasoning:

1. Tax statutes,
2. Interpretations and applications of the statutes in Treasury Regulations, court decisions and IRS rulings.

The analysis of these authorities leads to the selection and interpretation of the appropriate tax treatment which is the essence of tax research. The method of tax research (tax problem solving) can further be described as an iterative procedure (see Figure 1) in which the researcher identifies the objective, evaluates the authorities, and returns to request more facts or identify new issues before reaching any conclusions.

This method consists of four basic processes common to legal reasoning in general [Buchanan and Headrick, 1970]. In the first process, a goal is developed and evaluated. The second process involves the use of other instances to identify the relevant facts and to rank the importance of issues. The third process is the selection of the appropriate tax treatment from the set of statutes and authorities that can be applied to a fact scenario. The fourth process involves analogy. When, as is often the case, a situation with identical facts cannot be found, an analogy to either the facts or the treatment is used [Buchanan and Headrick, 1970; Gardner, 1987; Levi, 1949; MacCormick, 1978]. Thus, tax research is dependent upon the use of analogy since it is the basis for comparing and evaluating authorities and thereby interpreting and applying tax statutes.

A COGNITIVE MODEL OF TAX PROBLEM SOLVING

The tax research process as described above can be represented in terms of mental processes as a model of inductive inference. Holland et al. [1986] describe a pragmatic theory of induction which provides a natural framework for describing the four processes used in tax research and which highlights the use of analogy in inference. The gist of the Holland et al. [1986] theory is that people reason through manipulation of selected goals and knowledge. A goal is simply the achievement of some desired state, which might be as elementary as attaching a name to a known object or as complex as minimizing the tax liability associated with a corporate liquidation. These selected goals combined with the active subset of stored knowledge provide the necessary information for processing mechanisms that generate both expectations about the behavior of the environment and plans for action. Feedback regarding the success or failure of these expectations modifies the knowledge used in constructing the expectations. The nebulous nature of unstructured problems, such as those faced by the tax professional, requires manipulation of the goal relevant knowledge structure to generate solutions.

Mental Models and Knowledge Representation

Knowledge manipulation and problem solving takes place within the boundaries of a mental model. A mental model is a dynamic representation of a situation or problem. These models are constructed by integrating knowledge in various ways depending on the selected goals. For example, consider the two concepts of "income exclusion" and "trade or business." Both of these basic concepts would be represented by knowledge structures containing information about their attributes. Now consider the notion of "income excludable by trade or business." This notion would not be likely to have a ready made knowledge representation; instead a mental model would be constructed integrating the two base concepts.[1] The mental model would contain the necessary information about the joint concepts to generate expectations and problem solution. In addition, the mental model provides the mechanism for simulating alternative plans for reaching the desired state through the integration of previously unrelated concepts.

A mental model's components can be flexibly used and interrelated so that the manipulation mechanisms can effectively generate plans and expectations. The raw materials of mental models are rules which relate conditions and actions. There are three basic kinds of rules: empirical, inferential, and system operating principles [Holland et al. 1986, pp. 41-46].

Empirical rules describe the current state and possible future states. These rules are of two types. The first type represents relations between states such as between current and desired (future) states; for example, "if the shareholders of a closely-held corporation wish to avoid double taxation, then they should elect S corporation status." The second type represents organizational relationships such as the relationships within categories. For example, "if interest income is received from a municipality, then it is an exclusion."

Inferential and system operating rules are content-free rules which provide the mechanisms for knowledge manipulation and rule modification. Inferential rules are specifically concerned with the modification of existing rules or the generation of new rules based on feedback concerning expectations. There are a number of different kinds of these basic reasoning rules. The "law of large numbers" is one such type of rule which provides for the creation of a new rule about a population on the basis of an observed sample.[2] For example, if one observes that the IRS audited 20 out of 50 returns in which a deduction for home office expense was taken, then one would create a rule that the IRS audits 40% of the returns claiming a deduction for a home office. System operating principles are the innate procedures through which the system is manipulated. These include procedures for retrieving relevant rules, a bidding system for competing rules (described below), and procedures for action initiation.

While rules are the basic building blocks of mental models they must be organized into larger units in order for processing to be efficient. Clusters of rules may be formed into a number of different organizational types such as categories, schemata, scripts, and default hierarchies.[3] When two rules (or bundles of rules) are frequently activated together, during the construction of a mental model, they will eventually become associated in a new rule cluster such as a category. For example, "hobby" and "for profit" are distinct categories whose features are defined by experience with the various authorities. Reg. Sec. 1.83-2(b) identifies nine factors that are indicative of a "hobby" such as expertise of the taxpayer, elements of personal pleasure, and time devoted to the activity. Categories formed from such rule clusters are composed of a set of probabilistic relationships between features and the set of consequences given the presence of various features.

Rule clusters that form a category do not absolutely define the category. Instead, rule clusters provide a set of expectations about the environment, known as default expectations, which are held to be true until contradicted by specific new information. Default expectations provide the basis for organizing default hierarchies, which are combinations of rule clusters based on their superordinate and subordinate relations. The default hierarchy allows events to be represented using these default expectations so that the system is able to make predictions in the face of incomplete information. Holland et al. [1986, p. 37] argue that when expectations fail and an exception is identified, the default hierarchy is maintained and the exception is accommodated by creating a more specific category.

To illustrate, tax practitioners may have a rule cluster regarding deferred compensation for employees. A traditional rule of thumb is that an employee can reduce lifetime taxes by deferring compensation to his or her retirement years. This rule is based in part on the expectation that the employee's taxable income and, in turn, his or her marginal tax rate will be lower during retirement. However, this default expectation may have been changed by the Tax Reform Act of 1986 which reduced marginal tax rates to their lowest level in decades. With the worsening federal budget deficit, practitioners may now expect marginal rates to drift upward in the near future. Tax practitioners accommodate such exceptions by creating a more specific category, for example, a cluster of rules that addresses deferred compensation planning immediately after the Tax Reform Act of 1986.

The activated default hierarchies provide the mental model with expectations about future states and associations to related events. Within the mental model, the manipulation of these default expectations using goal-directed inference mechanisms is the basis for generating problem solutions.

Inference Mechanisms and Tax Problem Solving

The tax researcher determines the goal by identifying the desired state for a given problem. The mental model preserves only those aspects of the environment that have a direct goal-related value. The researcher will then generate models that lead from the initial problem state to a goal satisfied state by limiting the model to those aspects of the problem that are goal relevant. The development and manipulation of the mental model during problem solving is goal-directed and the knowledge segments to be activated in model formation are goal-determined.

Given a goal, the tax researcher must identify those facts and issues that are necessary for problem resolution. Rules, or clusters of rules, compete for the opportunity to represent the problem state. Holland et al. [1986] describe four criteria which in combination, determine the outcome of rule competition: (1) match, (2) strength, (3) specificity, and (4) support. *Matching* is a goodness of fit criteria that determines whether a rule may enter a competition. A rule is matched when the conditional component of the rule matches some goal-relevant feature of the environment. Two rules which are matched by the same feature in the environment might vary greatly in their likelihood. This factor is captured by the *strength* of a rule which is a measure of how well the rule has represented the environment in the past. *Specificity* captures the degree to which a rule completely describes the environment. The more complete the rule as a description of the environment the greater the degree of specificity. The final factor in rule competition is the level of *support* the rule gets from other rules. This factor measures how compatible the rule is with other rules generated in the mental model and thus is a measure of the coherence of the model. Based on these four factors each of the competing rules enters a bid for activation with the rule entering the highest bid earning the right to post a message to the current model.

Once the rule, or rule cluster, that has the highest bid is activated, then the researcher will manipulate the mental model to generate a conclusion to the tax problem by selecting and applying the appropriate tax treatment. Expectations are formed based on the selected tax treatment and a plan for action is generated. If feedback indicates that these expectations are not met, then some process for revising the selected rule must be used. The refinement of a selected rule or generation of a new rule can be achieved by a number of different mechanisms. One mechanism for rule refinement is generalization.

Instance-based generalization modifies rules by combining instances or examples that share properties into a more global rule. For example, suppose that on several occasions a tax researcher has observed that a Subchapter S election maximizes after-tax income for the owner of a small corporation. Under these circumstances, the tax researcher might conclude that a Subchapter S election is optimal for any owner of a small corporation. Condition simplifying generalization modifies rules by deleting some part of their attributes. For instance, suppose a researcher observes that advertising expense for self-employed individuals engaged in retail merchandising is deductible and that promotional expenses are deductible for professionals. The researcher might generalize that an expense incurred to sell goods or services is deductible.

Another mechanism is specialization. When rules result in unacceptable expectations then the old rule might not be abandoned. Instead, a rule for the special case is created by augmenting the attributes of the existing rule or by adjusting the expectations generated by the existing rule to include the observed outcome. Suppose that the tax researcher observes a client incurring expenses associated with advertising the sale of his or her personal automobile. Based on the generalization in the preceding paragraph, the researcher might conclude that this is a deductible expense incurred to sell goods; upon further investigation, however, the researcher would determine that the expense is not deductible as a business expense. From this incident, the researcher would modify the existing rule to state that expenses incurred to sell goods or services are deductible unless associated with the sale of personal items.

Analogy is the most complex mechanism for rule modification. Modifying a rule through analogy involves both generalization and specialization which lead to the generation of a new analogy-based mental model. Analogy is used to generate new rules applicable to the problem by transferring knowledge from a domain that is well understood to one which is not. In tax problem solving, and legal reasoning in general, analogy plays an especially critical role. Further discussion of this role of analogy in tax problem solving is presented below.

The Model In A Compliance Setting

Two general strategies can be identified that utilize the four basic processes of legal reasoning [Buchanan and Headrick, 1970]. These strategies, compliance and planning, define the parameters of the cognitive processes inherent in tax problem solving. The first strategy, compliance, emphasizes the interpretation of both the facts and relevant law for the benefit of the client [Buchanan and Headrick, 1970, p. 49] and consists of the following basic steps:

1. Specify objective.
2. Identify facts.
3. Search for cases that include a rule that leads to the desired consequences given the identified facts.
4. Evaluate and compare the facts and legal issues in these cases. Test the facts against the given rule.
5. Accept, reject or modify rule.

This strategy is comparable to the tax research process conducted in a compliance setting where the transactions are already completed [Black, 1981, p. 301].

Consider the following example of a tax research problem which illustrates the operation of the inductive framework described in the previous section. Suppose that the researcher is presented with a client who has made support payments to a spouse before the issuance of a divorce decree. Depending upon his or her expertise, the researcher may draw upon his or her knowledge of the tax laws to identify the pertinent issue as the deductibility of the payments as alimony under I.R.C. Sec. 71. However, since some of the payments preceded the issuance of the divorce decree, the researcher may have found it necessary to consult the tax authorities to ascertain if all of the payments qualified for deduction. As the researcher analyzed the authorities, he or she may have also found it necessary to inquire about additional facts, such as whether any written agreement existed prior to the issuance of the divorce decree and whether the client was living apart from his spouse. As Figure 2 indicates, the relevant messages are encoded by the perception system (the detector) and forwarded to working memory where certain categories are activated. The facts are sufficient to establish an immediate goal of generating an opinion as to the proper tax treatment of alimony paid before a divorce decree has been issued.

The facts and the researcher's knowledge may not provide the researcher with enough information for the specific type of situation to be identified and a hypothesis generated. The categories that are currently active and represent the researcher's current mental model might include the general level category "divorce and alimony," a mid-level category relating to "separation agreements," and the active goal of "determining the deductibility of the payments." No specific level category has been activated. This model represents a subset of the tax professional's domain specific knowledge. Domain specific knowledge of the tax professional would include basic concepts, procedural skills and contextual attributes [Anderson, Marchant, and Robinson, 1989], and forms a critical component of the tax professional's expertise [Chiesi, Spilich, and Voss, 1979; de Jong and Ferguson-Hessler, 1986]. The mental model comprises a set of associated categories at various levels of abstraction. These categories form the active default hierarchy which implies expectations

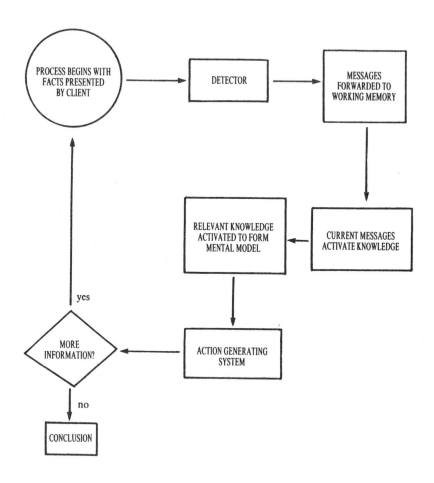

Figure 2.   Knowledge Activated To Form A Mental Model

about the client's scenario based upon the assumed subordinate/superordinate relationships between categories. These default expectations can be overridden by specific information but otherwise they provide the best guess as to the current state [Minsky, 1975]. These hierarchies represent the variability and uncertainty in the environment as well as capturing the generalities.

For the purpose of this example assume that the messages forwarded to the model are all equally compatible with respect to the four possible specific categories: "oral agreement," "written agreement," "decree retroactive," and "no agreement." The rule competition process is operationalized by assigning strength to each category. The competition between rules for activation is

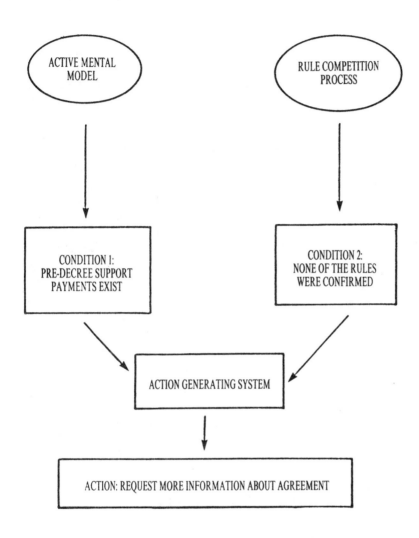

Figure 3.   Analysis of Issues

necessary to ensure that only useful rules are triggered. Success in this competition is determined by how well the rules match the current situation, how strong the rules are (which is determined by past usefulness), how specific the description is, and how much support other rules provide for inclusion.

To be activated a rule must meet a minimum confirmation threshold. In this case, the tax researcher's preferred interpretation of the facts is either that an oral agreement exists or no agreement was made regarding payments. But neither category passes the minimum threshold so a message is issued indicating no confirmation. The current state is identified by two conditions. The first condition, that there are pre-decree support payments, combines with the second condition, no confirmation message, to signal the selection of an action. This state is designed to assist confirmation of a specific category. In this case, the combination of conditions leads the action generating system (effector), as shown in Figure 3, to generate the action "Request more information about agreement from client." For the purpose of illustration assume that the situation is relatively unambiguous and that the proper tax treatment is straightforward once the type of agreement is identified.[4] The client might indicate in response to the request for more information that the agreement was oral and that no written document existed prior to the issuance of the divorce decree. This response results in a new set of messages being forwarded to the active mental model. The additional input gives a specific level category, "oral agreement," the support necessary for the category to exceed the threshold and be confirmed. Since this specific level category is goal relevant, the mental model now moves toward problem resolution.

The activation of the goal-relevant category, "oral agreement," prompts the forwarding of a message indicating the features of that category. The combination of this message with the goal of generating a hypothesis about the proper tax treatment of the alimony leads to the generation of the action/ response that "alimony is not deductible." The combination of the generated response and the goal-relevant category also leads to the production of expectations about future outcomes, such as the response will lead to higher taxes or will lower the risk of an audit by the IRS. These expectations could also be revised based upon observed future events, such as an IRS audit. This process allows the professional to learn and revise clusters of rules on the basis of outcomes.

The Model In A Planning Setting

The second basic research strategy, emphasizing planning and risk assessment, concerns the recommending of actions that satisfy the client's goals while avoiding unfavorable consequences [Buchanan and Headrick, 1970 p. 49]. The three stages of the planning strategy are:

1. Identify possible actions for client.
2. Match facts and generalizations from cases with the possible fact scenarios generated in the first stage and determine potential risk.
3. Predict how the court is likely to rule on possible fact scenarios and rank order alternatives.

This strategy varies from compliance in that the facts are controllable over some range of alternatives which meet a broad set of objectives, including business objectives as well as a favorable legal outcome. The planning strategy corresponds to the tax planning process which is described by Black as "an open fact situation where tax practitioners assess alternative tax strategies for structuring contemplated events" [1981, p. 301].

Consider the following example of an open fact tax research problem. Suppose that the researcher is approached by a client who intends to incorporate his or her existing business by contributing the assets of the business to a new corporation in exchange for stock. Depending upon his or her expertise, the researcher may suggest the issuance of debt in addition to the stock or, alternatively, the election of Subchapter S status. The researcher recognizes the potential of double taxation of the business's profits and assumes that the client wishes to avoid it. The principal advantage of debt is that the payment of interest to the client would be deductible by the corporation, whereas dividend payments are not. A Subchapter S election more or less avoids the corporate tax.

In terms of cognitive processes, the appropriate knowledge segments are activated through messages forwarded from the detector which encodes the scenario presented by the client (see Figure 2). The scenario, as encoded, leads the researcher to identify as the relevant processing goal the maximization of after-tax income within the corporate form. This generated goal then directs, within the active mental model, the search for goal-relevant knowledge and the generation of plausible alternatives. Based on the goal of maximizing after-tax income, the tax expert will activate the categories related to incorporation. The default hierarchy related to these categories will provide expectations as to taxability depending on the alternative scenarios for incorporating a business. The default hierarchy for incorporating a business contains a number of plausible alternatives including Subchapter S election and the use of debt in the capital structure. The rule competition procedure will operate to generate a goal-satisfying alternative. From this alternative, the mental model will generate expectations that will form the tax advice to the client.

Assume that a Subchapter S election is the strongest goal-relevant alternative and is activated to form the basis of the tax researcher's mental model used to generate expected consequences of incorporation.[5] The activation of the Subchapter S election category allows the researcher to conclude that this alternative minimizes taxes and thus meets the goal of maximizing after-tax income of the business. The mental model will then manipulate the active state, based on the activated knowledge of a Subchapter S election and the goal of maximizing the after-tax income of the business, to generate a set of expectations as to the taxability and the constraints imposed by using this election. This planning scenario is communicated to the client as the best alternative given the provided information.

The tax researcher's mental model could be modified if additional information were provided by the client. Suppose that the client indicated that he or she wishes to issue a second class of stock to relatives. This additional information would necessitate a revision of the researcher's mental model because one of the constraints in electing Subchapter S is that the corporation have only one class of stock [I.R.C. Sec. 1361(b)]. The researcher will search at a more detailed level to ascertain under what circumstances a Subchapter S election is consistent with the existence of two classes of stock. Relevant authorities are retrieved so that the mental model may be adjusted to fit the selected goal. The appropriate authority is selected through rule competition where strength of the rule containing the authority and match of the authority to the client's scenario determine the winner.

The selection of an appropriate authority requires the comparison and evaluation of existing authorities with the presented or prospective facts. In the situation where no authority is specifically on point the researcher must resort to analogy to reach a conclusion.

ANALOGY AND THE ANALYSIS OF AUTHORITIES

One of the essential components of tax problem solving is the comparison of the facts and issues in tax authorities with prospective or actual fact situations. This comparison is particularly important where the application of the law is ambiguous.[6] Analogy is a mechanism for integrating various segments of knowledge into a model of the current state particularly in ambiguous situations. The usefulness of an analogy depends upon recognizing the "significant similarity" [Holland et al., 1986, p. 287] between the source of the analogy and the problem requiring solution. Holland et al. indicate that often the role of analogy is to make situations that seemed unrelated seem more similar by a process of selectively abstracting the appropriate elements of the source analog.

Consider a more ambiguous version of the alimony example discussed above. In this version, suppose the client responds to the tax professional's request for more information by indicating that, although no "written agreement" exists, an agreement was made on videotape. Whether the videotape will qualify as a "written agreement" under I.R.C. Sec. 71 is uncertain. The specific category ("written agreement") has no goal relevant information and, therefore, no solution is possible. To arrive at a solution requires the use of one of the mechanisms for rule modification. In legal reasoning, particularly in statute-based areas such as taxation, comparing and evaluating decided cases through the use of analogy is the primary means for the modification of rules. The researcher will use analogy to conduct a search of both goal and agreement type categories.

In this case the researcher might attempt to analogize the treatment of a videotape agreement under the tax law to the treatment accorded a videotape contract under the statute of frauds. This would lead to the generation of the rule that a videotaped agreement may be evidence of an agreement, and thus, the alimony may be deductible. As before, this response would also lead to the generation of expectations based on this rule which could be revised upon litigation of the case. In addition, a new rule has been developed and associated with unwritten agreements in alimony.

As Einhorn and Hogarth [1982] point out, analogies provide a model of a problem, thereby directing attention to a specific set of features. Analogical reasoning is a comparison of the structure of complex systems. An analogy exists when the relationships of two systems, from different domains, are the same, even though the objects of the systems are different [Gentner, 1982]. Sternberg [1977, p. 353] argues that we "reason analogically whenever we make a decision about something new in our experience by drawing a parallel to something old." Sternberg has simply highlighted the practical relevance of analogical reasoning in our everyday experience. The use of analogical reasoning can be seen in the interpretation of metaphor, the construction of new scientific models, the making of predictions and diagnoses, and in any situation which requires a novel problem solution [Gick and Holyoak, 1983]. Tax problem solving is such a situation when the application of the statutes is unclear.

The process of mapping two analogs involves the search for a set of one-to-one correspondences at some level of abstraction. Gick and Holyoak [1980, 1983] describe analogical problem solving as a five-step process.

1. The representation of the two analogs in memory.
2. Recognition of the potential analogical relationship.
3. The initial mapping of the base analog to the target problem.
4. The extension of the mapping by constructing new knowledge about the target and thereby completing the analogy.
5. Testing of the hypothesized solution.

Gentner [1982] describes analogies as "structure mappings" where identical relations among different objects are mapped. This mapping process may, as Gick and Holyoak [1983] indicate, involve features of the analogs that are not explicit. Completing most analogies involves a search for an alternate view of the base analog, where the object relations of the target analog are matched [Schon, 1979]. The propositions of the base and target analogs must be decomposable into identities and differences [Tversky, 1977; Tversky and Gati, 1978], with the mapping reflecting the identities of the matched relations but not the differences. As an example, consider the goals of the radiation and military problems used by Gick and Holyoak [1983]. For the military problem the goal is "capture fortress with army" and for the radiation problem the goal is "destroy tumor with ray." Both of these goals are abstracted to "overcome target with force." This abstraction maps the similarities in the relations of the two analogs and reduces their differences.

As Gick and Holyoak [1983] show, a mapping may either be a success or a failure. A successful mapping has two components: mapped identities and structure-preserving differences. A structure-preserving difference is a difference associated with a mapped identity. For example, consider the mapping of the components of the two goals "capture" from the military problem and "destroy" from the radiation problem. "Capture" and "destroy" are mapped into the concept "overcome": the identity within the two goal components. The portion of the components not contained in the concept "overcome" is the structure-preserving difference. This difference does not affect the cause-effect relations within the two analogs.

A failed mapping also has two components: structure-violating differences and indeterminate correspondence. Structure-violating differences are differences between the two analogs that are inconsistent with the general transfer relations. These differences lead to failure of the analogy if any of the causal relations within the base analog are altered during transfer. For example, if a more specific level of the military and radiation problems were analyzed, the role of the army and the rays would not correspond. A direct attack on the fortress endangers the army, but a direct attack on the tumor does not endanger the rays. This lack of role parallelism is a structure-violating difference [Gick and Holyoak, 1983]. Indeterminate correspondence occurs when the propositions of the base analog cannot be conclusively mapped to the propositions of the target analog. For example, the solutions to both the military problem and the radiation problem require the assumption that the forces of the small groups of soldiers and the lower intensity rays when combined are equivalent in intensity to the army as a whole and a single high intensity ray. This assumption is not explicitly stated in either of the problems. Indeterminate correspondence occurs when this type of assumption cannot be made: The analogy is incomplete and fails.

To illustrate this structural mapping process in the tax setting, consider two such seemingly disparate tax laws as I.R.C. Sec. 267 (Losses, Expenses, and Interest With Respect to Transactions Between Related Parties) and I.R.C. Sec. 354 (Exchanges of Stock and Securities in Certain Reorganizations). A goal of Sec. 267 is to "disallow losses on sales between related parties." A goal of Sec. 354 is to "make exchanges of stock that accompany corporate reorganizations nontaxable events." Both of these goals can be abstracted to "defer recognition until a bona fide disposition occurs." Thus, although these two code sections differ in many respects, a decided court case regarding one of these code sections may be useful in resolving an issue regarding the other.

Gentner [1983] outlines the characteristics of the mapping. These characteristics can be divided into internal and external characteristics. The internal characteristics of analogy are:

1. *Clarity*, which refers to the specificity with which base propositions are defined. When a base proposition maps onto two or more target propositions, it indicates a lack of clarity.
2. *Richness*, which is the total number of base propositions that are applied to the target analog.
3. *Systematicity*, which is the degree to which each of the base propositions is related to the other base propositions.
4. *Abstractness*, which is the hierarchical level of the propositions mapped from the base analog.

The external characteristics of analogy are:

1. *Validity*, which is the degree to which base propositions mapped to the target analog are correct.
2. *Scope*, which is the number of situations to which an abstracted analogy can be applied.

These characteristics form the criteria upon which an analogy can be evaluated. As Gentner and Toupin [1986] point out, systematicity is the criterion for deciding which relations will be mapped. A relation that belongs to a mappable system of interconnected relationships is more likely to be mapped into the analogy than an isolated relation. Therefore, analogy is the process of mapping past experiences to new problem situations through the transfer of a set of interconnected relations.

IMPLICATIONS

The model of tax problem solving presented is a descriptive model of the cognitive processes used by tax professionals. Tax problem solving was broken down into its four fundamental processes which generate and modify mental models. First, goal development forms the basis for using specialized tax knowledge and directs fact and issue identification, selection of the appropriate tax treatment and analogy. Second, goal-relevant knowledge is retrieved to form the mental model comprising the appropriate facts and issues. Third, manipulation of the mental model towards the desired state provides the basis for selecting the appropriate tax treatment. Fourth, analogy is used in ambiguous or uncertain situations where an appropriate mental model cannot be easily identified.

The model provides a comprehensive account of the cognitive mechanisms underlying tax problem solving. Previous research into tax judgments has lacked a sound theoretic basis and has concentrated on isolated psychological phenomena. This model provides an explanation of how tax practitioners make professional judgments in both compliance and planning. By examining the entire problem solving process rather than concentrating only on choice where outcomes and probabilities are taken as a given, the theory enhances the understanding of tax expertise and the skills required to solve tax problems. Furthermore, the model is particularly valuable in the tax domain, where the ability to utilize inference mechanisms, such as generalization and analogy, is of critical importance because of the broad scope of the tax knowledge base.

The model provides a basis for conducting empirical research in a number of directions. First, this model posits the importance of analogy in the use of tax authorities. Research into the use of analogy and its role in the development of tax expertise will increase understanding of the selection and use of authorities in tax reasoning. Second, the model provides insight into the structure and content of the tax expert's knowledge which is an important component of expertise [Libby, 1985]. Determining the organizing principles of tax experts' knowledge, such as whether experts organize their knowledge by entity type or by transaction type, will increase our understanding of what it takes to be a tax expert and of what is required to bring tax expertise to bear on a problem. Further, the dynamic nature of tax practice provides a unique opportunity for studying how experts, with a high level of domain knowledge, update and revise their knowledge. Finally, the theory offers an opportunity to investigate the skills of tax experts in manipulating tax knowledge and generating inferences from tax authorities.

The model has at least two basic limitations. First, the model does not fully capture the role of advocacy in the tax professional's judgment process. Second, it ignores the strategic nature of the tax professional's relationship with the Internal Revenue Service. Both of these may influence the translation of professional judgments into action and thereby limit the model's ability to predict behavior. Despite these deficiencies, the model furnishes an appropriate framework in which to begin exploration into the complex nature of tax expertise.

ACKNOWLEDGMENTS

The authors gratefully acknowlege the comments and suggestions of our colleagues Steve Limberg and Anna Fowler, as well as those of the participants in the accounting colloquium at The University of Texas at Austin. Financial support was provided to Robinson and Anderson by The University Research Institute,The University of Texas at Austin.

NOTES

1.   For example, income from the rental of a vacation home may be excluded under certain circumstances [I.R.C. Sec. 280A].
2.   Holland et al. [1986, p. 43] define this rule as: "If S is a sample providing an estimate of the distribution of property P over some population, then create a rule stating that the entire population has that distribution with the strength of the rule varying with the size of S."
3.   The types of rule clusters vary by the relationships on which they are organized. Categories are rules organized around set and subset memberships [Rosch, 1975]. Schemata are rule clusters based on shared themes such as causal theories [Anderson, 1981]. Scripts are event-based schemata in which the propositions and images are linked by the temporal order of occurrence [Shank and Abelson, 1977]. Default hierarchies are abstracted expectations based on the hierarchical relationship of categories [Minsky, 1975].
4.   This is what legal theorists would call the "easy" case [Gardner, 1987; Levi, 1949; MacCormick, 1978].
5.   If, on the other hand, a goal satisfying alternative is not strong enough to be generated then the tax researcher will go back to the client and seek additional information about the client's situation.
6.   For a discussion of such situations, see Sommerfeld and Streuling [1981], pp. 135-155.

REFERENCES

Anderson, J., "Concepts, Propositions, and Schemata: What are the Cognitive Units?" in J. H. Flowers, ed., *1980 Nebraska Symposium on Motivation: Cognitive Processes* (University of Nebraska Press, 1981), pp. 121-162.

Anderson, J. and B. McIntosh, "An Analysis of the Tax and Incentive Considerations Involved in Employee Leasing," *Journal of the American Taxation Association* (Spring 1988), pp. 19-30.

Anderson, U., G. Marchant, and J. Robinson, "Instructional Strategies and the Development of Tax Expertise," *Journal of the American Taxation Association* (Spring 1988), pp. 7-23.

Black, R. L., "The Problem with Tax Problems," *The Tax Executive* (July 1981), pp. 299-313.

Buchanan, B. G. and T. G. Headrick, "Some Speculations about Artificial Intelligence and Legal Reasoning," *Stanford Law Review* (November 1970), pp. 40-62.

Chang, O., D. Nichols, and J. Schultz, "Taxpayer Attitude Toward Tax Audit Risk," *Journal of Economic Psychology* (September 1987), pp. 299-309.

Chiesi, H. L., G. J. Spilich, and J. F. Voss, "Acquisition of Domain-Related Information in Relation to High and Low Domain Knowledge," *Journal of Verbal Learning and Verbal Behavior* (June 1979), pp. 257-73.

De Jong, T. and M. G. M. Ferguson-Hessler, "Cognitive Structures of Good and Poor Novice Problem Solvers in Physics," *Journal of Educational Psychology* (August 1986), pp. 279-88.

Einhorn, H. J. and R. M. Hogarth, "Prediction, Diagnosis and Causal Thinking in Forecasting," *Journal of Forecasting* (January-March 1982), pp. 23-36.

Fellingham, J. and M. Wolfson, "Taxes and Risk Sharing," *The Accounting Review* (January 1985), pp. 10-17.

Gardner, A. L., *An Artificial Intelligence Approach to Legal Reasoning*, (MIT Press, 1987).

Gentner, D., "Are Scientific Analogies Metaphors?" in D. S. Miall, ed., *Metaphor: Problems and Perspectives* (Humanities Press, 1982), pp. 106-132.

_____, "Structure-Mapping: A Theoretical Framework for Analogy," Cognitive Science (April-June 1983), pp. 155-170.

Gentner, D. and C. Toupin, "Systematicity and Surface Similarity in the Development of Analogy," Cognitive Science (July-September 1986), pp. 277-300.

Gick, M. L. and K. J. Holyoak, "Analogical Problem Solving," Cognitive Psychology (July 1980), pp. 306-355.

_____, "Schema Induction and Analogical Transfer," Cognitive Psychology (January 1983), pp. 1-38.

Helleloid, R. "Hindsight Judgments About Taxpayers' Expectations," Journal of the American Taxation Association (Spring 1988), pp. 31-46.

Holland, J. H., K. J. Holyoak, R. E. Nisbett and P. R. Thagard, Induction: Processes of Inference, Learning and Discovery (MIT Press, 1986).

Jackson, B. and S. Jones, "Salience of Tax Evasion Penalties Versus Detection Risk," Journal of the American Taxation Association (Spring 1985), pp. 7-17.

Levi, E. H., An Introduction to Legal Reasoning (University of Chicago Press, 1949).

Libby, R., "Availability and the Generation of Hypotheses in Analytical Review," Journal of Accounting Research (Autumn 1985), pp. 648-667.

MacCormick, N., Legal Reasoning and Legal Theory (Clarendon Press, 1978).

Minsky, M., "A Framework for Representing Knowledge," in P. H. Winston, ed., The Psychology of Computer Vision (McGraw Hill, 1975), pp. 211-277.

Raabe, W., A., G. E. Whittenburg and J. C. Bost, West's Federal Tax Research (West Publishing, 1987).

Rosch, E., "Cognitive Representations of Semantic Categories," The Journal of Experimental Psychology: General (September 1975), pp. 192-233.

Sanders, D. L. and R. W. Wyndelts, "An Examination of Tax Practitioners' Decisions Under Uncertainty," in S. Jones, ed., Advances in Taxation (JAI, Press, 1989), pp. 41-71.

Schank, R. C. and R. P. Abelson, Scripts, Plans, Goals and Understanding: An Inquiry into Human Knowledge Structure (Erlbaum, 1977).

Schoemaker, P. "The Expected Utility Model: Its Variants, Purposes, Evidence and Limitations," Journal of Economic Literature (June 1982), pp. 529-563.

Schon, D. A. "Generative Metaphor: A Perspective on Problem-Setting in Social Policy," in A.Ortony. ed., Metaphor and Thought (Cambridge University Press, 1979), pp. 254-283.

Sommerfeld, R. M. and G. F. Streuling, Tax Research Techniques, 2nd ed. (AICPA, 1981).

Sternberg, R.J., "Component Processes in Analogical Reasoning," Psychological Review (July 1977), pp. 353-378.

Tversky, A. "Features of Similarity," Psychological Reveiw (July 1977), pp. 327-352.

Tversky, A. and I. Gati, "Studies of Similarity," in E. Rosch and B. B. Lloyd, eds., Cognition and Categorization (Erlbaum, 1978), pp. 79-98.

Waller, W. and J. Jiambolvo, "The Use of Normative Models in Human Information Processing Research in Accounting," Journal of Accounting Literature (1984), pp. 201-226.

CAPITAL GAIN TAXATION:
A CRITICAL ANALYSIS OF HISTORICAL
AND CURRENT ISSUES

Marshall A. Geiger and Herbert G. Hunt, III

ABSTRACT

This paper examines the issues surrounding the taxation of capital gains from both an historical perspective and in light of recent attempts at tax reform in the United States. The capital gain controversy continues to be debated in the wake of the elimination of preferential treatment for long-term capital gains by the Tax Reform Act of 1986. We first examine the rationale for capital gains taxation from an historical perspective, including legislative intent surrounding the capital gains tax provisions. Next, the advisability of continuing preferential capital gains rates is critically examined in light of historical, theoretical, economic, and tax reform issues. The analysis leads us to conclude that while preferential capital gain taxation was warranted in the past, the same is not true today. Furthermore, at least three of the basic goals of tax reform, increased equity, economic neutrality, and perceived fairness, will be furthered by the elimination of the tax-favored treatment of capital gains.

Advances in Taxation, Volume 2, pages 21-39.
Copyright © 1989 by JAI Press Inc.
All rights of reproduction in any form reserved.
ISBN: 0-89232-783-9

INTRODUCTION

Since the Revenue Act of 1913 began levying a tax on "all income from whatever source derived" [IRC, Sec. 61 (a)], capital gains have been included in the taxable income base along with other types of income not specifically excluded. Since the effective date of the Revenue Act of 1921, however, capital gains have received preferential tax treatment of some form or another. While the exact nature of this preferential treatment has varied over the years, the net effect has always been to tax capital gain income at a rate lower than for other types of income. This favored treatment has not been without controversy in the past and again is currently at the forefront of political and economic debate. The current debate is the result of the recently enacted Tax Reform Act of 1986 (P.L. 99-514) that totally eliminates the preferential treatment of capital gains and returns them to their pre-1922 tax status.

The purpose of this paper is to review the legislative intent of the original capital gains provisions and subsequent changes in them, and to examine the current economic, financial, and tax reform environment with respect to this original intent. Two factors motivate this examination. First, the significant role that tax considerations play in capital formation and economic growth requires ongoing analyses of the tax laws. Second, those opposing the full taxation of capital gains argue strongly that such treatment is unfair and will harm the economy. The merits of these arguments should be examined in light of original Congressional intent with respect to capital gains and in light of new factors that may have legitimately entered into the debate. Allowing special tax treatment for capital gains should result from compelling economic and equity considerations rather than political gamesmanship and special interest pressure.

The next section of this paper briefly examines the economic and tax environment that gave rise to the original capital gain legislation, and reviews the legislative history and Congressional intent of subsequent revisions of the capital gains statutes. The third section examines current issues in the capital gains controversy and the last section presents a summary and conclusion.

HISTORICAL ANALYSIS
OF THE CAPITAL GAINS PROVISIONS

A detailed analysis of the existing social, political and economic atmospheres affecting the enactment and each change of the capital gain provisions is in the nature of a major work and is clearly beyond the scope of this paper. However, these factors are important and to ignore them entirely would restrict understanding of the intent of the capital gain legislation. This section provides a review of the political and economic conditions that prevailed when capital gains were first afforded preferential tax treatment, identifies the major subsequent revisions of the capital gain legislation, and examines the Congressional intent surrounding the revisions.

Conditions Leading to the Revenue Act of 1921

The Revenue Act of 1913 treated income from all sources as equally taxable and applied the normal and surtax rates to all income not otherwise specifically excluded. This tax position prevailed until the enactment of the Revenue Act of 1921, which was the first tax legislation to make a distinction between gains from capital asset transactions and all other forms of income. In retrospect, this law was a radical departure from the original income tax policy. We now examine the conditions that promoted such a shift in tax policy in 1921.

The most notable aspect of this period was that it immediately followed the end of World War I. The United States was a prosperous nation during and directly following the end of the war. The agricultural industry was extremely strong, and the banking and savings and loan industries showed considerable growth during the period [Trani and Wilson, 1977, p. 7]. However, these indicators of economic prosperity were relatively short-lived.

The national economy took a severe downturn in the early 1920s as the economics of the war caught up with the nation [Hicks, 1960; Trani and Wilson, 1977]. Part of the economic deterioration was precipitated by high unemployment which had soared from 1.4 % in 1917-1918 to 5.2% in February 1919 [Trani and Wilson, 1977] and nearly 11.7% by early 1921 [Hicks, 1960]. The major contributor to the tremendous economic slump, however, was the national changeover from wartime to peacetime production. For example, by the early 1920s, the European farmer was again producing crops, thus lowering the demand for U.S. agricultural products abroad. In 1920, the U.S. government eliminated price supports for agricultural products and prices decreased two-thirds by May 1921 [Trani and Wilson, 1977]. Perrett [1982, p. 32] notes that, following the War:

> The administration clung resolutely to a utopian belief that everything would take care of itself. Business and labor, they believed, would resist any effort to direct reconversion. This assumption set the stage for a trial of strength.

The "trial of strength" occurred because the industrial readjustment from wartime goods production to peacetime goods production did not occur rapidly or smoothly. As a consequence, capital dried up, and from 1920 to 1921, many bankruptcies occurred in both business and agriculture [Hicks, 1960; Trani and Wilson, 1977].

Another major factor contributing to the economic decline was the government's curtailment of wartime spending [Perrett, 1982, pp. 31-32].

President Wilson believed that half of the spending for the war could be financed by borrowing through Victory bond issues and deficit spending [Paul, 1954, p. 114]. However, the actual war costs exceeded original expectations, and the government policy of deficit spending during and following the war played a substantial role in the U.S. economy. For instance, total government expenditures were $21.8 billion and $35.2 billion in 1918 and 1919, respectively, compared to $62.5 billion for all manufactured goods in 1919 [U.S. Department of Commerce, 1923]. When government expenditures were curtailed in 1920, total federal expenditures fell 33% to $23.6 billion for fiscal 1920, and continued to decline another 40% in 1921 to only $14.1 billion—a level only 40% of that two years earlier [U.S. Department of Commerce, 1923]. This drastic reduction in government spending accelerated the decline in the U.S. economy.

High levels of government spending, during and immediately following the war, were instrumental in creating inflationary pressures in the U.S. economy [Perrett, 1982, p. 31]. From 1914 to 1919, the money supply increased by 75% due mainly to government borrowings. However, over the same period of time, outputs of goods and services only rose by 2%, causing prices to virtually double [Perrett, 1982, p. 31]. In addition to government borrowings, inflation was also fueled by individuals' use of savings accumulated during the war, including the service and bonus pay of returning soldiers [Perrett, 1982]. Unfortunately, these sources of money began to run out in 1920 at the same time the federal government began to significantly reduce the spending [Perrett, 1982]. Further, due to the lack of labor organization and a plentiful supply of willing workers, wages during the postwar period remained stagnant [Perrett, 1982]. By the end of 1920, U.S. citizens were faced with high price levels, stagnant wages, and low levels of savings.

Perhaps the most salient factor during this period was the tax structure that existed in 1921. In attempting to fund the war effort, Congress had passed legislation that restructured individual tax rates, and resulted in a maximum combined (normal plus surtax) rate of 77% for 1918 and 73% for 1919 and 1920. Many felt that these high tax rates overburdened individual taxpayers [Wells, 1949, pp. 14-15]. It appears that the high rates, combined with the deteriorated economy, were instrumental in prompting the changes instituted by the Revenue Act of 1921.

This was the economic environment into which Warren G. Harding was elected as president in 1921. Harding's administration will be remembered as being favorable to business interests [Murray, 1969, pp. 170-172]. Hicks [1960, p. 50] indicates that

> ... as nearly as a leaderless administration could said to have had a policy, the policy of the Harding Administration was to do with alacrity whatever business wanted to have done ... (and) business called for a return to free enterprise.

Accordingly, this laissez-faire political atmosphere included the appointment of Andrew Mellon as Secretary of the Treasury. Mellon believed that the Treasury "was a business and should be so run, staffed by men intimately acquainted with business practice" [Trani and Wilson, 1977, p. 46]. Hicks [1960, pp. 53-54] espouses Mellon's documented philosophy of taxation:

> ... he (Mellon) contended earnestly against burdensome taxes on 'wealth in the making.' The result of such a system he argued, was to drive money that should be put to better use into 'safe but unproductive forms of investments.' If the wealth producers were left alone, he reasoned, they would create more jobs for more people, and add to the country's prosperity. But if the government continued to take away so large a share of their profits, they would refuse to take chances necessary to the proper expansion of business, and so everyone would suffer.

Thus, the political climate of 1921 was in tune with the needs of the nation's businesses and the administration appeared ready to institute tax relief that would come to their aid. However, as argued in the Hearings before the House Ways and Means Committee, Congress found itself in the unenviable position of realizing both that taxes were overburdening the economy, and that tax rates could not be drastically lowered without restricting the government's ability to meet $2.6 billion in outstanding debt requirements [U.S. Congress, 1920].

The economic and political state of the nation led the House Ways and Means Committee [U.S. Congress, 1921, p. 2] to the following conclusion in their Report on the Revenue Bill of 1921:

> ... the committee has sought out methods of reducing rather than shifting tax burdens ... the exacting of the present excessive sums of taxes from the country contributes in no small degree to the depressing influences under which business and industry in general are staggering as an aftermath of the World War. The cost of the war, the extent of its destruction, and the financial loss it occasions, is felt, not during the period of combat but after the cessation of hostilities, at which time the demand for war supplies terminates, with a resulting shrinkage of values. The nation is now passing through the trying time of liquidation and readjustment. The reduction of the tax burdens is essential to business recovery, and such reduction can only be based on a rigid enforcement of a policy of the strictest economy in the running expenses of the Government.

As finally enacted, the Revenue Act of 1921 eliminated the excess-profits tax, reduced the top surtax rate from 65% to 50%, and instituted the first preferential treatment of capital asset transactions. The Act divided capital gains into long-term gains (on assets held for more than two years) and short-term gains (on assets held two years or less). Short-term gains were fully includable in taxable income along with all other ordinary gains. For long-term capital gains, the taxpayer could elect to include them as ordinary income and pay the normal and surtax rates, or have them taxed at a flat rate of 12.5%.

The initial preferential treatment of long-term capital gains appears to have been a Congressional response to the fundamentals of the tax law imposing a tax on "income." The income tax law was, and is, based on the realization concept; taxes are imposed only when a transaction has been consummated and any gain or loss associated with an asset is realized. The realization concept, in its taxing of transactions, tends to "bunch" all of the associated gains or losses accrued over a period of years into one tax year. Congress viewed this "bunching" phenomenon as retarding the flow of capital and distorting the efficient allocation of capital assets. The House Ways and Means Committee [U.S. Congress, 1921, p. 3], in commenting on the capital gain provision, stated:

> The sale of farms, mineral properties, and other capital assets is now seriously retarded by the fact that gains and profits earned over a series of years are under the present law taxed as a lump sum (and the amount of surtax greatly enhanced thereby) in the year in which profit is realized. Many such sales, with their possible profit taking and consequent increase of tax revenue, have been blocked by this feature in the present law.

Thus, the initial capital gain preference was intended to help spur the capital markets to be more efficient in resource allocation by reducing the tax penalty on realizing long-term capital gains, and, accordingly, to stimulate economic growth during the postwar adjustment period. It is important to note that Congress' treatment of capital gains was not intended to create new incentives for capital formation, but rather to alleviate the economic penalties exacted by a progressive tax rate structure and high tax rates.

Major Revisions of Capital Gain Taxation

Several adjustments have been made to the capital gains provisions since the Revenue Act of 1921. The following paragraphs briefly describe these changes and examine the related Congressional intent. It is interesting to note that, as the capital gains provisions became more liberalized over the years, rationales in addition to concern with the bunching phenomenon, helped motivate lawmakers.

The Revenue Act of 1934 brought a major redrafting of capital gain legislation. The holding period for long-term capital gains treatment was reduced to one year, and the 12.5% alternative tax was replaced with a capital gains deduction. The deduction was a variable percentage of the realized capital gain with the percentage based on the holding period of the asset as follows:

Period Assests Held	% of Gain Included in Ordinary Income
1 year or less	100%
Over 1 year but not over 2 years	80%
Over 2 years but not over 5 years	60%
Over 5 years but not over 10 years	40%
Over 10 years	30%

Critics of the original capital gains legislation argued that no distinction was made for the length of time assets were held beyond two years, and that the two-year holding period encouraged taxpayers to postpone gains and accelerate losses to accomplish the best tax result [U.S. Congress, 1929]. Further, a report by the staff of the Joint Committee on Taxation found that the 12.5% alternative tax on capital gains gave substantial relief to only one-fourth of 1%, and no relief to 98.5%, of all filing taxpayers [U.S. Congress, 1929]. According to the House Ways and Means Committee, the prime motivation behind the 1934 Act was to develop a more equitable system designed, in part, to (1) alleviate the legislatively promoted "lock-in" effect feared as hampering the flow of capital assets, and (2) give tax relief to lower income taxpayers [U.S. Congress, 1934a].

According to the Congressional reports, the substitution of the percentage exclusions for the alternative tax was an attempt to make the capital gains rules more equitable across the various income tax brackets [U.S. Congress, 1934b]. Furthermore, the use of the graduated percentage exclusions was an attempt at reducing the heightened bunching effect of gain/loss realization. The percentages parallel those suggested by the 1929 Congressional report cited above and thus were apparently intended to approximate what the result would have been had the gain/loss been taxed in equal portions over the holding period of the asset. The Senate Finance Committee Report states that the new law was intended not only to provide increased incentives for gain realization and improved vertical equity, but also to stabilize the capital gains provisions as a revenue source [U.S. Congress, 1934b].

Four years later, the Revenue Act of 1938 was passed in response to criticisms of the existing capital gain provisions, and, according to Wells [1949, p. 25], to "minimize the effects of the capital gains tax upon the free flow of capital funds into productive enterprises." One criticism was that the sharp step-down in percentages of capital gains includable in income only encouraged deferring gains and accelerating losses. To adjust for this, the 1938 Act reduced to two the number of classes of long-term assets: (1) gains on assets held over 18 months, but not over 24 months, received a 33.3% percent exclusion from income, and (2) gains on assets held over 24 months received a 50% exclusion. Thus, the holding period for preferential capital gain treatment was effectively increased to 18 months.

Another criticism prompting the 1938 legislation was that the capital gains tax was too high based on existing rates [U.S. Congress, 1938]. This led to the reenactment of the alternative tax at a rate of 30%.

The Revenue Act of 1942 increased the alternative minimum tax to 50% and replaced existing holding periods for long-term treatment with one six-month holding period. Due to the demand for revenue to fund the World War II effort, all personal taxes were raised, along with the capital gains alternative tax. The effect of taxes on the free flow of capital was again a major issue surrounding the enactment of the 1942 law. For example, it was argued in Senate Finance Committee hearings that holding periods were superficial and unsound, and that they should be eliminated because they interfered with the free flow of capital and reduced tax revenue by discouraging transactions [U.S. Congress, 1942a]. The six-month holding period was introduced to both simplify capital gain taxation and to minimize tax interference on capital transactions. A single six-month holding period was deemed by Congress to be long enough to separate short-term speculators from long-term capital investors [U.S. Congress, 1942b]. The intent was not to eliminate the bunching of income effect, but to lessen the lock-in effect by shortening the required holding period for preferential tax treatment. Thus, the shortening of the holding period was intended to encourage realization of capital gains and thus increase overall tax revenue [U.S. Congress, 1942b].

The next amendment of significance was the Revenue Act of 1969. Between 1942 and 1969, a few minor adjustments to the capital gain provisions were enacted (e.g., extending the provision to include dealings in timber), but these changes had relatively little impact on the character or intent of capital gain taxation.

Prior to 1969, individuals in tax brackets higher than 50% were permitted to use the 50% alternative tax computation for long-term capital gains. Thus, with the 50% exclusion, the maximum tax rate was 25% on all long-term capital gains. The Revenue Act of 1969 provided for the phase-out and eventual elimination in 1972 of the alternative tax on long-term capital gains in excess of $50,000. In a report from the House, it was argued that the then present alternative tax rate may be considered as "going beyond the fundamental purpose of the 50% inclusion provision of not taxing income accrued over several years as though it were earned in a single tax year" [U.S. Congress, 1969, p. 144]. The alternative rate was used by only a few upper-class taxpayers and was considered inconsistent with the "ability to pay" principle inherent in the progressive tax rate structure [U.S. Congress, 1969].

The Tax Reform Act of 1976 raised the long-term holding period from six months to nine months for assets sold in 1977 and to one year for assets sold thereafter. The Joint Committee report related to this legislation indicates that Congress believed that the six-month holding period was too short and did not properly segregate speculators from long-term investors [U.S Congress, 1976]. The report also pointed out that the preferential treatment of capital gains was intended to reduce the penalty of currently taxing income that had accrued over a period of years, and therefore should not apply to income accruing over any less than one full year [U.S. Congress, 1976].

The Revenue Act of 1978 eliminated the remaining alternative tax provisions and increased the long-term capital gain deduction from 50% to 60%. The reason for the increased percentage deduction, according to the Senate Finance Committee Report, was that the existing capital gain provisions appeared to have "slowed the rate of economic growth" [U.S. Congress, 1978, p. 192]. In order to stimulate new growth, the deduction was increased in the hope of increasing the sales of appreciated assets. Congress noted that, in addition to lessening the bunching of income effect, the increase in the capital gains deduction would help to offset some of the effects of inflation by reducing the portion of gain that was taxable [U.S. Congress, 1978].

The Deficit Reduction Act of 1984 again reduced the holding period for long-term capital gain treatment from one year to six months. According to the Joint Committee, the holding period was decreased in an attempt to reduce the lock-in effect and correspondingly reduce the adverse impact of tax policy on capital market efficiency [U.S. Congress, 1984].

Summary of Capital Gain Legislation and Congressional Intent

In summary, preferential treatment for capital gain income was first legislated in the United States by the Revenue Act of 1921. During this period of time, the economic climate was suffering from several postwar effects including high unemployment, declining industrial and agricultural production, and bankruptcies. Sensing that the high individual tax rates and the progressive rate structure that existed in 1921 were having a negative impact on the flow of capital and the efficient allocation of resources, Congress included provisions in the Revenue Act of 1921 designed to alleviate the tax penalties caused by having capital gains which had accumulated over a series of years taxed in the year of realization.

Since 1921, there have been several significant revisions of the capital gain provisions. These revisions have generally liberalized the preferential treatment of capital gains to the point where, in recent years, only 40% of capital gains on assets held for at least six months was includable in taxable income. The rationales given by Congressional committees for the continued preferential treatment and the liberalization of capital gain taxation have generally included a "free flow of capital" argument in one form or another; the effect of bunching was mentioned in Congressional reports on the 1934, 1969, 1976, and 1978 tax revisions. Similarly, the lock-in phenomenon (where taxpayers wait to realize gains until the statutory long-term holding period has passed) was mentioned several times, including 1934, 1938, 1942, and 1984. Other rationales for preferential capital gain treatment have centered more on providing incentives for gain realization than on removing tax barriers. For example, the 1942 law was intended not only to lessen the lock-in effect, but specifically to increase tax revenue. The Revenue Act of 1978 was expressly designed to stimulate capital investment in addition to relieving the bunching effect. Similarly, the Deficit Reduction Act of 1984 was intended to improve capital market efficiency by lessening the lock-in effect on capital gains.

CURRENT ISSUES IN CAPITAL GAIN TAXATION

The Tax Reform Act of 1986 (P.L. 99-514) effectively eliminates all preferential treatment for capital gain income. Beginning in 1988, for the first time in 65 years, U.S. taxpayers will owe tax at their marginal rate on 100% of realized capital gains.[1] This dramatic change in the taxation of capital gains is an attempt at tax reform and tax simplification on the part of the 99th Congress and the Reagan Administration.

Two provisions of the Tax Reform Act of 1986 that have particular relevance to capital gain taxation are the sharp reduction in the top marginal tax rate from 50% to 28% (38.5% in 1987), and the reduction from 14 to 2 in the number of tax brackets. Thus, when the new law is fully phased in (after 1987), capital gains will be taxed at either 15% or 28%, depending on the taxpayer's income level.[2] In effect, the new law means an increase in the rate at which capital gains are taxed for most taxpayers since the highest effective rate under prior law was 20 percent.

Although many arguments have been used in the past to justify preferential treatment for capital gains [e.g., see Blum, 1957], opposition to the 1986 tax law has centered mainly on the alleged negative impact that full taxation of capital gains will have on risk-taking and investment [e.g., Conda, 1986; Gupta, 1986; Lindsey, 1986; Murray and Gutfeld, 1986]. The arguments advance two general themes. First is the notion that a differential tax rate between ordinary and capital gain income is necessary to encourage risk-taking. Murray and Gutfeld [1986] report that business and investor groups argue that "no matter how low the top rate on ordinary income is, the capital gains rate should be lower to provide an incentive for investing in risky enterprises." Without the potential for lower tax rates on risky investments, investors will no longer commit capital to risky investments. Similarly, Gupta

[1986, p. 8] states that "many entrepreneurs say the single most important incentive for starting a new venture is the different tax treatment of earned income and capital gains." Since entrepreneurs can take a large portion of their compensation in the form of increased firm ownership, the opportunity existed under the old law to earn tax-preferred capital gain income.[3]

The second general theme focuses on the effect on investment behavior of a significant increase in the capital gains tax. Lindsey [1986] cites several published studies, including one of his own, that indicate capital gains are more sensitive to tax rates than other types of income. The studies suggest that an increase in the tax rate tends to cause investors to delay selling assets beyond the point of economic efficiency. Lindsey states that "higher capital-gains rates will discourage entrepreneurship, impede capital formation and retard economic growth." Arguing along the same lines, Conda [1986, p. 411] concludes that "sound economics and irrefutable empirical evidence make a powerful case for reducing—and even abolishing—the tax on capital gains."

While these arguments present an intuitively appealing case for the tax-favored treatment of capital gains, the premises on which they are founded must be examined within the larger context of the current economic and financial environment, and with respect to the objectives of tax reform. The arguments raise important issues such as whether economic policy should be set using the U.S. income tax system, whether taxpayers affected by capital gain provisions provide a significant portion of the invested capital in the current economic environment, the extent to which the current economic conditions compare to those that gave rise to preferential capital gain treatment, and the relationship between the tax treatment of capital gains and the objectives of tax reform. Our basic conclusion is that the arguments favoring continued preferential treatment for capital gains are not convincing when examined in light of other considerations. The reasons for this conclusion are outlined in the following paragraphs.

Original Congressional Intent

As discussed previously, the bunching problem created by the realization principle was the single most important reason for the initial tax-favored treatment of capital gains. While there were other means available for alleviating the inequities created by the bunching phenomenon (e.g., income averaging),[4] taxing capital gains at rates effectively lower than ordinary income was certainly justified on equity grounds in an environment of high, and steeply progressive, tax rates (as existed in the 1920s). This is true to only a limited extent in the post-1986 period. Indeed, under the new law, capital gains will be taxed at either 15% or 28%. The maximum tax penalty that a taxpayer would incur by bunching capital gains into one tax year is 13% (as opposed to several times this rate under the previous law).

In addition to the sharp reduction in tax rate progressivity accomplished by the Tax Reform Act of 1986, the bunching argument has lost much of its legitimacy in recent years as the holding period for tax-favored capital gain treatment decreased from several years to only six months. Indeed, allowing taxpayers to exclude 60% of the gain on an asset held for only six months illustrates the departure that Congress has taken over the years from the original intent of the capital gains provisions.

The lock-in problem, created when taxpayers hold capital assets longer than is economically efficient, was another rationale used by Congress in the past to justify tax-favored treatment for capital gains. This problem will still exist under the new law, although it has been ameliorated to some extent. On the one hand, since the holding period for assets is considerably less important after the 1986 changes, the motivation to time sales of capital assets in order to minimize taxes has been largely removed.[5] On the other hand, the fact that the federal estate tax still allows a "step-up" in asset basis to fair market value at the date of death will continue to provide an incentive to hold assets until death and allow them to pass through an estate. However, the lock-in effect created in this situation is relevant only for those taxpayers who can afford not to liquidate their investments during their lifetime.

Incentives and Economics

As pointed out earlier, several of the legislative changes in the capital gains provisions in the past were enacted ostensibly to benefit the U.S. economy by providing incentives for taxpayers to realize gains on capital assets. An important and relevant question is whether the tax system should be used at all to set economic policy. Although the history of capital gains taxation shows that Congress does use the tax system to provide economic policy incentives, some would argue that the main objective of a tax system is to raise revenue for the operation of government in as unobtrusive and neutral a manner as possible [e.g., Musgrave and Musgrave, 1976; U.S. Treasury, 1984]. Indeed, much of the motivation for recent attempts at tax reform arose from the realization that economic tax incentives had, in part, created a system that was both complicated and unfair, and that retarded savings, investment, and economic growth [U.S. Treasury, 1984]. In addition to the mismatching of revenues and expenses and the deferral of income, the differential between the tax rates on ordinary income and long-term capital gains was an important element in the tremendous growth and popularity of the tax shelter industry [U.S. Treasury, 1984].

Because many tax shelters were economically inefficient and were only designed to allow investors to artificially reduce their tax liability, shelters became a highly visible target of tax reformers. The recent Treasury Department study [U.S. Treasury, 1984, pp. 6-7] states the following:

The well-advertised boom in the tax shelter industry in recent years has had particularly adverse effects. Even perfectly legal tax shelters distort the allocation of scarce capital because they produce highly visible inequities in taxation. Perhaps most importantly of all, they undermine taxpayer confidence in the integrity and fairness of the tax system. Tax shelter losses typically result from a combination of current deductions for future expenses, deferral of taxable income, and conversion of ordinary income to preferentially taxed long-term capital gains.

In order to ensure economic efficiency, decisions to invest in business ventures should be based on compelling business factors, not tax considerations. As the Treasury Report points out, "many shelter activities that offer attractive after-tax yields have little social value, as evidenced by before-tax yields that are low and sometimes even negative" [U.S. Treasury, 1984, p. 7]. In cases where investments are undertaken only to obtain tax benefits, all taxpayers share in subsidizing these investments as well as the other negative side effects created by unproductive investments. The mere existence of tax-favored treatment for capital gains does not necessarily lead to unproductive activities. However, the fact that this has occurred on a significant scale in the past requires a careful examination of the cost-benefit trade-offs of the capital gain provisions.

Even if it is assumed, for the sake of argument, that the tax system is an appropriate tool to use in setting economic policy, the question remains whether elimination of the tax-favored treatment of capital gains will significantly hinder capital formation and the economic health of the nation. As pointed out earlier, there was deep concern in 1921 that high tax rates discouraged entrepreneurial activity and risk-taking. This concern, led to the initial capital gain legislation. Further, the fact that the top marginal tax rate on ordinary income has exceeded 50% for most of the period since the income tax was imposed in 1913 appears to have supported the case for maintaining a capital gains rate lower than the regular tax rate. In the current environment, however, the top marginal rate has dropped to 28% (33% over some income ranges) and this argument has lost much of its credibility. Indeed, "the capital gains exclusion was repealed on the theory that the very low tax rates removed the need for any tax-rate distinction between earned income and income from capital investment" [Arthur Anderson, 1986, pp. 33-34].

There are those who counter by arguing that a "risk differential" is still required between capital gain and ordinary income tax rates to ensure adequate capital formation [Gupta, 1986; Murray and Gutfeld, 1986]. Murray and Gutfeld [1986] quote a corporate lobbyist as stating that without a tax incentive for investing in risky enterprises, "people will just invest in Treasury bills. Why should they invest in a new company or stocks or anything with ascertainable risk if there is no capital gains differential?" One answer to this and similar questions is that people should, and in fact will, invest in risky ventures when the expected rate of return is high enough to compensate for the added risk. Investment bankers seem to have had no problems in recent years selling extremely risky "junk bonds" even though the interest from such bonds is fully taxed. Add to these points the one made earlier that economic efficiency is enhanced by allowing investments to stand on their own without tax subsidies, and the case for a differential tax rate for capital gains is further weakened.

A fact often overlooked by those who argue that venture capital will dry up with the elimination of capital gain preferences is that a significant portion of the capital currently invested in new and emerging firms comes from investors who do not benefit from the capital gain provisions. For example, pension funds, individual retirement accounts, and foreign investors have all become significant sources of capital in recent years. Murray [1985] reported that,

> Most of the new venture capital has come from tax-exempt pension funds and foundations, and foreign sources not subject to U.S. tax, all of which haven't any reason to respond to lower capital-gains taxes ... only 15 percent of the new venture capital last year came from individual U.S. investors, who are supposedly the most sensitive to capital-gains cuts.[6]

Similarly, the Treasury study estimates that "roughly one-half of the funds committed to so-called venture capital firms come from tax-exempt entities, such as pension funds, endowments and foundations" [U.S. Treasury, 1984, p. 104]. Gupta [1986] writes that,

> of the approximately $3 billion raised by the (venture capital) industry last year, only 13 percent came from individuals and families. And with over 40 percent of the funds coming from tax-exempt investors like pension funds and foundations and another 23 percent from foreigners, investors are not as influenced by tax rates.

Thus, although the estimates vary somewhat, the amount of venture capital coming from sources unaffected by capital-gains taxes is clearly significant, and contradicts the claims that preferential capital-gains rates are needed to encourage investment in new and emerging companies.[7]

Not surprisingly, pension funds also own a substantial amount of the equity in more established companies as well. A recent study by the Employee Benefit Research Institute reported that pension plans hold 18% of all equities in the U.S. economy [Deloitte Haskins and Sells, 1986]. Further, Drucker [1986] reports that "pension funds now own a third of the equity of all publicly traded companies in the U.S., and 50 percent or more of the equity of the big ones." What this evidence suggests is that the economic environment has changed dramatically from what it was when Congress first accorded preferential tax treatment to capital gains. The phenomenal growth in tax-exempt investors in the equity markets has significantly decreased the importance, and thus the potential economic impact, of investors for whom the capital gains tax provisions affect investment decisions.

Overall, the case for the continued tax-favored treatment of capital gains from an economic and incentive viewpoint is extremely weak. From a theoretical viewpoint, the value of administering economic policy through the tax system is questionable, and, in fact, has proven detrimental in the past. While this latter point may be debatable (but subject to empirical verification), there is mounting evidence that an adequate supply of investment capital will continue to be available regardless of the presence or absence of tax-favored treatment for capital gains.

Other Considerations

Another argument often used to justify lower capital-gains tax rates is that some adjustment is necessary on equity grounds to compensate for inflation [e.g., see Royster, 1987]. The basic argument is that when nominal capital gains are fully includable in income, but contain a significant inflationary component, it is unfair to tax the entire gain because to do so results in an effective tax rate higher than the nominal rate. The problem is compounded by a progressive tax rate structure because inflationary gains may also boost the taxpayer into a higher tax bracket than would be the case in the absence of inflation. While these are legitimate concerns that have been empirically documented by other researchers [e.g., Feldstein and Slemrod, 1978], the solution is not the total or partial exclusion of capital gains from the income base.[8] Any exclusionary percentage agreed upon by policymakers would be arbitrary since there is no way to predict inflation with any accuracy [Feldstein and Slemrod, 1978]. It can be argued that the 60% exclusion allowed under prior law was much too generous for assets held for the minimum six-month holding period during low inflation, while it was inadequate for assets held over longer and higher inflationary periods [U.S. Treasury, 1984]. Alternatively, allowing taxpayers to precisely adjust the basis of their capital assets for the effects of inflation is a theoretically and intuitively appealing option for handling this problem[9] [Feldstein and Slemrod, 1978]. This alternative was proposed as part of the recent Treasury study on tax reform [U.S. Treasury, 1984]. Unfortunately, the Tax Reform Act of 1986 did not include a provision for indexing capital asset bases.

A final point that needs to be made relates to one of the major goals of recent tax reform efforts—simplification. Few would argue with the notion that the capital gain provisions of the Internal Revenue Code are among the most extensive, complex, and confusing [Blum, 1957; Klein, 1976]. To eliminate these provisions would rid the tax system of a significant amount of complexity and help accomplish the basic goals of tax reform. If the capital gains structure were completely removed from the Internal Revenue Code, most of Subchapter

P (Sections 1201-1288) would be eliminated, including the complicated depreciation recapture provisions contained in Sections 1245 and 1250.[10] Further, miscellaneous code sections that tie into the Subchapter P provisions would also be affected. For example, Section 166 which accords short-term capital loss treatment to nonbusiness bad debts could be simplified, as could the parts of Section 170 dealing with contributions of capital gain property.

Although Congress has effectively eliminated the tax-favored treatment of capital gains, and thus reduced the significance of the distinction between capital gain income and other income, it chose to retain all of the statutory mechanisms relating to capital gain computations. This can be viewed in both a positive and a negative light. On the positive side, the Congressional conference report states that the capital gain provisions were retained to "facilitate reinstatement of a capital gains rate differential if there is a future tax rate increase" [U.S. Congress, 1986, p. 106]. In light of the continuing high budget deficits and the temptation of Congress to raise tax rates to help alleviate them, a legitimate need for preferential treatment of capital gains, may develop. In this regard, Congress was prudent to retain the capital gain provisions.

On the other hand, the rationale that led Congress to retain the capital gain provisions will always exist as long as we have an income tax. Thus, despite the intuitive appeal of a tax code that does not discriminate between different types of income, the significance of the capital gain provisions over the past 65 years ensures their survival in the Internal Revenue Code.

SUMMARY AND CONCLUSION

The appropriate taxation of capital gains continues to be debated on several fronts, especially since the Tax Reform Act of 1986 effectively eliminates the tax-favored treatment for capital gains that has existed in one form or another since 1921. This paper examines the economic and political environment that led to the original capital gain provisions and the legislative intent of those provisions and the subsequent changes that have occurred since 1921. The paper then examines the current economic and financial environment and the reasoning offered by those advocating the continued tax-favored treatment for capital gains with a focus on both original legislative intent and economic incentives.

At best, we find that the arguments of proponents of preferential treatment for capital gains are not compelling,and in fact, incorrect in some cases. While a weak case can be made for the tax-favored treatment of capital gains from an equity perspective (to offset the effect of the bunching of income into one tax year), the disadvantages of according some types of income-favored tax treatment over other types outweigh any possible benefits. Indeed, such favored tax treatment was one of the contributing factors to the inefficient, complex, and inequitable tax system that has been the target of concentrated tax reform efforts in recent years. According to many, the major purpose of a tax system is to raise revenue for the efficient functioning of government. The fewer the number of exceptions to the tax rules, the greater the revenue-producing ability of the provisions and the greater the perceived equity among the taxpaying public.

While the economic and financial environment of the 1920s, and the early structure of the tax laws created conditions under which the preferential treatment of capital gains was justified on both equity and economic grounds, the same is not true today. The major goals of tax reform include increased equity, economic neutrality, and perceived fairness [U.S. Treasury, 1984]. The elimination of preferential tax treatment for capital gains by the Tax Reform Act of 1986 is a move toward the attainment of these goals.

NOTES

1. The preferential treatment of capital gains is reduced, but not eliminated for 1987. While the top marginal tax rate is 38.5% for 1987 and 33% for years after 1987, the 1986 law limits the rate of tax on individual capital gains in 1987 to 28%. For years after 1987, the 28% limitation still applies, although the existence of capital gain income, in some cases, will result in other income being effectively taxed at 33%. See Gardner and Stewart [1987] for a more complete discussion.

2. Ibid.

3. For example, certain stock options received as compensation could effectively increase the entrepreneur's ownership of the firm and result in tax-favored capital gains on the subsequent disposition of stock acquired through exercise of the options.

4. For an excellent discussion of the advantages of averaging as opposed to partial or total exemption of capital gains as a cure for the bunching problem, see Blum [1957].

5. Of course, to the extent that the taxpayer expects to be in a lower (higher) tax bracket in a subsequent tax year, the motivation to delay (accelerate) gain recognition still exists.

6. An anonymous reveiwer pointed out that one potential explanation for the relatively low percentage of venture capital coming from individuals in 1984 is that the U.S. savings rate is the lowest it has been for years. Indeed, the reduced savings rate is being increasingly cited as a negative factor in U.S. captial formation and it undoubtedly has affected the availability of venture capital.

7. However, as one reveiwer pointed out, the evidence cited may present a case for arguing that perhaps the capital gain tax rates were not *low enough* under previous law and that even more of a differential is required.

8. See Klein [1976, pp. 76-77] for further discussion on this point.

9. See Klemperer and O'Neil [1986] for various analyses examining the impact on the value of assets of substituting a basis inflation-adjustment for the capital gains tax prefernece.

10. The provisions for capital loss carrybacks and carryforwards would need to be revised and retained to allow taxpayers to benefit from any unused capital loss carryforwards.

REFERENCES

Arthur Andersen & Company, *Tax Reform 1986: Analysis and Planning* (Arthur Andersen, 1986).
Blum, W. J., "A Handy Summary of the Capital Gains Arguments," *Taxes–The Tax Magazine* (April 1957), pp. 247-266.

Conda, C.V., "Next Year's Tax Bill: Fix Capital Gains," *Tax Notes* (October 27, 1986), pp. 409-412.

Deloitte, Haskins, and Sells, "Nation's Pension Plan Assets Approach $2,000,000,000,000!," *DH&S Review* (November 24, 1986), p. 4.

Drucker, P. F., "A Crisis of Capitalism," *The Wall Street Journal* (September 30, 1986).

Feldstein, M. and J. Slemrod, "Inflation and the Excess Taxation of Capital Gains on Corporate Stock," *National Tax Journal* (June 1978), pp. 107-118.

Gardner, R. L. and D. N. Stewart, "Capital Gains and Losses After the Tax Reform Act of 1986," *Taxes–The Tax Magazine* (February 1987), pp. 125-132.

Gupta, U., "Tax Bill Would Discourage Formation of New Firms, Venture Capitalists Say," *The Wall Street Journal* (May 12, 1986), p. 8.

Hicks, J. D., *Republication Ascendency 1921-1933* (Harper and Row, 1960).

Klein, W. A., *Policy Analysis of the Federal Income Tax* (Foundation Press, 1976), pp. 75-78.

Klemperer, W. D. and C. J. O'Neil, "Trading the Capital Gains Tax Preference for An Inflation-Adjusted Basis," Presented at the American Accounting Association Annual Meeting, New York, August 1986.

Lindsey, L. B., "Misguided Capital Gains Levy," *The Wall Street Journal* (September 10, 1986).

Murray, A., "Congressional Tax Writers Are Likely to Reject Reagan Proposal to Reduce Capital-Gains Levy," *The Wall Street Journal* (August 23, 1985), p. 32.

Murray, A. and R. Gutfeld, "Some Old Backers of Lowering Tax on Capital Gains Now Favor a Rise," *The Wall Street Journal* (May 8, 1986).

Murray, R. K., *The Harding Era* (University of Minnesota Press, 1969).

Musgrave, T. A. and P. B. Musgrave, *Public Finance in Theory and Practice* (McGraw-Hill, 1976).

Paul, R. E., *Taxation in the United States* (Little, Brown and Company, 1954).

Perrett, G., *America in the Twenties: A History* (Simon and Schuster, 1982).

Royster, V., "The Tax Revenue Act of 1987?" *The Wall Street Journal* (January 14, 1987).

Trani, E. P. and D. L. Wilson, *The Presidency of Warren G. Harding* (The Regents Press of Kansas, 1977).

U.S. Congress, Hearings Before the Committee on Ways and Means—Revenue Division, 67th Congress, 1st Session, Volume 282 (December 13, 1920).

————, Committee on Ways and Means, *Report on Revenue Bill of 1921,* House Report No. 350, 67th Congress, 1st Session (August 6, 1921).

————, *Report to the Joint Committee on Internal Revenue Taxation: Supplemental Report on Capital Gains and Losses,* 71st Congress, 1st Session (June 8, 1929).

————, *Report of the House Ways and Means Committee on the Revenue Bill of 1934,* House Report No. 704, 73rd Congress, 2nd Session (February 12, 1934a).

————, *Report of the Senate Finance Committee on the Revenue Bill of 1934,* Senate Report No. 558, 73rd Congress, 2nd Session (March 28, 1934b).

————, *Report of the Subcommittee of the Committee on Ways and Means on Proposed Revision of the Revenue Laws,* 75th Congress, 3rd Session (January 1938).

————, Hearings Before the Senate Committee on Finance, House Report No. 7378, 77th Congress, 2nd Session, Volume 1 (July 23, 1942a).

————, *Report of The Senate Committee on Finance on The Revenue Bill of 1942,* Senate Report No. 1631, 77th Congress, 2nd Session (October 2, 1942b).

————, *Report of The Committee on Ways and Means on The Tax Reform Act of 1969,* House Report No. 413, 91st Congress, 1st Session (August 2, 1969).

————, *Report of the Staff of the Joint Committee on Taxation, House Report No. 455, 94th Congress, 2nd Session [December 29, 1976].*

————, *Report of the Senate Committee on Finance on The Revenue Bill of 1978,* Senate Report No. 1263, 95th Congress, 2nd Session (October 1, 1978).

_____, *Report of The Joint Committee on Taxation,* House Report No. 4170, 98th Congress, 2nd Session (December 31, 1984).

_____, *Tax Reform Act of 1986: Conference Report to Accompany H.R. 3838,* House Report 841, 99th Congress, 2nd Session, Volume II (September 18, 1986).

U.S. Department of Commerce, Bureau of Census, *Statistical Abstracts of the United States: 1922* (Washington, D.C., 1923).

U.S. Treasury, *Tax Reform for Fairness, Simplicity, and Economic Growth,* The Treasury Department Report to the President, Volume 1 (U.S. Department of The Treasury, November 1984).

Wells, A., "Legislative History of Treatment of Capital Gains Under the Federal Income Tax," *National Tax Journal* (March 1949), pp. 12-32.

AN EXAMINATION OF TAX PRACTIONERS' DECISIONS UNDER UNCERTAINTY

Debra L. Sanders and Robert W. Wyndelts

ABSTRACT

This study empirically examined the decisions of two groups of tax practioners under conditions of uncertainty. Of specific interest was whether decision framing affects the choice preferences of practitioners when giving tax advice to their clients. Prospect theory was employed as a framework for examining the effects of contingency and outcome framing on decision choices. The "certainty effect" for contingency framing predicted by prospect theory was found. The outcome framing effect (risk averse for gains and risk seeking for losses), however, cannot be completely supported by the findings of this study. Factors other than the outcome frame affected the tax practitioners' decision choices.

In recent years, the U.S. income tax system has become increasingly complex. This growing complexity is the result of a rapid succession of five major tax acts within the last six years. Each act has added a new law as well as amending a substantial portion of the existing law. This inundation of tax changes has increased the uncertainty under which tax practitioners must make decisions. These decisions of tax practitioners have important consequences

Advances in Taxation, Volume 2, pages 41-72.
Copyright © 1989 by JAI Press Inc.
All rights of reproduction in any form reserved.
ISBN: 0-89232-783-9

not only for themselves (reputation) but also to their clients (cash flows). Despite the importance of these decisions, little is known about how tax practitioners make decisions under conditions of uncertainty.

This paper reports the findings of experiments that investigated the decision making of tax practitioners under conditions of uncertainty. Before the description of the experiment a general discussion of the theories of decision making under conditions of uncertainty is presented.

DECISION THEORIES

Expected Utility Theory

The foremost economic theory of decision making under uncertainty is the expected utility model of von Neumann and Morgenstern [1947]. It has general acceptance as the normative model for rational behavior and is used predictively and descriptively in many of the decision sciences. According to the theory, rational behavior is evidenced by a preference for the prospect with the highest expected utility. The focus of the decision maker is on the ultimate outcome of the decision choice rather than changes in wealth positions. Preference choice ordering should not be affected by the contextual presentation of the problem. The decision maker should demonstrate consistency in preference choice ordering over repetitive trials.

Because expected utility theory is the foremost theory of decision making under uncertainty, it has been the focus of extensive theoretical and empirical research [Mosteller and Nogee, 1951; Allais, 1953; Simon, 1955; Ellsberg, 1961; Tversky, 1969; Lindman, 1971; Lichtenstein and Slovic, 1971, 1973; Bar-Hillel, 1973; Tversky and Kahneman, 1974, 1982; Kunreuther et al., 1978; Cooms, 1975; Yaari, 1979; Kahneman and Tversky 1979, 1984; and Schoemaker, 1980]. The overwhelming conclusion drawn from this extensive research is that individuals' choice patterns systematically violate the axioms of the expected utility model. Thus, while the mathematical simplicity and conciseness of expected utility makes it a very attractive normative model, its descriptive validity is questionable [Newman, 1980].

Prospect Theory

The model of decision making most directly in competition with expected utility theory is the relatively new model called "Prospect Theory" [Uecker, Schepanski, and Shin, 1985]. It was created by Kahneman and Tversky [1979] to provide a more descriptive model of individuals' choice preferences under conditions of uncertainty. The theory's development was based on simple decision choices with explicitly stated probabilities; nevertheless, prospect theory may be useful in explaining a variety of decision choices.

One of the underlying principles of prospect theory is that the framing of a decision may influence the decision choice. The frame of a decision includes the presentation of the decision (the act), the possible outcomes of the decision (prospects), and the probability associated with each possible outcome (contingency). The social norms and personal characteristics of the decision maker as well as the formulation of the decision will also have an impact on the ultimate frame assumed. Consequently, it is possible for decision makers to frame the same decision in more than one manner just as it is possible to view an object from more than one vantage point. The framing of a decision affects the decision maker's perception of that problem and, thus, its ultimate solution.

Prospect theory envisions decision choice as a two-step process. The first step, editing, is not represented in the expected utility model, whereas the second step, evaluation, is common to most decision models. The editing phase is a preparatory step for the subsequent evaluation phase. The function of the editing phase is to reduce the cognitive requirements of the evaluation step. This simplification is accomplished by the reformulation of the decision choice through editing operations. Due to individuals' limited cognitive abilities in processing voluminous information, prospect theory assumes that decision simplification is performed whenever possible. These simplifying editing operations are, according to prospect theory, the basis for the systematic violations of rational behavior.

The editing operation of interest in this study is coding. Coding is the assignment of gain or loss status to each possible decision prospect. The same prospect can be edited as either a gain or a loss depending on the reference point selected for the decision. The decision maker focuses on the changes in wealth or welfare from the reference point rather than focusing on the ultimate outcome of the decision.

Example 1:   Imagine that you have had $6,000 of taxes withheld from your paychecks.

A.   If action X is taken, $2,000 of your withholding will be refunded to you (gain).
B.   If action X is taken, $4,000 of your withholding will be kept by the government (loss).

Notice that A and B provide the same information: you will receive a $2,000 refund and the government will retain $4,000 of your withholding. However, the foci of prospect A and B are quite different. The focus of prospect A is on the change in current wealth position, receipt of a $2,000 refund (gain).

The $6,000 of withholding is treated as a sunk cost and not considered relevant to the decision. Whereas, the focus of prospect B is on the amount of the withholding forgone, $4,000 (loss). The $6,000 of withholding is relevant to the decision for prospect B. Thus, the manner in which the prospects are presented (framed) reflects the reference point selected by the decision maker.

In the second step of the decision process, the evaluation phase, the edited prospects are compared and the prospect with the highest expected utility is selected. This phase does not differ from its counterpart in expected utility theory. The formula for expressing the expected value of edited outcomes in prospect theory, $[d(P)][v(X)]$, superficially resembles that of the expected utility model, $(P)(X)$. Both multiply the value of the prospect by its probability of occurrence. However, in prospect theory the value and the probability are subjectively weighted $[d(P)$ and $v(X)]$ by the decision maker. The subjective weights (d and v) are the products of the editing phase. It is these subjective weights, and therefore the editing phase, which cause decision makers to violate expected utility's rational behavior axioms.

Value Weights

The value weight (v) is a function of the reference point, and the magnitude of the change from this point. Although the subjective values weights may differ across individuals, prospect theory maintains that the value weight function is "S" shaped, concave for gains and convex for losses. The slope of the value function is considerably steeper for losses than for gains. This steepness of the loss slope suggests that the anxiety associated with losses is stronger than the pleasure associated with a gain of equal magnitude.

The asymmetry of the value function may induce preference choice reversals merely by changing the decision domain from gain to loss while holding all other variables constant. This phenomenon is called the "reflection effect" [Kahneman and Tversky, 1979].

Example 2:   Select one prospect for each choice

Choice 1:   A. a sure gain of $1,000, or

B. a 20% chance of a $5,000 gain.

Choice 2:   C. a sure loss of $1,000, or

D. a 20% chance of a $5,000 loss.

Consistency would require that a decision maker preferring prospect A in choice 1 should prefer prospect C in choice 2. However, the reflection effect produces inconsistency in the preferences for choices 1 and 2. Due to the shape of the value function, decision makers demonstrate risk aversion in the gain domain (choosing prospect A over prospect B) and risk seeking in the loss domain (choosing prospect D over prospect C).

Decision Weights

Example 2 above also reveals that outcomes which are certain are overweighted relative to those which are merely probable. This prospect weighting behavior is explained by Tversky and Kahneman through the use of decision weights [Kahneman and Tversky, 1979]. A decision weight (d) is a monotonic function of a probability but is not a probability. It is a nonlinear subjective weight formulated during the editing phase of decision making process. These subjective weights, however, should not be considered as indicating a degree of belief or perceived likelihood of occurrence by the decision maker. According to Tversky and Kahneman [1981], the weighting function has the following properties: Extremely low probabilities are treated as zero; extremely high probabilities are treated as certain; low probabilities are overweighted; and, moderate to high probabilities are underweighted. The underweighting of high probabilities is more pronounced than the overweighting of low probabilities.

The characteristic of the decision weights that is of interest in this study is the certainty effect; probable prospects are underweighted relative to certain events [Allais, 1953]. In the gain domain, the certainty effect intensifies risk aversion. Individuals will prefer a riskless prospect to a risky prospect of equal or greater expected value. Similarly, in the loss domain, the certainty effect heightens risk seeking behavior and the anxiety felt over losses. The decision maker will prefer a risky prospect to an equal or smaller certain loss.

The certainty effect suggests that reducing the probability of a prospect by a constant factor will have more impact on the decision choice when the outcome was initially certain than when it was merely probable.

Example 3: Treat each of the two games as seperate decisions.

Game 1: Choose one of the following prospects:
   A. sure win of $60.
   B. 80% chance to win $75.

Game 2: Choose one of the following prospects:
   A. 50% chance to win $60;
   B. 40% chance to win $75.

Consistency would require that if prospect A is chosen in game 1 then prospect A should be chosen in game 2. However, the overweighting of certain prospects makes option A more attractive in game 1 than in game 2. Thus, the reduction of the probabilities by a constant factor may lead to inconsistent decision preferences. This certainty effect has been observed by many researchers [Allais, 1953; Ellsberg, 1961; Schoemaker, 1980; Kahneman and Tversky, 1979].

Tversky and Kahneman [1981 and 1982] have created preference choice reversals through superficial modifications in the context (framing) of decision choice. These reversals are the product of two sets of factors: the framing of the decision acts, outcomes and contingencies; and the nonlinearities of the value and decision weight functions. Although expected utility theory would consider these preference reversals as irrational behavior, prospect theory does not define preference reversals as irrational [Tversky and Kahneman, 1982]. Humans have cognitive limitations and the inconsistent preferences are the results of these limitations. Thus, acting on the most readily available frame can be justified under the "bounded rationality" concept [Simon, 1955].

THE EXPERIMENT

The purpose of this research project was to examine decisions made by tax practitioners under conditions of uncertainty. Specifically, the experiments examined the effects of contextual decision frames on tax practitioners' decision choices. The framing effects tested were the reflection effect and the certainty effect (described in the Decision Theory section). These factors have been shown to cause inconsistent decision choices preferences and violations of the rational behavior axioms [Tversky and Kahneman, 1982].

The decision task selected for testing the framing effects involved a common decision of tax practitioners: advising clients on the tax treatment of a specific income or expense item. Each case involved a single tax issue upon which the subjects were asked to give advice to their client. The possible advice was limited to a single decision choice between two plausible tax treatments (prospects). Associated with each plausible prospect was a probability estimation of its ultimate outcome.

Every subject received two such independent cases and thus, made only two decision choices. Since the manipulation of the independent variables generally involved mere changes in the wording of the scenarios, a within subject design was not practical. The tests of the hypotheses are of a between subject design.

Hypotheses

Three Hypotheses were developed for testing the contextual framing effects advanced by prospect theory. Hypotheses 1 and 2 concern the reflection framing effect and Hypothesis 3 concerns the certainty framing effect.

H_1:   Subjects will not have the same preference choice ordering for decisions with withholding positions framed as gains as for those framed as losses (withholding framing effect).

Tversky and Kahneman [1982] operationalized the framing of outcomes (gain and loss) by merely changing certain words in their decision problems. In a tax setting, this type of operationalization can be accomplished by manipulating the withholding position of the taxpayers. A refund withholding position represents a gain (increase from the present wealth position) and a tax payment represents a loss (decreases from the present wealth position). Therefore, the testing of this hypothesis required only the actual words "refund" or "payment" and "increase" or "decrease" to differ between the cases. All other wording of the cases was held constant (see Appendix 1).

The two cases each subject received were consistent in their withholding framing positions; either both were framed as refunds or both were framed as tax payments. No subjects received cases with inconsistent withholding decision frames positions (i.e., one refund and one tax payment).

Prior research has found a withholding framing effect among taxpayer subjects [Chang, Nicholas, and Shultz, 1987]. Tax practitioners, however, presumably would be cognizant of the fact that refunds or payments are created merely by the amounts of withholdings and/or estimated payments made by the taxpayer during the year. A refund is nothing more than the receipt of taxpayer's own money and not an actual gain. The operationalization of gains and losses as refunds and payments has been employed in this experiment to determine whether tax practitioners are subject to the same withholding framing effect as taxpayers.

H_2:   Subjects will not have the same preference choice ordering for decisions with outcomes framed as gains as for those framed as losses (outcome framing effect).

The framing of outcomes was manipulated through the type of tax issue utilized in the decision choices. A tax expense issue was selected for operationalizing of the gain frame. A tax expense decreases taxable income thereby reducing the tax liability of the taxpayer. Reduction of the tax liability increases an expected refund or decreases an expected payment. Therefore, a tax expense issue would meet prospect theory's definition of a gain [Kahneman and Tversky, 1979]. Following the same logic, an income issue was chosen for operationalizing the loss frame.

An expense case was matched with an income case on all factors other than the tax issue in question. Thus, the two cases were identical except for the manipulation of the tax issue involved (see Appendix 2). Two separate sets of matched expense and income cases were developed. Each subject received either two expense issue cases or the two income issue cases (see Appendix 2). No subjects received both outcome decision frames (expense and income cases).

H₃: Reducing the probabilities of a certain and a probable prospect by a constant factor will effect the preference choice ordering of prospects by the subjects (contingency framing effect).

For all of the experiments in this study, the contingency (probability) associated with each possible prospect (tax treatment) represented an estimate of its outcome; that is, its acceptance or rejection as the correct tax treatment for the issue in question. The two contingency frames utilized in testing Hypothesis 3 were the certainty decision frame and the probable decision frame. In the certainty frame, one of the two prospects presented with the decision choice had a probability of one (certainty). Whereas, in the probable frame both of the two prospects offered to the subjects had probabilities of less than one. The probabilities of the latter decision were obtained by reducing the probabilities of the former by a constant 50% (See Appendix 3). Thus, the only difference in the certain and probable decision frames was the magnitude of the probabilities. All other wording of the cases was held constant.

Each subject received either two cases incorporating certain decision frames or two incorporating a probable decision frame. No subject received both contingency decision frames.

In summary, the three independent variables developed for testing the three hypotheses described in this section were:

H₁: withholding framing effect—refund/tax payment;

H₂: outcome framing effect—expense/income; and

H₃: contingency framing effect—certain/probable.

The dependent variable for the hypotheses' tests was the single decision choice required for each case. This was the only dependent measure for this research.

Subjects

The practitioners participating in the experiments were from two distinct groups. The first experiment was performed during tax training sessions conducted by one of the national CPA firms for their employees. This group consisted of 116 staff and senior accountants from the firm (National Group). Most of the National Group subjects were under the age of 31 and had less than five years experience. The second test occurred at a continuing education

Table 1. Demographic Data
(In percent)

	National Group	Local Group
Age		
23 through 30	94	0
31 through 39	5	24
Older than 39	0	76
Not given	1	0
Total	100	100
Gender		
Female	36	9
Male	64	91
Total	100	100
Highest Degree Held		
Bachelor's	63	63
Masters	23	18
Law Degree	10	14
Masters Law Degree	4	3
Doctorate Degree	0	2
Total	100	100
Rank		
Staff	29	0
Senior	67	0
Manager	4	9
Partner/Owner	0	77
Industry/Other	0	14
Total	100	100
Tax Experience		
Less than 5 years	98	0
5 through 10 years	2	18
more than 10 years	0	82
Total	100	100
Type of Firm		
Local	0	68
Regional	0	2
National	100	16
Industry/Other	0	14
Total	100	100

Table 2. Comparison of National and Local Group's Demographic Data

Desription	P-Value
Age	
ANOVA	<.0001
Gender	
Pearson chi-square	<.0001
Highest Degree Held	
Pearson chi-square	.7819
Rank	
Pearson chi-square	<.0001
Tax Experience	
ANOVA	<.0001
Firm Size	
Pearson chi-square	<.0001

program sponsored by the National College of Tax Practice.[1] This group consisted of 46 subjects who were mainly sole proprietors or partners in local CPA firms (Local Group). All of Local Group subjects were over the age of 30 and had at least five years experience. The differences between the two groups in age, gender, experience, rank, and type of firm were found to be statistically significant. A summary of the subjects' demographic characteristics is presented in Table 1. The results of statistical comparisons of the two groups are given in Table 2.

Design

Table 3 illustrates the experimental design of this research project. Note that the research does not incorporate a fully crossed 2 x 2 x 2 factorial design. The tenets of prospect theory predict a withholding framing effect only in the certain framing situation. Therefore, the withholding framing variable (refund/tax payment) was crossed only with the certain level of the contingency framing variable. The outcome framing variable (expense/income), on the other hand, was fully crossed with the contingency framing variable (certain/probable).

Since the manipulation of the independent variables entailed mere changes in the wording of the scenarios, a between subject design was selected in order to minimize the hypothesis guessing by the subjects. The between subject design was augmented by the development of two expense (education and travel) and two income (award and sale of business) scenarios. Further, four independent cases were employed in hopes of avoiding issue specific findings. Table 4 gives all of the possible case combinations that subjects could have received.

Table 3.   Experimental Design

	Expense		Income	
	Refund	Payment	Refund	Payment
Certain	1[a]	2[a]	3[b]	4[b]
Probable	5	xxxxxxxxxx	6	xxxxxxxxxx

Notes: [a] Collapsed into 1 cell for Hypothesis 2.
      [b] Collapsed into 1 cell for Hypothesis 2.

Research Instrument

The nature of the study and the general instructions for completing the test instrument were explained in a cover letter. In addition, the letter informed the subjects that there were no right or wrong answers to the cases and that their responses would be kept strictly confidential.

The cases began with a listing of the clients' names (taxpayer and spouse), the number of years as clients, the clients' occupations, and an explicit statement of the tax item in question. The clients, in all cases, were married couples with both spouses having full-time employment. To insure that the scenarios were perceived as independent cases, the two cases given to each subject concerned different taxpayers.

The body of each case described the particulars of the tax issue in question. This description was approximately one page in length. To guarantee that there were no right or wrong answers to the cases, the tax issues chosen involved gray areas of the 1985 tax law.[2] Each decision choice required the subject to consider the particular facts and circumstances when resolving the issue in question. The cases were reviewed by a number of expert judges to ensure that they fell within gray areas of the law.[3] The cases were also pretested in a pilot study using Masters of Taxation students.

To avoid findings that would be considered issue specific (tax item specific), four tax issues were selected. The expense issues chosen concerned the deductibility of employee travel expenses or employee educational expenses. The income issues involved the taxability of an award from an employer or the allocation of the sales proceed of a business between a covenant not to compete and goodwill (see Appendix 2). The particular facts of each case were designed to be novel. The subjects should have been familiar with the decision task but should not have been familiar with the specific decision facts. The tax law and authoritative literature pertaining to the issues were briefly articulated to ensure that all subjects were aware of the legal standing of the problem.

Table 4.   Possible Case Combinations

---

1. Certain, Refund Educational Expense Case and
   Certain, Refund Travel Expense Case

2. Certain, Payment Educational Expense Case and
   Certain, Payment Travel Expense Case

3. Certain, Refund Award Income Case and
   Certain, Refund Sale of Business Case

4. Certain, Payment Award Income Case and
   Certain, Payment Sale of Business Case

5. Probable, Refund Educational Expense Case and
   Probable, Refund Travel Expense Case

6. Probable, Refund Award Income Case and
   Probable, Refund Sale of Business Case

After a discussion of the tax issue in question, the clients' taxable income, tax, and expected refund (payment) were presented. The decision choice was the last component of the case. The choice required the subjects to select one of the two tax treatment presented to recommend to the client for the tax item in question. Associated with each offered treatment was a probability estimation of its ultimate outcome. This was the only decision choice requested of the subjects for each case.

The final section of the test instrument requested the demographic data from subjects. It also contained questions concerning the subjects' risk preferences and manipulation checks. The risk preference questions required the subjects to make a simple choice for a client and for themselves regarding the possibility of receiving a refund/tax payment. The simple choice gave two possible actions: one risk averse (probability of 100%) and one risk seeking (probability of less than 100%). The two prospects had the same expected value. The design of these decision choices were very similar to those developed by Kahneman and Tversky [1979].

DATA ANALYSIS

Most of the data analysis for this experiment was accomplished by using the following tests of association: Pearson chi-square; Fisher's exact test; and McNemar test of symmetry. The correction for continuity proposed by Yates was not applied to any of the samples. Empirical evidence has shown that the correction for continuity is overly conservative [Grizzle, 1967; Conover, 1974; Feinberg, 1985]. Nonparametric statistical methods were chosen for the data analysis because the dependent variable, the decision choice, was a dichotomous variable.

As described in the Experimental Task section, the subjects' decision choice was to select one of two possible tax treatments (prospects) for the single tax issue specified in the case. Of the two prospects offered for each decision choice, one prospect was framed as being a more risky treatment than the other. However, the expected values for both prospects of the decision choice were equal. For example, one case involved the following prospects:

A. tax treatment which will decrease the taxpayer's refund by $2,475 (-2475 x 100%); and

B. tax treatment which will not change the refund. However, there is a 75% chance of this treatment being disallowed. If disallowed, the taxpayer will have to pay $3,300 in back taxes and interest (-3300 x 75% = 2,475).

Treatment A is less risky than treatment B because its probability of occurrence is 100%. However, both treatments have the same expected value of $(2,475).

The subjects made one decision choice for each of the two independent cases they received. As noted previously, the manipulation of the independent variables merely entailed changes in the wording of the scenarios. All tests of the hypotheses were, therefore, of a between subject design in order to avoid hypothesis guessing by the subjects.

Hypothesis 1 Results

Hypothesis 1 tested the withholding framing effect on decision choices of the subjects. Each case contained either a refund or a tax payment withholding frame. As previously discussed, the two cases each subject received were consistent in withholding framing, that is, either both were refund or both were payment cases (see Table 4). A difference across subjects in the decision choice responses for cases framed as refunds from those framed as tax payments would indicate a withholding framing effect. Consistency in responses across withholding positions would mean that the subjects' decision choices were not affected by the withholding framing. Consistency in responses was defined as no statistically significant differences in the subjects' responses to the refund frames and to the tax payment frames.

With one exception, no significant differences in responses (at the $p < .1$ level) were found between decision choices framed as refunds and those framed as tax payments. The one scenario evoking significant differences in responses was the educational expense scenario (Pearson chi-square $p = .0182$; Fisher exact test $p = .0302$). As a group, the Local Group subjects were risk averse for the refund case (gain) and risk seeking for tax payment case (loss). These responses follow the risk preference pattern predicted by prospect theory. The

National Group demonstrated no statistically significant differences in responses.

The results of Hypothesis 1 tests suggest that the subjects, for the most part, did not consider the withholding position of the clients when making their decisions. Rejecting Hypothesis 1 provides support to the notion that tax practitioners understand the economic realities of withholding positions. Rejection of this hypothesis also allowed the experimental cells for Hypothesis 2 to be collapsed over the withholding position in all cases with the exception of the educational expense cases for the Local Group of subjects (see Table 3).

The educational expense scenarios were the only cases in which the Local Group and the National Group of subjects had significant differences in their responses (Pearson chi-square for refund p = .0337; for loss p = .0159). Therefore, the tax practitioners were treated as one group of subjects for the majority of Hypothesis 2 and Hypothesis 3 tests. Only in those tests containing educational expenses scenarios were the subjects segregated into two groups.

Hypothesis 2 Results

The independent variables for testing the outcome framing effects of Hypothesis 2 were the tax issues presented in the cases. Gains were operationalized as expense issues (educational expenses and travel expenses) and losses as income issues (award from employer and sale of a business). The educational expense case was identical to the award case on all factors other than the tax issue in question. Similarly, the travel expense was identical to the sale of business case (see Table 5). The subjects either received both of the expense cases or both of the income cases.

Each expense case was compared with each income case in order to detect the outcome framing effect. Consistent responses to the decision choices across gain and loss framing would demonstrate a lack of outcome framing effect whereas inconsistent responses would support Hypothesis 2. Inconsistent responses were defined as statistically significant differences in the number of subjects selecting, for example, the risk averse prospect for each outcome frame (gain and loss).

As Table 6 discloses, responses to the gain frames were significantly different ($p < .1$) from responses to the loss frames in approximately one-half of the tests performed. The travel expense/sale of business test in which female responses of the National Group were separately tested provided nonsignificant results (Pearson chi-square p = 1.000). The other tests lacking significant findings involved the educational expense/award comparisons and the tax payment frame for the educational expense/sale of business test (see Table 6). Thus, the findings are inconclusive with regard to the influence of outcome

Table 5.   Attributes of Case Scenarios

Description	Type X	Type Y
Tax gain	Educational Expense	Travel Expense
Tax loss	Award from Employer	Sale of Business
Clients' names	Allen & Kathy Andrews	Rex & Pam Clifford
Occupations	A: Research Scientist K: Staff Financial Analyst	R: Union Welder P: Self-Employed
Taxable income	$37,500	$45,000
Tax	$ 7,041	$ 9,516
Probabilities of prospects	100/25%	100/50%

framing on tax practitioners decision choices. Hypothesis 2 cannot be rejected for all tax issue comparisons performed.

The results of a stepwise regression on the demographic data indicated gender as an explanatory variable for the National Group's responses to the cases. None of the demographic variables were selected as explanatory variables for the Local Group. Further tests identified only one case, the certain, travel expense case, as demonstrating gender differences in responses. Therefore, Hypothesis 2 (and Hypothesis 3) tests containing this travel case were analyzed by gender (see Table 6).

Hypothesis 3 Results

The last hypothesis tested the contingency framing effect (certainty effect) by comparing the subjects' decision choice responses to cases framed as certain and those framed as probable. In the certain frame, only one of the prospects had a certain outcome. In the probable frame, both tax treatment prospects had probabilities of occurrence of less than one. The certain and probable cases were identical except for the magnitudes of their probabilities. The two cases each subject received were consistent in contingency framing, that is, either both cases were certain or both were probable.

A statistically significant difference in the subjects' decision choice preferences for the certain frame and for the probable frame would demonstrate the contingency framing effect. Only one of the five tests for Hypothesis 3 did not reveal significant differences (at the .05 level) in the subjects' responses. The test lacking significance involved the females' responses to the travel expense scenarios (Pearson chi-square p = .3613; Fisher exact test p = .3250). As a group, females exhibited risk neutral preferences for both the certain and the probable frames. A risk neutral preference for the female group was

Table 6.   Hypothesis 2 Findings
(Pearson Chi-Square P-Values)

Description	National Group P-Values[a]		Local Group P-Values[b]	
Type X: gain = loss		.6148	refund	.3194
			payment	.1596
Type Y: gain = loss	female	1.0000		
	male	.0047		.0237
Type X gain = Type Y loss		.0123	refund	.0105
			payment	.9493
Type X loss = Type Y gain	female	.0946		
	male	<.0001		.0002

Notes: Type X gain—educational expense
   Type Y gain—travel expense
   Type X loss—award from employer
   Type Y loss—sale of business
   a.   Blocked by gender for Type Y gain cases. See Hypothesis 2 Results section for explanation.
   b.   Blocked by withholding position for Type X gain cases. See Hypothesis 1 Results section for explanation.

evidenced by 50% of this group selecting the risk averse prospect for the certain frame and the remaining 50% selecting the risk seeking prospect for the same frame.

Thus, changing the contingencies of prospects from certain to merely probable affected the decision choice preferences of most tax practitioners in this experiment. The results provide support for Hypothesis 3 and the tenets of prospect theory.

Additional Analysis

Due to the inconclusive findings for Hypothesis 2 (outcome framing effect), additional comparisons of decision choice responses were performed. Specifically analyzed was the consistency of decision choice responses within the gain frame (expenses issues) and within the loss frame (income issues). Besides the outcome framing, the other attributes of the cases (clients' names, occupations, taxable income, tax, and probabilities of the possible outcomes) could have affected the subjects' decision choices. Therefore, these other attributes were also examined. Lastly, the subjects' risk preferences were evaluated to ascertain their contributions to the inconclusive findings for

Hypothesis 2. The subject's risk preference was demonstrated through the prospect selection of the decision choice, that is, by which tax treatment the subject selected for the tax issue in question.

The use of two expense and two income issues permitted an analysis of the effect of the specific tax issue on the subjects' choice preference responses within the gain or loss outcome frame. For the gain outcome frame, responses to the travel expense cases were compared to the responses to the educational expense cases. In the same manner, the loss frames, award from employer and sale of business, were also compared.

Because each subject received either both expense cases or both income cases, a within subject experimental design was possible. The McNemar test of symmetry revealed that neither the expense nor the income issues were treated in a consistent manner (see Table 7). Subjects exhibited both risk aversion and risk seeking behavior for expense issues (gains) and for income issues (losses). The tax issue attribute (expense vs income) was, therefore, not the factor influencing the decision choices or risk preferences of the subjects. The specific tax issue (travel, education, award, or sale of business) or one of the other attributes of the scenarios (see Table 5) influenced the subjects' responses.

Table 6 revealed that similar (not statistically different) responses were given to educational expense and award from the employer cases. These two cases were matched on the taxpayer attributes of client's name, occupation, dollar amount of taxable income, dollar amount of tax, and magnitude of the prospect probabilities (see Table 5). On the other hand, Table 6 also noted that statistically different responses were given to the travel expense and sale of business cases. The taxpayer attributes in these two cases were also held constant. Given these contradictory findings, it is unlikely that the client's name, occupation, dollar amount of taxable income, dollar amount of tax, and magnitude of the prospect probabilities were the sole factors influencing the subjects' decision choice responses to the outcome framing cases. Further research on the aforementioned attributes is needed in order to determine the effect of each of these attributes on tax practitioners' decision choice preferences.

The remaining trait of the scenarios, the specific tax issue, was unique for each scenario. A comparison of all possible combinations of the tax issues revealed no particular pattern of responses. By virtue of the fact that the experiment was not specifically designed to test this characteristic, it is difficult to determine to what extent the particular tax issue utilized is the governing factor in decision choices preferences of tax practitioners. Additional research on the tax issues may reveal that tax practitioners' decision choices are based on the facts and circumstances of each client's problem rather than framing of the task.

Prospect theory postulates that individuals will be risk averse in a gain setting and risk seeking for losses, the outcome framing effect. Risk seeking behavior

Table 7.   Scenario Comparisons
(McNemar Tests of Symmetry P-Values)

Description	National CPA		Continuing ED	
Gain: Type X = Type Y	female	.0946	refund	.0005
	male	.0002	payment	.9493
Loss: Type X = Type Y		.0046		.0317

Notes: Type X gain—educational expense
Type Y gain—travel expense
Type X loss—award from employer
Type Y loss—sale of business

for Hypothesis 2 was defined as selecting the tax treatment that contained both the highest absolute dollar benefit to the client and the highest probability of ultimately being disallowed. Risk averse behavior was choosing the tax treatment with the certain probability of ultimately being accepted. Absolute dollar benefit associated with this choice was lower than that of the risk seeking choice. These definitions are consistent with the prospect theory parameters for gain and losses [Tversky and Kahneman, 1982].

Overall risk preferences of the subjects did not follow the pattern suggested by prospect theory. As a group, subjects were risk averse for the educational expense (gain) and award from employer (loss) scenarios. Similarly, the responses to the travel expense (gain) and sale of business (loss) were risk seeking. The apparent pattern was risk aversion for the scenarios with the lower taxable income, tax and probabilities, and risk seeking for those with the higher levels of these traits (see Table 5). Additional research is needed in order to determine whether any one of these factors or a combination thereof could be the cause of the divergent choice preferences of tax practitioners.

Finally, the subjects were asked, in the demographic questionnaire, to make a choice between two tax refund or two tax payment situations. The decisions were made for a client and for the tax practitioners themselves. The subjects were, on average, risk averse regarding clients returns and risk seeking for their own returns in both the refund and tax payment settings.

IMPLICATIONS AND SUMMARY

Prospect theory suggests that certain outcomes will be overweighted relative to those that are merely probable. This implies risk aversion/risk seeking preferences for certain prospects and more neutral risk preference for probable outcomes. The findings of this experiment suggest that tax practitioners do overweight those tax treatments approved by the Internal Revenue Service (certain outcomes) relative to those not sanctioned by the Internal Revenue Service. Therefore, the risk preference of the tax practitioners affected their decision choices. Tax practitioners may be able avoid the influence of their personal risk preference when giving advice to clients by considering that no outcome is certain. Decisions could be viewed as a choice among only probable outcomes, and thereby not evoke strong risk preferences.

The framing of withholdings as refunds or payments, in most of the cases, did not affect the advice tax practitioners selected for their clients. The majority of subjects recognized the economic realities of the withholding positions of the clients. This illustrates a sophistication beyond that of taxpayers who have demonstrated withholding framing effects in their decision choices [Chang, Nicholas, and Shultz, 1987]. Based on the findings of this study, tax practitioners did not consider the withholding position of the client when giving tax advice.

The operationalization of gains/losses as expenses/income provided limited support for prospect theory. Approximately one-half of the tests found significant differences in the treatments of expenses and income. Further, it was found that the expense issues were treated differently from each other. The same can be said for the income issues. It must be conceded that the factor governing the subjects' tax treatment decision choices was not outcome framing as operationalized in this research.

When evaluating the findings of this study consideration should be given to the manner in which the decision tasks were operationalized. Tversky and Kahneman [1982, 1984] used simple, brief decision tasks. The cases in this experiment, on the other hand, were more complex. They consisted of approximately one page of information giving the background of the problem and its legal significance.

Payne et al. [1980] found that individuals rely on heuristics when making simple decisions under uncertainty and when the task complexity is high. The information content of these cases was perhaps sufficient but not overwhelming. Thus, the cases may not have required the subjects to rely on the risk preference heuristics described in prospect theory.

In the demographic questionnaire, the subjects were asked to make simple decisions regarding clients' returns. The decision choice designs were very similar to those used by Tversky and Kahneman [1982]. The subjects, on average, were risk averse for clients' returns in both gain and loss scenarios. These results of the simple decision task did not coincide with the subjects' responses to the main cases. This discovery is also consistent with the findings of Payne et al. [1980]: Individual behavior is highly adaptive to the demands of the task. It appears that simple risk questions may not be reliable indicators of behavior in more complex tax decision settings. However, further research in this area is needed before definite conclusions can be reached.

Finally, the National and Local groups of practitioners employed in this experiment were statistically different on the demographic characteristics of age, rank within firm, tax experience, and type of firm. It was contemplated that these dissimilarities could lead to response inconsistencies between the groups. Specifically, those subjects affiliated with local or regional firms were considered to have more direct contact with clients. This could yield responses to the decision choices more in line with the taxpayer responses established by Chang, Nicholas, and Shultz [1987].

In only one instance (certain, educational expense cases) was a statistical difference found between the National and the Local groups' responses. In this one situation, the Local group followed the risk preference pattern found for taxpayers. These findings imply that local and national tax practitioners make decisions in similar manners.

LIMITATIONS

The prevailing limitation associated with research of this design is the lack of task realism. Although the cases provided the essential information required for the decision task, more information would be available for use in an actual decision. Information considered important by the decision maker may have been omitted from the cases. The case approach lends itself to effective manipulation of the independent variables, making it a useful research tool. Nevertheless, realism may have been sacrificed for controllability.

This research employed four scenarios in operationalizing gains and losses. Four scenarios were used to insure that the findings would not be situation specific. However, it was found that the type of scenario may have been the controlling factor in the decision choices of the subjects. This finding limits the external validity of this research to the tax issues involved.

Each decision task involved suggesting to clients a tax return treatment for an expense or an income issue. This is only one type of decision that tax practitioners must make on a daily basis. Generalizations of these findings to other types of decisions would be suspect. Other decision tasks should be investigated. Due to the difference in information associated with other types of decisions, prospect theory might be more predictive of decision makers' behavior in these settings.

The last limitation that should be mentioned is the effect of small cell frequencies for the female/male and refund/payment samples. The small sample sizes caused the magnitude of differences required for detecting significant results to be high (for some tests as high as .70 based on Fleiss, [1973]). In spite of this limitation, significant results were found.

CONCLUSION

The purpose of this research was to attain knowledge about factors influencing practitioners' decision choices. It was designed to discover whether the framing of decision contingencies and outcomes influence the decision choice preferences of tax practitioners when giving tax advice. The overall results of this experiment lead to three conclusions.

First, the certainty effect predicted by prospect theory and Allais [1953] is germane to the decisions of tax practitioners. Certain outcomes are overweighted relative to those that are merely probable. The risk preferences of the tax practitioners influence their decisions more when one outcome of the decision is known with certainty than when all of the prospects are merely probable. Tax practitioners should be made aware of the possibility that their decisions may be inconsistent when the certainty effect is in play.

Second, the tax advice a practitioner gives is not contingent on the withholding position (refund or tax payment) of the client. Clients need not worry that the tax practitioners will suggest riskier treatments of items solely because the client is in a tax payment position. This finding suggests that the risk preference of the tax practitioner maybe in conflict with that of the client. Chang, Nicholas, and Schultz [1987] found that taxpayers' risk preferences are influenced by their withholding position. Tax practitioners should be aware of this potential conflict when giving advice to their clients.

Third, tax practitioners were generally able to avoid the irrational decision choices predicted by prospect theory concerning outcome framing. The outcome frame, operationalized as an expense or an income issue, was not the controlling factor in determining the tax practitioners' risk preferences in these experiments. The findings of this research suggest that tax practitioners are less susceptible to outcome framing effects than the general public, at least when making decisions within their field. Further research is needed to determine what characteristics of the tax issues influence decision choice preferences and to provide a better understanding of the tax practitioner's decision choice process.

APPENDIX 1

REFUND

Clients: Allen and Kathy Andrew
Years as Clients: 4 years
Occupations: Allen: Research Scientist
                 Kathy: Staff Financial Analyst
Item in Question: $7500 received from employer

In reviewing the Andrews' tax data for 1984, you discover that Allen received $7,500 from his employer in addition to his regular salary. Allen tells you that the amount was given to him as a surprise for his 65th birthday. The plaque accompanying the cash said, "This award is to honor the totality of Allen Andrew's special achievements and scientific contributions over the last 40 years in the area of robotics."

A search of the authoritative literature on awards fails to provide you with a conclusive answer as to the proper tax treatment of the $7,500. In a few of the court cases you read, awards received by employees from employers were treated as nontaxable. However, you also found several cases where awards given by employers to employees were treated as ordinary taxable income. None of these cases were directly on point with the Andrews' factual situation.

Based on your analysis of the authoritative literature plus your assessment of the probability of being audited, you estimate that the Andrews have a 25% chance of being allowed nontaxable treatment for the award, and a 75% chance of the nontaxable treatment ultimately being disallowed, thus causing the award to be ordinary income.

The Andrews' taxable income without considering the $7,500 award is $37,500. The tax on this amount is $7,041 and the Andrews' expected refund is $2,600.

While the Andrews do not like to take too risky of a stance on their tax return, they nevertheless like to take advantage of the existing tax laws. Which tax treatment would you suggest to the Andrews for the $7,500? Please circle your choice.

A.   Treat as a nontaxable award and not change the Andrews refund. There is a 25% chance of this treatment being accepted and a 75% chance that this treatment will be ultimately disallowed. If disallowed, the Andrews will have to pay $3,300 in back taxes and interest.

B.   Treat as ordinary income and decrease the Andrews' refund by $2,475.

PAYMENT

Clients: Allen and Kathy Andrew
Years as Clients: 4 years
Occupations: Allen: Research Scientist
                          Kathy: Staff Financial Analyst
Item in Question: $7,500 received from employer

In reviewing the Andrews' tax data for 1984, you discover that Allen received $7,500 from his employer in addition to his regular salary. Allen tells you that the amount was given to him as a surprise for his 65th birthday. The plaque accompanying the cash said, "This award is to honor the totality of Allen Andrew's special achievements and scientific contributions over the last 40 years in the area of robotics."

A search of the authoritative literature on awards fails to provide you with a conclusive answer as to the proper tax treatment of the $7,500. In a few of the court cases you read, awards received by employees from employers were treated as nontaxable. However, you also found several cases where awards given by employers to employees were treated as ordinary taxable income. None of these cases were directly on point with the Andrews' factual situation.

Based on your analysis of the authoritative literature plus your assessment of the probability of being audited, you estimate that the Andrews have a 25% chance of being allowed nontaxable treatment for the award, and a 75% chance of the nontaxable treatment ultimately being disallowed, thus causing the award to be ordinary income.

The Andrews' taxable income without considering the $7,500 award is $37,500. The tax on this amount is $7,041 and the Andrews' expected tax payment is $2,600.

While the Andrews do not like to take too risky of a stance on their tax return, they nevertheless like to take advantage of the existing tax laws. Which tax treatment would you suggest to the Andrews for the $7,500? Please circle your choice.

A. Treat as a nontaxable award and not change the Andrews tax payment. There is a 25% chance of this treatment being accepted and a 75% chance that this treatment will be ultimately disallowed. If disallowed, the Andrews will have to pay $3,300 in back taxes and interest.

B. Treat as ordinary income and increase the Andrews' tax payment by $2,475.

APPENDIX 2

Clients: Allen and Kathy Andrew
Years as Clients: 4 years
Occupations: Allen: Research Scientist
                     Kathy: Staff Financial Analyst
Item in Question: Educational expenses

The Andrews tell you that Kathy received her MBA degree in December of 1984. All of the courses necessary to obtain this degree were taken at night during 1984. The cost for books, supplies, transportation and tuition was $2,500. From questioning Kathy you learn that she did *not* obtain the MBA in order to meet the minimal educational requirements of her job.

Kathy's employer encourages, but does not require, its employees to maintain and improve their skills by taking continuing education classes. The company does reward successfully completed courses with increases in salary. For this reason, several of Kathy's fellow workers also take classes. Kathy also tells you that upon completing her MBA she was offered a position in the management advisory service department of a national CPA firm. This local office hires only individuals with masters degrees directly into the department. Kathy has decided to accept the position and will start May 1, 1985.

The authoritative literature on educational expenses indicates that Kathy's expenses are deductible if they are for maintaining her skills but are not deductible if they qualify her for a new position or profession. In most of the court cases you read, the costs of obtaining a graduate degree were not deductible. However, you did find a small number of cases where the graduate degree expenses were deductible even when the taxpayer accepted a new position upon completion of the degree. Unfortunately, none of these cases had the same facts as Kathy's.

From your analysis of the authoritative literature plus your assessment of the audit probability, you estimate that the Andrews will have a 25% chance of being allowed to deduct the educational expenses, and a 75% chance that the deduction will ultimately be disallowed.

The Andrews' taxable income before considering the educational expenses is $37,500. The tax on this amount is $7,041 and the Andrews' expected refund is $2,600.

While the Andrews do not like to take too risky of a stance on their tax return, they nevertheless like to take advantage of the existing tax laws. Which tax treatment would you suggest to the Andrews for the educational expenses? Please circle your choice.

A.   Treat as deductible and increase the Andrews' refund by $825. There is a 25% chance of this treatment being accepted, and a 75% chance that this treatment will be ultimately disallowed. If disallowed, the Andrews will have to pay $1,100 in back taxes and interest.

B.   Treat as not deductible and not change the Andrews' refund.

Clients: Allen and Kathy Andrew
Years as Clients: 4 years
Occupations: Allen: Research Scientist
                 Kathy: Staff Financial Analyst
Item in Question: $7,500 received from employer

In reviewing the Andrews' tax data for 1984, you discover that Allen received $7,500 from his employer in addition to his regular salary. Allen tells you that the amount was given to him as a surprise for his 65th birthday. The plaque accompanying the cash said, "This award is to honor the totality of Allen Andrew's special achievements and scientific contributions over the last 40 years in the area of robotics."

A search of the authoritative literature on awards fails to provide you with a conclusive answer as to the proper tax treatment of the $7,500. In a few of the court cases you read, awards received by employees from employers were treated as nontaxable. However, you also found several cases where awards given by employers to employees were treated as ordinary taxable income. None of these cases were directly on point with the Andrews' factual situation.

Based on your analysis of the authoritative literature plus your assessment of the probability of being audited, you estimate that the Andrews have a 25% chance of being allowed nontaxable treatment for the award, and a 75% chance of the nontaxable treatment ultimately being disallowed, thus causing the award to be ordinary income.

The Andrews' taxable income without considering the $7,500 award is $37,500. The tax on this amount is $7,041 and the Andrews' expected refund is $2,600.

While the Andrews do not like to take too risky of a stance on their tax return, they nevertheless like to take advantage of the existing tax laws. Which tax treatment would you suggest to the Andrews for the $7,500? Please circle your choice.

A. Treat as a nontaxable award and not change the Andrews refund. There is a 25% chance of this treatment being accepted and a 75% chance that this treatment will be ultimately disallowed. If disallowed, the Andrews will have to pay $3,300 in back taxes and interest.

B. Treat as ordinary income and decrease the Andrews' refund by $2,475.

Clients: Rex and Pam Clifford
Years as Client: 4 years
Occupations: Rex: Union Welder
                          Pam: Self Employed
Item in Question: Travel expenses

Rex is a union welder in Junction, North Dakota. Construction was in a slump in Junction during 1984; therefore, Rex got a job through the union on a government work site located approximately 83 miles from Junction. Rex worked 10 weeks at the site before being laid off. During the layoff, Rex worked two weeks in Junction on a small job. Rex was recalled to the government site 5 weeks after his initial layoff. He worked at this site the remainder of the year (35 weeks). As of April 1, 1985, Rex was still employed at the government site. Rex views his position at the site as temporary even though he has worked there for more than 1 year. The reason for his view is that layoffs on government jobs are common and for indefinite periods of time. Due to budget cuts by the present administration, Rex cannot count on being rehired if he is laid off in the future. He is unsure as to whether the project will ever be completed. If he is laid off and the government does recall workers, Rex knows that he will be one of the first recalled because of his seniority.

Travel expenses incurred between home and a place of work are deductible if the employment is temporary. If the employment is indefinite rather than temporary, the travel expenses are not deductible. After examining Rex's data, you think that if the Cliffords claim a travel expense on their 1984 tax return, they could claim either $1,600 (10 weeks) or $5,500 (45 weeks) of expenses.

From your research on travel expenses and your assessment of the probability of being audited, you estimate that if the Cliffords claim 45 weeks of travel expenses, they have a 50% chance of obtaining the full deduction ($5,500) and a 50% chance that the number of weeks allowable will ultimately be reduced to 10 weeks ($1,600). If, on the other hand, the Cliffords claim only 10 weeks of travel expense, you figure they have a 100% chance of obtaining the deduction ($1,600).

The Cliffords taxable income without considering the travel expenses, is $45,000. The tax on this amount is $9,516 and the Cliffords' expected refund is $2,600.

While the Cliffords do not like to take too risky a stance on their tax returns, they nevertheless like to take advantage of the existing tax laws. In this case, the Cliffords wish to take a travel expense deduction. Which tax treatment would you suggest to the Cliffords for the travel expenses? Please circle your choice.

A. Claim 45 weeks ($5,500) and increase the Cliffords' refund by $1,815. There is a 50% chance of this treatment being accepted and a 50% chance of paying $2,574 in back taxes and interest, if only 10 weeks of travel expenses are ultimately allowed.

B. Claim 10 weeks ($1,600) and increase the Cliffords' refund by $528.

Clients: Rex and Pam Clifford
Years as Client: 4 years
Occupations: Rex: Union Welder
                 Pam: Self Employed
Item in Question: Sale of business

The Cliffords have owned the Linen Service Company for the past 20 years. The business consists of renting sheets, towels, tablecloths, and other cloth items to hotels and restaurants. As a result of Pam's hard work and pleasant personality, Pam has built a thriving business with about 750 loyal customers.

In 1984, Pam decided to retire from this business and sold the company to Tom Hawk.

The sales price of the business was $40,000. This covered the assets of the business as well as the goodwill and a covenant not to compete. Tom was willing to pay a premium for the company in order to obtain a going concern with numerous loyal customers. Client lists are very important in the linen service industry because the number of new customers is limited. Tom insisted on a covenant not to compete in order to protect this client list. Although the covenant not to compete was separately stated in the sales contract, no allocation of sales price was made to it or any other items. The fair market value of the assets is $30,000, leaving $10,000 to be allo   d between goodwill and the covenant not to compete.

It is necessary for the Cliffords to determine the proper allocation of the sales price between goodwill and the covenant not to compete. The sale of goodwill is treated as the sale of a capital asset, whereas the proceeds of a covenant not to compete are considered to be ordinary taxable income. A search of the authoritative literature indicates that if the covenant not to compete is considered to be necessary and not severable from the goodwill, the entire amount may be allocated to goodwill. However, if the covenant not to compete was instrumental in the sale of the business and/or was separately stated and negotiated, part of the sales price should be allocated to the covenant not to compete.

After applying your findings to the Cliffords' factual situation, you conclude that if the Cliffords allocate part of the sales price to the sale of goodwill, they could either allocate the entire $10,000 to goodwill or allocate $5,000 to goodwill and $5,000 to the covenant not to compete.

Based on your assessment of the audit probability and the strength of their position, you estimate that if the Cliffords allocate the entire $10,000 to goodwill they have a 50% chance that this treatment will be accepted and a 50% chance that ultimately $5,000 will be allocated to the covenant not to compete. If, on the other hand, the Cliffords allocate $5,000 to the covenant not to compete and $5,000 to goodwill, you figure they have a 100% chance of this treatment being accepted.

The Cliffords' taxable income without considering the questioned $10,000 is $45,000. The tax on this amount is $9,516 and the Cliffords' expected refund is $2,600.

While the Cliffords do not like to take too risky a stance on their tax returns, they nevertheless like to take advantage of the existing tax laws. In this case, the Cliffords wish to allocate part of the sales price to the sale of goodwill. Which tax treatment would you suggest to the Cliffords for the $10,000? Please circle your choice.

A.   Allocate the $10,000 to the sale of goodwill and decrease the Cliffords'
      refund by $1,320. There is a 50% chance of this allocation being accepted
      and a 50% chance of paying $1,980 in back taxes and interest, if $5,000
      is ultimately allocated to the covenant not to compete.

B.   Allocate $5,000 to the sale of goodwill and $5,000 to the covenant not
      to compete. This will decrease the Cliffords' refund by $2,310.

APPENDIX 3

Clients: Rex and Pam Clifford
Years as Client: 4 years
Occupations: Rex: Union Welder
                 Pam: Self Employed
Item in Question: Travel expenses

Rex is a union welder in Junction, North Dakota. Construction was in a
slump in Junction during 1984; therefore, Rex got a job through the union
on a government work site located approximately 83 miles from Junction. Rex
worked 10 weeks at the site before being laid off. During the layoff, Rex worked
two weeks in Junction on a small job. Rex was recalled to the government
site 5 weeks after his initial layoff. He worked at this site the remainder of
the year (35 weeks). As of April 1, 1985, Rex was still employed at the
government site. Rex views his position at the site as temporary even though
he has worked there for more than 1 year. The reason for his view is that layoffs
on government jobs are common and for indefinite periods of time. Due to
budget cuts by the present administration, Rex cannot count on being rehired
if he is laid off in the future. He is unsure as to whether the project will ever
be completed. If he is laid off and the government does recall workers, Rex
knows that he will be one of the first recalled because of his seniority.

Travel expenses incurred between home and a place of work are deductible
if the employment is temporary. If the employment is indefinite rather than
temporary, the travel expenses are not deductible. After examining Rex's data,
you think that if the Cliffords claim a travel expense on their 1984 tax return,
they could claim either $1,600 (10 weeks) or $5,500 (45 weeks) of expenses.

From your research on travel expenses and your assessment of the
probability of being audited, you estimate that if the Cliffords claim 45 weeks
of travel expenses, they have a 50% chance of obtaining the full deduction
($5,500) and a 50% chance that the number of weeks allowable will ultimately
be reduced to 10 weeks ($1,600). If, on the other hand, the Cliffords claim

only 10 weeks of travel expense, you figure they have a 100% chance of obtaining the deduction ($1,600).

The Cliffords taxable income without considering the travel expenses is $45,000. The tax on this amount is $9,516 and the Cliffords' expected refund is $2,600.

While the Cliffords do not like to take too risky of a stance on their tax returns, they nevertheless like to take advantage of the existing tax laws. In this case, the Cliffords wish to take a travel expense deduction. Which tax treatment would you suggest to the Cliffords for the travel expenses? Please circle your choice.

A. Claim 45 weeks ($5,500) and increase the Cliffords' refund by $1,815. There is a 50% chance of this treatment being accepted and a 50% chance of paying $2,574 in back taxes and interest, if only 10 weeks of travel expenses are ultimately allowed.

B. Claim 10 weeks ($1,600) and increase the Cliffords' refund by $528.

Clients: Rex and Pam Clifford
Years as Client: 4 years
Occupations: Rex: Union Welder
                Pam: Self Employed
Item in Question: Travel expenses

Rex is a union welder in Junction, North Dakota. Construction was in a slump in Junction during 1984; therefore, Rex got a job through the union on a government work site located approximately 83 miles from Junction. Rex worked 10 weeks at the site before being laid off. During the layoff Rex worked two weeks in Junction on a small job. Rex was recalled to the government site 5 weeks after his initial layoff. He worked at this site the remainder of the year (35 weeks). As of April 1, 1985, Rex was still employed at the government site. Rex views his position at the site as temporary even though he has worked there for more than 1 year. The reason for his view is that lay-offs on government jobs are common and for indefinite periods of time. Due to budget cuts by the present administration, Rex cannot count on being rehired if he is laid off in the future. He is unsure as to whether the project will ever be completed. If he is laid off and the government does recall workers, Rex knows that he will be one of the first recalled because of his seniority.

Travel expenses incurred between home and a place of work are deductible if the employment is temporary. If the employment is indefinite rather than temporary, the travel expenses are not deductible. After examining Rex's data, you think that if the Cliffords claim a travel expense on their 1984 tax return, they could claim either $1,600 (10 weeks) or $5,500 (45 weeks) of expenses. Either position is likely to be questioned by the IRS.

From your research on travel expenses and your assessment of the probability of being audited, you estimate that if the Cliffords claim 45 weeks of travel expenses, they have a 25% chance of obtaining the full deduction ($5,500), a 25% chance that the number of weeks allowable will ultimately be reduced to 10 weeks ($1,600), and a 50% chance that all of the travel expenses will ultimately be disallowed. If, on the other hand, the Cliffords claim only 10 weeks of travel expense, you figure they have a 50% chance of obtaining the deduction ($1,600), and a 50% chance that all of the travel expenses will ultimately be disallowed.

The Cliffords taxable income, without considering the travel expenses, is $45,000. The tax on this amount is $9,516 and the Cliffords' expected refund is $2,600.

While the Cliffords do not like to take too risky of a stance on their tax returns, they nevertheless like to take advantage of the existing tax laws. In this case, the Cliffords wish to take a travel expense deduction. Which tax treatment would you suggest to the Cliffords for the travel expenses? Please circle your choice.

A. Claim 45 weeks ($5,500) and increase the Cliffords' refund by $1,815. There is a 25% chance of this treatment being accepted, a 25% chance of paying $1,714 in back taxes and interest, if only 10 weeks of travel expenses are allowed, and a 50% chance of paying $2,417 in taxes and interest, if all of the travel expenses are ultimately disallowed.

B. Claim 10 weeks ($1,600) and increase the Cliffords' refund by $528. There is a 50% chance of this treatment being accepted, and a 50% chance of paying $700 in back taxes and interest, if all of the travel expenses are ultimately disallowed.

NOTES

1. The National College of Tax Practice is a nonprofit organization associated with the School of Accountancy at Arizona State University.
2. The experiments were performed in 1985 and thus were based on the tax laws in force at that time.
3. The expert judges were six tax faculty members and three doctoral students at Arizona State University.

REFERENCES

Allias, M., "Le Comportement de l'Homme Rationnel Devant le Risque, Critique des Postulats et Axiomes de l'Ecole Americaine," *Econometrica* (October 1953), pp. 503-546.
Bar-Hillel, M., "On the Subjective Probability of Compound Events," *Organizational Behavior and Human Performance* (June 1973), pp. 396-406.

Barns, J.D. and J.E. Reinmuth, "Comparing Imputed and Actual Utility Functions in a Competitive Bidding Setting," *Decision Sciences* (October 1976), pp. 801-812.

Chang, O., D.R. Nicholas, and J.J. Schultz, "Taxpayer Attitudes Toward Tax Audit Risk," *Journal of Economic Psychology* (August 1987), pp. 299-309.

Cohen, J., *Statistical Power of Analysis for the Behavioral Sciences* (Academic Press, 1969).

Conover, W.J., "Some Reasons for Not Using the Yates Continuity Correction on 2 x 2 Tables," *Journal of the American Statistical Association* (June 1974), pp. 374-382.

Coombs, C.H., *A Theory of Data* (Wiley, 1964).

————, "Portfolio Theory and the Measurement of Risk," in *Human Judgement and Decision Processes.* Edited by M.F. Kaplan and S. Schwartz (Academic Press, 1975), pp. 63-86.

Ellsberg, D., "Risk, Ambiguity and the Savage Axioms," *Quarterly Journal of Economics* (November 1961), pp. 643-669.

Feinberg, S.E., *The Analysis of Cross-Classified Categorical Data* (MIT Press, 1985).

Fishburn, P.C. and G.A. Kochenberger, "Two-Piece von Neumann-Morgenstern Utility Functions," *Decision Sciences* (October 1979), pp. 503-518.

Fleiss, J.L., *Statistical Methods for Rates and Proportions* (John Wiley & Sons, 1973).

Grayson, C.J., *Decisions Under Uncertainty: Drilling Decisions by Oil and Gas Operators* (Harvard University, 1960).

Grizzle, G., "Continuity Correction in the X2-Test for 2 x 2 Tables," *The American Statistician* (October 1967), pp. 28-32.

Jackson, B.R. and S.M. Jones, "Salience of Tax Evasion Penalties Versus Detection Risk," *Journal of the American Taxation Association* (Spring 1985), pp. 7-17.

Kahneman, D. and A. Tversky, "Prospect Theory: An Analysis of Decision Under Risk," *Econometrica* (March 1979), pp. 263-291.

————, "Choices, Values, and Frames," *American Psychologist* (April, 1984), pp. 341-350.

Kunreuther, H., R. Ginsberg, L. Miller, P. Sagi, P. Slovic, B. Borkan, and N. Katz, *Disaster Insurance Protection: Public Policy Lessions* (Weley, 1978).

Laughhunn, D.J., J.W. Payne, and R. Crumm, "Managerial Risk Preferences for Below-Target Returns," *Management Science* (December 1980), pp. 1238-1249.

Lichtenstein, S. and P. Slovic, "Reversals of Preference Between Bids and Choices in Gambling Decisions," *Journal of Experimental Psychology* (July 1971), pp. 46-55.

————, "Response-Induced Reversals of Preference in Gambling: An Extended Replication in Las Vegas," *Journal of Experimental Psychology* (November 1973), pp. 16-20.

Lindman, H.R., "Inconsistent Preferences among Gambles," *Journal of Experimental Psychology* (August 1971), pp. 390-397.

Markowitz, H., "The Utility of Wealth," *Journal of Political Economy* (April 1952), pp. 151-158.

Mosteller, F. and P. Nogee, "An Experimental Measurement of Utility," *Journal of Political Economy* (October 1951), pp. 371-404.

Newman, D.P., "Prospect Theory: Implications for Information Evaluation," *Accounting Organizations and Society* (April 1980), pp. 217-230.

Payne, J.W. and M.L. Braunstein, "Preferences Among Gambles with Equal Underlying Distributions," *Journal of Experimenal Psychology* (January 1971), pp. 13-18.

Payne, J.W. and D.J. Laughhunn, and R. Crum, "Translation of Gambles and Aspiration Level Effects in Risky Choice Behavior," *Management Science* (October 1980), pp. 1039-1060.

Riley, D., "Individual Income Tax Returns: Selected Characteristics from the 1983 Taxpayer Usage Study," *Statistics of Income S.O.I. Bulletin,* 4 #1 (1984), pp. 45-61.

Russo, J.E. and B.A. Doshers, "An Information Processing Analysis of Binary Choice," Working Paper, Carnegie-Mellon University (1976).

Schoemaker, P.J.H., *Experiments on Decisions Under Risk: The Expected Utility Hypothesis* (Nijhoff Publishing, 1980).

————, "The Expected Utility Model: Its Variants, Purposes, Evidence and Limitations," *Journal of Economic Literature* (June 1982), pp. 529-563.

Simon, H.A., "A behavioral Model of Rational Choice," *Quarterly Journal of Economics* (February 1955), pp. 174-183.

Tversky, A., "Intransitivity of Preferences," *Psychological Review* (January 1969), pp. 31-48.

————, "Choice by Elimination," *Journal of Mathematical Psychology* (November 1972), pp. 341-367.

Tversky, A. and D. Kahneman, "Judgement under Uncertainty: Heuristics and Biases," *Science* (September 1974), pp. 1124-1131.

————, "The Framing of Decisions and the Psychology of Choice," *Science* (January 1981), pp. 453-458.

————, "The Framing of Decisions and the Psychology of Choice," in *New Directions for Methodolgy of Social and Behavioral Sciences,* R.M. Hogarth eds., (Jossey-Bass Inc., March 1982), pp. 3-19.

Uecker, W., A. Schepanski, and J. Shin, "Toward a Positive Theory of Information Evaluation: Relevant Tests of Competing Models in a Principal-Agency Setting," *Accounting Review* (July 1985), pp. 430-457.

von Neumann, J. and O. Morgenstern, *Theory of Games and Economic Behavior* (Princeton University Press, 1947).

Yaari, M.E., "Convexity in the Theory of Choice Under Risk," *Quarterly Journal of Economics* (May, 1979), pp. 278-290.

A COMPARATIVE ANALYSIS
OF TAX EXPENDITURE BUDGET TRENDS

W. Ron Singleton

ABSTRACT

Tax expenditures are used extensively by the federal government as a means to provide publicly favored goods. This study provides a discussion of the theoretical conditions necessary for the optimal use of tax expenditures. The role of tax expenditures in the budgetary process is then analyzed by comparative trend analysis. Specific issues of tax efficiency concerning the role of tax expenditures relative to direct expenditures, both in total and cross-sectionally by budget function, are investigated. The equity issue of tax entity incidence is also addressed.

The federal government employs two major fiscal tools to achieve desired social goals: direct expenditures and tax expenditures. Direct expenditures represent direct monetary outlays for specific activities, whereas tax expenditures are indirect subsidies in the form of tax incentives. Thus, policymakers not only must decide which social programs to provide, but also which fiscal instrument, a direct outlay or an indirect tax incentive, to use. Tax expenditures reflect public choices because they are used as decision variables to achieve predetermined public goals.

Advances in Taxation, Volume 2, pages 73-89.
Copyright © 1989 by JAI Press Inc.
All rights of reproduction in any form reserved.
ISBN: 0-89232-783-9

Tax expenditures and direct expenditures of the federal government are budgeted annually. Direct budget outlays have traditionally received major attention by policymakers, and tax expenditures often were "... not so well understood" [Ott and Ott, 1977, p. 15]. The role of tax expenditures in budget policy, however, has been receiving increasing attention. Arguments have been made for incorporating tax expenditures into the budget process [e.g., Surrey, 1970a, 1970b] and concern has been expressed about their increasing magnitude [e.g., Committee on the Budget, 1981]. Legislation has been suggested that tax expenditures be subjected to ceilings and more formal, rigorous review [e.g., U.S. Congress, Committee on Rules, 1986].

Analytics and normative standards have also been developed for determining when to use direct expenditures versus tax expenditures [e.g., Feldstein, 1980] and more recent efforts have been devoted to improving the estimation techniques employed in the preparation of the tax expenditure budget [Robinson and Renfer, 1985]. Ando et al. [1985] employed a revised tax expenditure approach for assessing issues of tax reform. In addition, there have been numerous studies of the effects of specific tax subsidies, such as the long-term capital gain deduction and the state/local tax deduction.

The purpose of this article is to provide an additional dimension to the analyses of tax expenditures. The focus is the relative role and compositional (cross-sectional) shifts of aggregate tax expenditures over time. Specifically, the emphasis will be to examine whether the use of tax expenditures relative to direct expenditures has changed significantly over time, both in total and by specific budget (functional) category. Additional issues to be investigated are whether cross-sectional shifts by budget function and shifts in tax entity incidence have occurred over time. The results of the analyses have important implications for fiscal issues such as assessing the relative use of tax and direct expenditures as budget tools. In addition, the results could be important for tax policy purposes when examining the magnitude and trends in the use of specific tax subsidies.

The paper addresses these issues with an initial discussion of the tax expenditure concept, and then reviews the theoretical justification for its use. The research design and methodology of the study are introduced, following by a presentation of the results. The final section discusses the implications of the results, and offers suggestions for future research.

THE TAX EXPENDITURE CONCEPT

Tax expenditures were formally defined in the Budget Act of 1974 as [U.S. Congress, Senate Committee on the Budget, 1978]:

... those revenue losses attributable to provisions of the Federal tax laws which allow a
special exclusion, exemption or deduction from gross income or which provide a special
credit, a preferential rate of tax or a deferral of tax liability.

Thus, the definition of tax expenditures is within the context of forgone
revenues associated with special incentives granted by Congress via the tax
system. They are usually identified as any tax provision that reduces a tax
liability, except those incurred in earning income. The tax expenditure budget
is simply a summary of the forgone tax revenues associated with activities in
which Congress elects to use the tax structure instead of direct outlays to
accomplish policy objectives.[1]

The initial development of the tax expenditure concept is generally attributed
to Stanley Surrey. He was particularly concerned with the increasing use of
tax subsidies and their lack of budgetary review [Surrey, 1973]. His views on
the necessity of including tax expenditures in the budgetary process prevailed,
and the Congressional Budget Act of 1974 required that a tax expenditure
budget be submitted as part of the annual budget report. Surrey's views on
the tax expenditure concept, however, have not been universally accepted. The
concept has been the subject of continuing controversy and debate among tax
policy theorists.

Numerous arguments have been advanced against various aspects of the
tax expenditure concept. Bittker [1969], Blum [1975], and Goode [1977] were
critical of the lack of an adequate standard for defining the baseline tax
structure which is inherent in defining a tax expenditure. Additionally, they
were critical of the many debatable value judgments and assumptions implicit
in such definitions. Also, difinitional differences arose in the tax expenditure
budgeting process. For example, the Treasury Department uses different
definitions of tax expenditures from those used by the Joint Committee on
Taxation.[2]

Additional questions relating to the methodology employed in estimating
tax expenditures have been raised. Bittker [1969] and Hanley [1976] stressed
the logical inconsistency of recognizing revenue losses of tax expenditures,
but not recognizing revenue gains (negative tax expenditures) associated with
taxing noneconomic income or disallowing economic losses (such as excess
capital losses). Bittker [1969] and Weidenbaum [1978] also criticized
weaknesses in estimation techniques due to the failure of the estimates to
account for indirect and secondary economic effects that would occur in
response to changes in tax laws. Jackson [1986] incorporated these criticisms
into a specific analysis of the tax expenditure estimates for pensions.

In summary, Wagner [1979, p. 21] viewed the tax expenditure budget
process as "... an exercise in fiscal impressionism ..." and argued that its
use was to mask political motives to broaden the tax base. Weidenbaum
[1978] suggested that an implication of the tax expenditure concept was that

the government controls all resources and has an unlimited right to a taxpayer's income. This is a governmental role inconsistent with the private property views of most U.S. taxpayers.

Proponents of tax expenditure reporting, such as the General Accounting Office (GAO) [1979] or Surrey and Hellmuth [1969], argued that the assumption of governmental ownership of all revenues was inconsistent with the intent of those who either originated or were using the concept. These proponents also argued that there is relatively broad agreement among policy makers and theorists as to the definition of a baseline tax system and that any items of disagreement were not of a magnitude that would warrant elimiation of tax expenditure information. In addition, they argued that even though decision makers are often forced to rely on estimated data that are not as complete as may be desired, such information can still be useful with proper consideration of the underlying assumptions and resulting limitations employed in the estimates. Finally, they noted that even budget estimates of direct expenditures often do not include secondary and indirect effects in the analyses. Therefore, the tax expenditure methodology of estmating only direct effects was not inconsistent with techniques often used in other areas.

In spite of the aforementioned controversy, most authors agree that tax expenditure estimates can provide useful information, and that estimating revenue impacts is important for evaluating tax policies. The tax expenditure budget provides a convenient catalogue of tax expenditures, for analyzing issues such as those in this paper. The expenditures, however, should be analyzed within the proper context and with due consideration of potential limitations in their use.

THEORY OF TAX EXPENDITURES

The previous section reviewed the role of tax expenditures from the macroeconomic perspective of their use in budget policy. The purpose of this section is to provide a general model of the optimal conditions necessary for specific tax expenditures, and establish that a solution exists to justify their use. The analysis is limited to a discussion of the basic principles and features of the model, and does not attempt to determine whether a given tax expenditure should be eliminated or increased. Such a conclusion would require a specific estimate of each expenditure on a case-by-case basis, which is beyond the scope of this paper.

The theory is based upon the idea of minimizing the cost of the government providing goods to society. After society (via the government) establishes a desired program or activity that will be publicly provided, the method of payment must be determined. Payment for the program can be made by either a tax expenditure or direct expenditure. A tax expenditure is justified when it costs less than a direct expenditure. The following discussion provides a more formal mathematical analysis of the theory and the conditions that justify the use of tax expenditures. Thus, the theory section provides the framework for addressing the hypotheses that are developed later in the paper.

The theory and model of tax expenditures presented here relies heavily upon the seminal work of Feldstein [1980]. The theory is an extension of Ramsey's [1927] optimal commodity taxation, and incorporates an explicit utilitarian social welfare function.[3] The analysis addresses the policy issue from the perspective of the de novo design of an optimal tax subsidy as opposed to changing an existing tax structure with tax subsidies in place. The basic issue is to determine the choice of policy instrument, direct expenditure or tax expenditure, that generates the least excess burden when providing a desired good or service. Thus, a tax expenditure or subsidy will be a desired alternative when the welfare cost of the new subsidy is less than the welfare cost of direct government spending for a desired project.

The concept can be illustrated by the case of an economy with n identical individuals who supply labor L at a wage rate w with income subject to constant tax rate t. Each individual uses his/her after-tax income to purchase a quantity c of the sole consumption good, whose price will serve as the numeraire, and quantity x of the sole publicly "favored" good at price p. Assuming that the favored good has a tax subsidy at rate s, and therefore a lower net price, then n individual's budget constraint is given as:

$$(1 - t) \, wL + a = c + (1 - s) \, px, \tag{1}$$

where a is exogenous nonlabor income

Assuming separable utility functions, and that each individual's utility u depends only on leisure, consumption of the general good, and consumption of the favored good f yields:.

$$u = h \, (c, 1 - L, f) \tag{2}$$

The government provides g of the favored good,[4] and the private sector x. In the case of purely private goods, that is, no externalities are present, consumption of the favored good is:

$$f = x + g/n \tag{3}$$

The expression for f can be extended to include the more probable case of many government subsidies where externalities are present:

$$f_i = x_i + \xi \, \Sigma \, x \, j + (g/n) \, [1 + \xi \, (n - 1)] \tag{3'}$$

Finally, the government faces a budget constraint:

$$n \, (twL + spx) - pg - r = z; \tag{4}$$

where r is revenue required for other activities and z is a residual term. z is a major constraint in that it reflects whether the government is operating within a balanced budget ($z = 0$) or whether there is a budget surplus/deficit. Thus, z is an indication of governmental budget policy.

When a government wants to increase consumption of the favored good by one unit; that is, ($df = 1$), it will be maximizing a social welfare function for *n* people, subject to the budget constraint given in (4). The government can either provide a tax subsidy s, thereby encouraging the private sector to purchase the favored good, or provide the good directly. The optimal solution will be the method yielding the lowest welfare cost, as determined by comparing the effects of each method on social welfare.

The welfare cost is measured in the tax subsidy case as:

$$dW' = n \lambda (dc - (1 - t) wdL), \qquad (5)$$

where W is the social welfare function, and λ is the Lagrangian multiplier associated with the standard first-order maximizing conditions. Dividing through by $-\lambda \eta$ provides a measure of welfare costs, C_t for providing one unit of f by a tax expenditure:

$$C_t = - (\partial c/\partial s - (1\text{-}t) w \, \partial L/\partial s) \, ds - (\partial c/\partial t - (1\text{-}t) w \, \partial L/\partial t) \, dt \qquad (6)$$

Similar maximization techniques for the case of a direct government provision of the good g result in a welfare cost of :[5]

$$C_d = - (\partial c/\partial g - (1\text{-}t) w \, \partial L/\partial g) \, dg - (\partial c/\partial t - (1\text{-}t) w \, \partial L/\partial t) \, dt \qquad (7)$$

The result is that whenever the relationship $C_t > C_d$ exists for a proposed change, the argument could be made that a tax subsidy, that is, a tax expenditure would be the more appropriate policy instrument.

The derivations of (5), (6), and (7) are given in Feldstein [1980, pp. 109-117]. In addition, details are provided of how the model can be expanded to include differences in efficiencies of government versus private sector purchases. Expressions are also presented in elasticity and budget share form. The formal criterion of when $C_t > C_d$ exists is more explicitly stated. Since the purpose of this section of the paper is only to provide a framework for a later analysis of the composition of tax expenditure budgets, a condensed version is presented for the sake of brevity.

This section and the preceeding section have surveyed the tax expenditure concept and the theoretical framework that provides conditions for the use of tax subsidies. The remainder of this study basically takes the optimizing conditions as given, and then analyzes the changes in the use of tax expenditures over a defined sample period.

RESEARCH DESIGN AND METHODOLOGY

Specification of Research Issues

The research issues of interest are grouped into two broad categories: efficiency and tax equity issues. The efficiency issues are concerned with the relative use of tax expenditures in a manner that affects excess burdens or welfare losses (C_t or C_d). The approach for addressing efficiency questions is limited to comparative analyses of changes in tax expenditures over time. The three research issues of interest are:

1. The change in use of the tax expenditures method TE relative to the direct expenditures method DE; that is: Has the use of TEs been increasing or decreasing relative to DEs?
2. Changes in use of TEs by budget function relative to functional DEs; that is: Has there been a change in use of TEs versus DEs for particular budget categories?
3. Functional shifts within the TE budget by budget function; that is: Has there been a change in emphasis from one type of TE relative to other TEs?

The questions focus on the extent to which one method is used relative to the other method over time. The data indicate that both TE and DE, and most of the budget functions, increased over the sample period. Thus, pure substitution between TE and DE is not readily apparent. However, substitution does exist to some extent, once a predetermined social goal is identified.[6] Achievement of the goal requires either TE or DE (or some combination); thus, choices must be made concerning which fiscal method to use. Use of TE versus DE implies substitution to some degree, even though use of both methods has been increasing. The extent of substitutions between methods is measured in this study as the rate at which the use of one method has been changing relative to others. If TE, for example, has been increasing at a significantly faster rate over the sample period than DE, the implications are that TEs reflect a public sector choice in use of fiscal tools for budget policy purposes.

The tax equity issue of concern is whether there has been a shift in the incidence of TEs by taxpayer entity; that is: Has there been a change in the amount of TEs enjoyed by corporate taxpayers.[7] relative to TEs received by individual taxpayers? This shift in relative incidence by tax entity is measured by changes in growth rates in corporate TEs versus individual TEs during the sample period. Significant differences in relative growth rates have important implications for income and wealth distribution policies. The equity and efficiency research issues are presented as specific hypotheses and tested in subsequent sections using a data base developed in the next section.

Data Source

The sample period for the analysis is fiscal year (FY) 1972 through FY 1986. This period is selected due to consistency in definitions, measurement, and reporting of data. The desired result is selection of a sample period that is minimally affected by confounding variances due to measurement and reporting differences. An issue could be raised that the data are not consistent due to changes in tax laws over time. Thus, tax expenditure estimates of different FYs are not comparable. Tax expenditure budgets usually change, holding economic assumptions constant, because of changes in existing tax expenditures or due to new tax preferences being added to the budget. It is the effects of these changes, however, that are most significant and that this paper attempts to capture. Thus, these changes are not a problem for consistency purposes.

The primary source of tax expenditure data TE is the annual *Estimates of Federal Tax Expenditures* prepared by the U.S. Congress Joint Committee on Taxation (or its predecessor, the Joint Committee on Internal Revenue Taxation). The Joint Committee's annual *Estimates* for FY 1977 and FY 1979 were not available. Accordingly, the related Senate Budget Committee estimates of tax expenditures for FY 1977 and FY 1979 were used. A comparison of tax expenditures by the Joint Committee and the senate Budget Committee in other years indicates that similar definitions and measurement techniques are used, thus, the FY 1977 and FY 1979 data are consistent with the remainder of the sample.

Data for direct expenditures (DE) for FY 1972 through FY 1986 are obtained from the *Budget of the United States Government* prepared by the Office of Management and Budget. Direct expenditures are represented by estimated budget outlays classified by budget function.

The functional budget classifictions for direct expenditures and for tax expenditures are the same for each fiscal year. The functional categories are further grouped into six categories for expositional convenience in testing hypotheses of functional shifts of tax expenditures. A judgmental criterion is used to classify budget functions. The five budget functions with the largest tax expenditures in FY 1986 are treated as specific variables, and the balance of the tax expenditures are combined to represent the sixth category. The specific categories are commerce and housing (CH), education, training, employment, and social services (ED), health (HE), income security (IS), and general purpose fiscal assistance (GP). Selection of the five largest budget categories seemed reasonable since the next largest budget function (energy at $3.3 billion) was distinctly smaller than the fifth category (general purpose

Table 1.   Classification of Functional Budget Categories
and Major Subcategories of Tax Expenditures
(in $ billions for FY 1986)

Total Tax Expenditures	$424.5
Commerce and Housing (CH)	$194.0
Exclusion of interest on life insurance	5.7
Deductibility of mortgage interest for homeowners	27.1
Deductibility of property taxes for homeowners	10.2
Deferral of capital gains on home sales	5.9
Excess depreciation on nonrental real property	10.9
Excess depreciation on equipment	20.3
Capital gains (other than agriculture, etc.)	24.4
Investment credit	35.8
Deductibility of nonmortgage interest	8.8
Nonrecognition of gain on liquidating property distributions	8.0
Reduced corporate tax rates on first $100,000	8.4
Other	28.5
Education, Training, Employment, and Social Services (ED)	$ 32.7
Deduction for two-earner married couples	6.8
Deductibility of charitable contributions	11.2
Other	14.7
Health	$ 31.0
Exclusions for medical insurance premiums	23.7
Other	7.3
Income Security (IS)	$ 99.3
Exclusion of untaxed social security benefits	18.6
Exclusion of pension contributions and earnings, including self-employed plans and IRAs	70.2
Other	10.5
General Purpose Fiscal Assistance (GP)	$ 41.4
Exclusion of interest on municipal debt	14.8
Deductibility of nonbusiness state and local governmental taxes	25.0
Other	1.6
Other Budget Categories (0) (1)	$ 26.1

Notes: 1. Major subcategories representing over $5 billion in tax expenditures are presented for descriptive
purposes only.
2. (1) Other budget categories are national defense, international affairs, general science, space and
technology, energy, natural resources and environment, agriculture, transportation, community and
regional development, veterans benefits and services, general government and interest.
Source: Joint Committee on Taxation, *Estimates of Federal Tax Expenditures For Fiscal Years 1986-1990*
[U.S. Government Printing Office, April 12, 1985].

at $41.1 billion). The five budget functions selected represent over 93% of the total tax expenditures for FY 1986 and are presented in Table 1. Subcategories of tax expenditures that were over $5 billion in FY 1986 are also presented for descriptive purposes.

Temporal Dimensions

The temporal attributes of data are important for analyzing the results and for making policy inferences. The data are estimates of future direct and tax expenditures, as opposed to actual expenditures.[8] Thus, the emphasis is on the ex-ante policy choices reflected in the budget process rather than either the political processes involved in passing a final budget[9] or the ex-post perspective of comparing actual results with some previously estimated amount. Since the focus of this analysis is on the social choices and trade-offs reflected in the tax expenditure budgets themselves, the use of estimated expenditures is the most appropriate data choice.

Limitation of Data

There are important limitations to be considered when analyzing the data and interpreting the results. Perhaps one of the most important issues concerns the measurement of tax expenditures. Tax expenditures represent estimates of the initial or direct effects of a change in a given tax provision while holding taxpayer behavior constant; that is, the estimates do not include interactive or feedback effects. Thus, the list of tax expenditures in the tax expenditure budget are not additive in a strict sense.[10] However, the sum of the tax expenditures does indicate, in a static framework, the importance of each specific expenditure relative to other expenditures, and their relative changes over time. Since the purpose of this study is to examine the relative importance and compositional changes of expenditures as reflected in a discrete choice budget model, limitations on measurements of absolute amounts become less critical. The issue is not to determine the absolute amount of given expenditures, but to evaluate the allocation of tax expenditures within the total budget constraint. Such allocations reflect the public choices made concerning the provision of certain goods through the budget process. Such an approach is consistent with most tax expenditure studies.

Methodology

The methodological approach focuses on determining the significance of rates of change in tax and direct expenditures, both in total and by various budget categories. Accordingly, growth rates for the sample period are estimated in log form, by ordinary least squares, as follows:

$$\ln Yi = \alpha + b_iT + e \qquad (8)$$

where Y is the variable of interest, $T =$ time and e is the error term. The coefficient b_i represents the growth rate for variable Y_i. Regression estimates of the resulting coefficients provide the basis for hypothesis testing. Hypotheses are developed for each research issue previously specified. The hypothesis in general form is:

$$H_n : b_{i1} = b_{i2} = b_{i3} \ldots = b_{in}$$

Failure to reject H_n implies that there are no significant differences in growth rates of the variables in question. The specific null hypotheses to be tested are as follows:

1. Relative use hypothesis: TE and DE have changed at the same rate over the sample period; that is,

$$b_{TE} = b_{DE};$$

2. Functional use hypothesis: TEs by budget function i have changed at the same rate as DE budget categories i for the sample period; that is

$$b_{TEi} = b_{DEi};$$

3. Functional shift hypothesis: within the TE budget, functional categories i have changed at the same rate for the sample period; that is,

$$b_{TECH} = b_{TEED} = b_{TEHE} = b_{TEIS} = b_{TEGP} = b_{TEO} \qquad \text{and}$$

4. Tax entity incidence hypothesis: TE by tax entity i have changed at the same rate for the sample period; that is,

$$b_{TEC} = b_{TEI}$$

Significant differences between b's are tested by the use of Student's t-test for all hypotheses except the functional shift hypothesis. An analysis of covariance is used for the functional shift hypothesis where coefficients for six cross-sectional regressions are compared.[11] Rejection of a null hypothesis implies that the growth rates of the variables of comparison are not equal. The policy implications of this result are discussed in a subsequent section.

RESULTS

This section presents the results of the study with related interpretations. Preliminary policy implications are noted, followed by additional policy comments in the Conclusion. The results of the estimations of b are shown at Table 2. Tax expenditures grew at a rate of almost 15% per year for the

Table 2.   Results of Regression Analyses

Parameter estimates from: $\ln Yi = \alpha + b_i T + e.$

Variable (1)	α	bi	sse
Total budgeted amounts			
TE	3.84	.148	.004
DE	5.31	.110	.003
Tax expenditures by budget function			
CH	2.99	.150	.006
ED	.44	.215	.026
HE	1.17	.160	.007
IS	2.28	.156	.009
GP	1.97	.118	.007
0	1.49	.126	.007
Direct expenditures by budget function			
CH	3.24	-.215	.050
ED	2.25	.091	.015
HE	2.96	.089	.023
IS	4.05	.130	.004
GP	1.85	.003	.020
O	4.62	.110	.003
Tax expenditures by tax entity			
Corporate	2.33	.156	.006
Individual	3.59	.146	.005

Note: 1. See Table 1 for explanation of variable abbreviations.

sample period, as compared to approximately 11% for direct expenditures. Tax expenditures for commerce and housing (CH), income security (IS), and health (HE) approximated the overall trend, with education (ED) increasing at a greater rate and general purpose fiscal assitance (GP) trailing. The results also inicate that there was less variability in tax expenditures during the sample period, whereas direct expenditures, except for income security (IS), exhibited more fluctuations. The direct expenditure category that was most stable during the sample period, IS, was also the budget function with the highest growth rate. Except for direct CH, both direct and tax expenditure categories increased during the sample period, although at different rates.

The significance of the differences in growth rates of the various expenditures are tested by hypotheses 1, 2, 3, and 4, and the results are presented at Table 3. The first hypothesis that TE and DE growth rates are not significantly different is rejected at the 1% level. Rejection implies that the rates of growth between the two policy instruments differ significantly. This difference reflects the relative emphasis on the use of tax policies to achieve social objectives. Although TE and DE both exhibited positive growth rates for the sample

Table 3. Summary Statistics of Tests of Hypotheses

Hypothesis	Test Statistic	Reject/ Fail	Significance Level
1. Relative Use Hypothesis			
$b_{TE} = b_{DE}$	t = 7.696	Reject	< .01
2. Functional Use Hypotheses			
$b_{TECH} = b_{DECH}$	t = 7.155	Reject	< .01
$b_{TEED} = b_{DEED}$	t = 4.150	Reject	< .01
$b_{TEHE} = b_{DEHE}$	t = 2.713	Reject	< .05
$b_{TEIS} = b_{DEIS}$	t = 0.817	Fail[a]	—
$b_{TEGP} = b_{DEGP}$	t = 5.760	Reject	< .01
$b_{TEO} = b_{DEO}$	t = 2.103	Reject	< .05
3. Functional Shift Hypothesis (for TE)			
$b_{CH} = b_{ED} = b_{HE} = b_{IS} = b_{GP} = b_O$	$F(5,78) = 18.81$	Reject	< .01
4. Entity Incidence Hypothesis (for TE)			
$b_{TEC} = b_{TEI}$	t = 0.104	Fail[a]	—

Note: [a] Fail to reject hypothesis at 5% level of significance.

period, TE grew at a more rapid rate, indicating the increasing role of tax subsidies in the budget process.

The use of TE relative to DE is analyzed in more detail by testing specific budget functions for significant differences in growth rates during the sample period. Functional use hypotheses for each budget function are rejected for all categories except income security (IS). The implictions of rejection are that not only has there been a significant shift in the use of TE relative to De, but that the increased emphasis occurs in all budget categories except income security. This shift in functional usage of TE is presented dramatically in the case of commerce and housing (CH). The rate of growth of CH as a tax expenditure has been increasing, yet direct expenditures for CH show a negative growth rate.

The relative changes by budget function are further analyzed by the test of the functional shift hypothesis. The cross-sectional test of hypothesis 3 indicates that there are significant differences in growth rates of functions within the tax expenditure budget. Subsequent tests support the results in Table 2 that tax expenditures for education have received the most relative emphasis, although not in absolute magnitude, during the sample period. In addition, commerce, health, and income security have increased significantly faster than other TE functions.

It is interesting to note the previous failure in rejecting the functional use hypothesis for income security. The implications are that not only is TE-IS increasing at a significant rate, but that this increase is being funded at approximately the same rate by both TE and DE budget policies. In addition, as previously noted, the IS coefficients DE and TE are relatively stable across the sample period.

Finally, the test of the entity incidence hypothesis indicates that the null hypothesis of equality of growth rates could not be rejected. Failure to reject indicates that the rate at which tax expenditures have been allocated between corporate and individual taxpayers, as groups, have not differed significantly for the sample period.[12] Thus, from a long-run policy perspective, the implications are that policymakers have not been significantly biased in granting tax subsidies to either corporate or individual taxpayers for the entire sample period.

CONCLUSION

This study has provided a detailed comparative analysis of the tax expenditure budget and investigated whether significant changes have occurred in its use. The evidence indicates that tax expenditures have increased, both in total and in most budget categories, at a faster rate than direct expenditures. Four of six tax expenditure budget categories exhibited faster rates of change than the most rapidly growing DE category of income security. In addition, certain categories of tax expenditures have increased more rapidly than others. Most notable was the 21% growth rate for education.

The equity issue of a bias in the rate of change of TE to either corporate or individual taxpayers is not supported by the results. Thus, evidence was not found to support a popular opinion that corporate taxpayers have been receiving an increasing share of TE during the entire sample period. This effect, however, may be present in subsequent years.

These reports have important implications for tax and budget policy issues. Tax expenditures, both in total and by budget function, appear to be becoming increasingly important as a means of accomplishing governmental objectives. The reason for their increased usage may be due to either political expediency as advocated by some theorists, or for efficiency reasons. Regardless of the motives for their use, the results suggest that due to the relative shift in budget emphasis to tax subsidies, increasing attention and review of the tax expenditure budget may be warranted. Analysis, not only of the magnitude of the amounts, but also of the composition and overall direction of tax expenditures, provide important information for budget purposes, and highlight the important role of tax policies.

Tax expenditures represent a rich area for future research. The evidence in this study suggests that deadweight losses may exist in the use of tax expenditures. For example, externalities or public goods may be present in some budget categories, such as health and education. These tax expenditure budget functions, however, increased at a significantly faster rate than did their direct expenditure counterparts. Such implications suggest that an important area for future research would be to develop hypotheses for testing the optimality of budget variable choice; that is, a tax expenditure or a direct expenditure. Then, estimates of the associated deadweight losses could be used to determine if the appropriate policy instrument is being employed. Additionally, studies of whether tax expenditures are achieving their predetermined policy objectives would provide important information concerning the efficiency of using tax subsidies. Such future studies and continued analyses are important since tax expenditures represent the allocation of resources in the economy, distributions of wealth and are reflections of public choice.

NOTES

1. A distinction is sometimes made between a "revenue loss" (E) and an "expenditure equivalent" (EQ) definition of tax expenditures. A revenue loss definition implies that a particular activity is subsidized with after-tax dollars. The expenditure equivalent approach, however, recognizes that a direct subsidy is made with pre-tax dollars. Thus, if the direct expenditures are included in a taxpayer's income, and the recipient with a tax rate (t) is to enjoy the same after-tax benefit, the necessary expenditure equivalent will be greater than the corresponding tax expenditure; that is,

$$EQ = E/ (1\text{-}t)$$

This difference is discussed further in *Special Analysis G* [U.S. Office of Management and Budget, 1982] and has important implications when evaluating the merits of a tax expenditure with a direct subsidy for funding a particular program. Since the focus of this paper is on the relative role of the tax expenditures, the more conventional "revenue loss" definition is used.

2. The Treasury Department differs somewhat with most studies in classifying certain tax provisions as tax expenditures. The Treasury classification requires that a given rule must apply to a narrow class of transactions or taxpayers *and* a general provision must exist for which the narrowly applied provision is a clear exception. The different classification criteria do not usually result in significant differences, although some notable differences do exist. For example, additional depreciation under the Accelerated Cost Recovery System and the two wage-earner deduction for married couples are not considered to be tax expenditures using the Treasury's classification. For a more extensive discussion, see *Special Analysis G* [U.S. Office of Management and Budget, 1982].

3. For a more complete critique and discussion of the ramifications of the use of a welfare optimization criteria as opposed to other standards, see examples such as [Feldstein, 1980].

4. For purposes of this analysis, the government provision of the favored good g by either goods-in-kind or by a direct cash outlay are treated as equivalent conditions.

5.   The model incorporates the adjustments necessary to reflect that an increase in g will result in a tax increase, and that many taxpayers' purchase of x will probably be reduced by the additional government provision of g. Thus, the individual's marginal propensity to consume x becomes an integral part of the solution. For a more detailed discussion, see Feldstein [1980], pp. 112-114.

6.   Implicit in the process is that the preference and value structure of the political establishment (and the electorate) are constant over the sample period.

7.   The issue simply addresses the allocation of (TE)s between corporate and individual taxpayers. The question of thte incidence of the corporate income tax (or inversely, tax benefits) is beyond the scope of this study. In addition, equity and social benefits are implicit in the preceding efficiency issues such as the functional shift issue for TEs. Equity issues are limited in scope of discussion to the tax entity incidence question for expositional convenience.

8.   Tax expenditures estimates represent the t +1 estimates obtained from Joint Committee reports at time (t). The estimates are based upon tax laws in effect at the end of the preceeding year t − 1. Corresponding estimates of direct expenditures reflect a similar lead-lag time structure for estimates and report dates.

9.   For an analysis of the optimality conditions and issues that would be important in the passage of a budget, such as "logrolling," see examples such as Atkinson and Stiglitz [1980].

10.   An example of interactive effects that could occur, but are held constant, would be the repeal of two or more itemized deductions. The revenue effects of concurrently repealing two deductions would be less than the sum of the two individual tax expenditures. This result is due to more taxpayers opting for the standard deduction after repeal of each individual deduction. Thus, the repeal of an additional deduction may not have as much revenue impact as the repeal of the first.

For a more extensive discussion of the data limitations in the measurement of tax expenditures, see the Joint Committee on Taxation annual estimates or *Special Analysis G* [1982]. Incorporating such interdependencies would require substantial expansion of the model. Such work is currently being conducted by Robinson and Renfer [1985].

11.   The F tests for homogeneity of regression coefficients assumes not only equality of sample means, but also equality of sample variances. Test for heterogeneity of residual mean squares, such as Bartlett's test, are often sensitive; thus, standard variance ratio tests were not conducted. However, the degrees of freedom were adjusted to reflect the additional constraints imposed on the pooled regression that:

$$\sigma_1^2 = \sigma_2^2 = \sigma_3^2 = \ldots \sigma_n^2$$

For a discussion of the comparative advantage of the F test for testing equality of regression coefficients and the power of the tests involved, see examples such as Zar [1974].

12.   This result does not suggest that specific major tax bills may not be biased to a particular type of taxpayer. Instead, the results indicate that for the *entire* sample period the hypothesis could not be rejected. The implications are that any taxpayer entity biases created by specific tax law changes within the sample period offset when analyzed over the entire sample period. Tests of such intraperiod biases, although interesting, are beyond the scope of this paper.

REFERENCES

Ando, A., M.E. Blume, and I. Friend, *The Structure and Reform of the U.S. Tax System*, (The MIT Press, 1985).

Atkinson, A.B. and J.E. Stiglitz, *Lectures on Public Ecnomics* (McGraw Hill, 1980), Chapter 10.

Bittker, B.I., "Accounting for Federal 'Tax Subsidies' in the National Budget," *National Tax Journal* 22 (June 1969).

Blum, W.J., "Review of Pathways to Tax Reform: The Concept of Tax Expenditures, by Stanley Surrey," *Journal of Corporate Taxation* 1 (1975), pp. 486-91.

Break, G.F., "The Tax Expenditure Budget—The Need For a Fuller Accounting," National Tax Symposium, *Emerging Issues in Tax Policy* (May 1985).

Committee on the Budget, U.S. Senate, *Tax Expenditure Limitation and Control Act of 1981* (November 24, 1981).

Feldstein, M., "A Contribution to the Theory of Tax Expenditures: The Case of Charitable Giving," *The Economics of Taxation* (The Brookings Institute, 1980).

Goode, R., "The Economic Definition of Income," *Comprehensive Income Taxation* (The Brookings Institute, 1977).

Hanley, T.R. and G.G. Bauernfeind, "The Tax Expenditure Budget," *The Tax Advisor* (October 1976).

Jackson, P.H., "Pensions as Tax Expenditures: How the Figures Mislead," *Journal of Compensation and Benefits* (January-February 1986).

Ott, D.J. and A.F. Ott *Federal Budget Policy* 3rd ed. (The Brookings Institute, 1977).

Ramsey, F.P., "A Contribution to the Theory of Taxation," *Economic Journal* (March 1927), pp. 47-61.

Robinson, J.P. and K.M. Renfer, *An Alternative Tax Expenditure Model,* A Final Report submitted to the Arthur Young Research Program in Taxation (July 1985).

Surrey, S., "Tax Incentives as a Device for Implementing Government Policy: A Comparison with Direct Government Expenditures," *Harvard Law Review* (1970a).

———, "Federal Income Tax Reform: The Varied Approaches Necessary to Replace Tax Expenditures with Direct Governmental Assistance," *Harvard Law Review* 84 (1970b).

———, *Pathways to Tax Reform* (Harvard University Press, 1973).

Surrey, S.S. and W.F. Hellmuth, "The Tax Expenditure Budget—Response to Professor Bittker," *National Tax Journal* (December 1969).

U.S. Congress, House of Representatives, Committee on Rules, H.R. 4882, *A Bill to Include Tax Expenditure Ceilings in the Congressional Budget Resolutions* (U.S. Government Printing Office, December 1981).

U.S. Congress, Joint Committee on Taxation, *Estimates of Federal Tax Expenditures* (U.S. Government Printing Office, various years).

U.S. Congress, Senate Committee on the Budget, *Tax Expenditures* (U.S. Government Printing Office, 1976).

———, *Tax Expenditures* (U.S. Government Printing Office, 1978).

U.S. General Accounting Office, *Tax Expenditures-A Primer* (U.S. Government Printing Office, 1979).

U.S. Office of Management and Budget, *Budget of the United States Government*, fiscal years 1972 through 1986 (U.S. Government Printing Office, various years).

———, *Special Analysis G: Tax Expenditures, the Budget of the United States Government, 1982* (U.S. Government Printing Office, 1981).

———, *Special Analysis G: Tax Expenditures, the Budget of the United States Government, 1983* (U.S. Government Printing Office, February 1982).

Wagner, P.E., The Tax Expenditure Budget: An Exercise in Fiscal Impressionism (Tax Foundation Inc. 1979).

Weidenbaum, M.L., "The Case for Tax Loopholes," *A New Tax Structure for the United States,* D.H. Skadden, ed. (Bobs-Merrill Educational Publishingm 1978).

Zar, J.H., *Biostatistical Analysis* (Prentice-Hall, 1974), Chapter 12.

AN EMPIRICAL EXAMINATION OF THE INFLUENCE OF SELECTED ECONOMIC AND NONECONOMIC VARIABLES ON DECISION MAKING BY TAX PROFESSIONALS

William A. Duncan, David LaRue, and P.M.J. Reckers

ABSTRACT

The following study examines the judgement processes of 133 professional tax managers as they render advice to clients. Subjects examined hypothetical tax scenarios and made income reporting recommendations to clients. Beyond the facts of the case, the authors hypothesized that five factors would influence the professionals' advice. Those factors included the probability of IRS audit, the risk preferences and the year-end payment status of the client, and the technical knowledge and the recent experiences of the professionals, themselves, with other client audits. Only the probability of audit failed to register significance in the experiment. This variable was, however, manipulated at more modest and realistic levels than in several other recent studies of taxpayer compliance.

Advances in Taxation, Volume 2, pages 91-106.
Copyright © 1989 by JAI Press Inc.
All rights of reproduction in any form reserved.
ISBN: 0-89232-783-9

INTRODUCTION

Tax evasion is clearly a problem of significance [Jackson, 1985], and efforts to capture the tax revenue associated with the "underground economy" absorb much of the Internal Revenue Service's (IRS) enforcement budget. Additional and significant revenue losses result from activities which cannot be characterized as evasion. The legal minimization of the tax burden, through such legal activities as taking other investment and business deductions, is the subject of enforcement effort when it encroaches on the "gray" area separating evasion and acceptable tax avoidance.

As the tax law has grown in complexity, distinguishing between tax evasion and tax avoidance has become more difficult. In many instances, the legal right to a deduction turns on technical determinations which are clearly beyond the expertise of taxpayers. Some determinations test the knowledge and judgment of even the most experienced practitioners. This may be one reason that approximately half of the tax returns in the United States are completed by paid preparers [Department of the Treasury, 1985-1986].

Since preparers must make compliance decisions for taxpayers when technical issues arise, they represent an important third element in the relationship between the taxpayer and the government. However, while much research has recently been directed at examining issues of taxpayer evasion/compliance, very little of that research has considered the influence of the professional tax preparer.

Historically, CPAs and other preparers have acted as advocates for taxpayers and have been expected to recommend the most advantageous possible legal position for their clients, perhaps subject to the client's expressed preferences. That is, it is arguable that a preparer would adopt less aggressive legal positions for those clients who lack temerity, are faced with an unstable financial position or who greatly fear the audit process.

Recognizing the influence of tax preparers on compliance and believing that enforcement efforts have been inadequate, Congress and the IRS have acted to shift a portion of compliance monitoring to practitioners. As a result, tax preparers may be subject to fines or other sanctions for failing to properly apply the law or for failing to disclose positions taken in opposition to stated IRS policy, as well as for other actions. To date, relatively few preparers have run afoul of these provisions, and the fines for those who have done so have been modest. Still, the economics of adopting or recommending an aggressive position have been altered and may be altered more in the future. In this new environment, it is unknown whether, and/or to what extent, professional tax preparers' judgments may be influenced by client preferences and/or by the tax preparer's personal disposition or experience. As the study of the general compliance/evasion problem develops, and as we begin to study the efficacy of various new governmental efforts to improve compliance, we may be well advised to consider the place of professional tax preparers, and the relation of their recommendations to current and potential levels of sanctions and fines and to varying client attitudes and preferences.

For these reasons, preparer behavior and some of the factors which may influence this behavior are the subject of this work. The research reported in this paper builds on fundamental economic utility theory. But the analysis goes beyond that theory to consider the influence on the advice rendered by the preparer of (1) client preferences, (2) the year-end payment status of the taxpayer client, and (3) individual preparer characteristics. The next section discusses the reasons specific factors were selected for inclusion in the experiment and frames testable hypotheses.

BACKGROUND AND HYPOTHESES

Kinsey [1986] discusses the use of economic theory to understand an individual's tax compliance/noncompliance behavior and to determine the optimal level of tax evasion (see also Allingham and Sandmo [1972]; Srinivasan [1973]; Weiss [1976]; and Lewis [1982]). Within the traditional economic framework, an optimal level of evasion is a function of the potential costs and benefits of the action. Economic benefits and costs, in turn, are a function of the amount of nonreported income, the tax rate, the probability of detection (audit), and the size of the penalty. Further, it is generally assumed that the taxpayer's behavior conforms to the Von Neumann-Morganstern axioms for behavior under uncertainty, which specify that the taxpayer's cardinal utility function has income as its only argument, and that marginal utility is everywhere positive and strictly decreasing, so that the person is generally risk averse.

This model may also apply to tax professionals who act on behalf of taxpayers. Madeo, Schepanski, and Uecker [1987] recently examined tax preparer reactions to experimentally manipulated income levels, tax rate progressivity, size of penalty, and likelihood of detection (the last manipulated through varying the source of income.) The probability of detection was found to exert by far the strongest influence. It must be noted, however, that the tax preparers in Madeo, Schepanski, and Uecker's study role-played as taxpayers, not as professional advisors. Kaplan, Reckers, Boyd, and West [1988] also report that experimentally manipulated probability of audit registered a significant influence on the advice rendered by their professional tax preparer subjects.

Other authors have challenged the adequacy of the economic model (see reviews and discussions by Lewis [1982]; Kinsey [1986]; and Jackson and Milliron [1986]). Recent advances in utility theory, especially prospect theory, proposed by Kahneman and Tversky [1979] suggest a very different view of behavior under uncertainty than is represented by the traditional model.

Among important departures are observations that: (1) Income may not be the only argument in the taxpayer's utility function; (2) The taxpayer's utility function may be different for perceived opportunities for gain versus perceived potential for loss reduction (thus, marginal utility for income is not always positive and decreasing); and (3) High probabilities and low probabilities are often over-weighted. Accordingly, in the following study we attempt both to incorporate traditional economic theory and consider other recent advances.

In this study we manipulated the probability of audit (evasion detection) in testing the comparative strength of the fundamental economic model. As noted above, this was the most significant factor found by Madeo, Schepanski, and Uecker [1987] in their recent modeling of taxpayer compliance, and is a significant factor in the Kaplan et al. [1988] study. Further, it is also the element of the general economic model most easily changed by government regulators and legislators. In fact, recent Congressional action has significantly increased the IRS operational budget to provide for more audits, for the purpose of increasing revenues through evasion deterrence and capture of "lost" taxes.[1] In recent studies of taxpayer behavior, the influence of the probability of audit was examined by Witte and Woodbury [1985] and Chang, Nichols, and Schultz [1987], and in both instances the influence was found to be highly significant. However, the levels of manipulation of this variable in prior studies have frequently been great, perhaps extreme, and this may account for the high significance observed for this variable.

As an example, Chang, Nichols, and Schultz [1987] manipulated the variable at levels of 10%, 50%, and 90% probability of audit, and Kaplan et al. [1988] at 10% and 50%. Madeo et al. [1987] also effected an extreme manipulation by contrasting the probability of audit that develops from not reporting salary income with that which develops from not reporting self-employment income. In this study we employ more realistic levels of audit probability. We expected that at more realistic levels, given the factual case used, manipulations of the probability of audit would either not significantly influence professionals' judgments or would influence them less than has been suggested in prior studies. This finding would be especially relevant given the government's focus on this method as a means to improve compliance.

Another reason for using less extreme levels of audit probability is the propensity to overweigh high and low probabilities. That is, high probabilities tend to be interpreted as approaching certainty, and low probabilities tend to be totally dismissed. This does not conform with classical Von Neumann-Morganstern modeling of decision making under uncertainty, but it is consistent with prospect theory and recent tests of that theory by Chang et al. [1987]. Hence, this related research suggests that subjects categorically interpret very low and very high probability manipulations as exhibiting greater certainty than is warranted and that they thus overreact to the factor.

Further, the need to use more realistic rates than 10% and 50% [Kaplan et al., 1988] or 10% and 90% [Chang et al., 1987] was deemed critical in this study because our subjects were professional tax preparers. Their knowledge of actual levels would limit the breadth of believable manipulations.

In summary, then, a number of recent empirical, experimental studies using taxpayers have found that the probability of audit significantly influences compliance decisions. In addition, two studies using tax practitioners supported this finding, although in one of these studies the tax practitioner subjects role-played taxpayers. Practical and theoretical arguments suggest: (1) The need to use more "realistic" rates than have been common to these prior studies, and (2) The need to consider the role of professional tax preparers in the compliance decision process. Our first hypothesis, thus, is:

H_1: Professional tax preparers will provide more aggressive advice to taxpayer clients when the probability of audit is relatively lower.

As an alternative to relying exclusively on the factual elements of the tax case and economic information concerning the probability of audit, the professional tax preparer might offer advice in keeping with the expressed desires or orientation of the tax client. It might be speculated that the tax advisor would render different advice to a risk-seeking client than would be rendered to a risk-averse client. Such varying professional responses might be a conscious strategy or an unconscious bias on the part of the tax professionals and the response may either be supportive or may try to mitigate (or dampen) the client's biases in deciding tax issues. The influence of client biases on tax professionals' decisions/advice have been examined with mixed results by Roark [1985], Sanders [1986], and Kaplan, Reckers, West, and Boyd [1988]. These authors attempted to examine the influence of client bias by manipulating, within case scenarios, client risk profiles. Roark [1985] found significant results; Kaplan et al. [1988] found nonsignificant results; and Sanders' [1986] results appear potentially uninterpretable. The negative findings of Kaplan et al., may be attributable to the presence of other very strong manipulations as the client preference factor alone was manipulated between subjects. It is arguable that artificially enhanced reactions to strong within subject manipulations may have swamped the relatively pallid client preference manipulation. These considerations lead to the assessed need to further explore this variable, and to our second hypothesis:

H_2: Professional tax preparers will provide more aggressive advice to taxpayer-clients who are relatively more risk-seeking.

In addition to examining the influence of client preference, from the perspective of a general client propensity, we also attempted to manipulate related phenomena at a situation-specific level. Specifically, we examined whether advice to taxpayers who overpaid estimated taxes and withholdings during the year was different than advice given to those who were underpaid at that point. Logically, the necessity of making a large payment on April 15 can be quite disruptive to family budget and cash flows—and intuitively, this certainly represents a more odious prospect than that of receiving a smaller refund. It can be conjectured that individuals facing the prospect of large payments will seek relief by more aggressively approaching tax reporting alternatives. This conjecture, further, may have roots in selected elements of prospect theory, previewed above. That is, taxes saved through the underreporting of income variously could be viewed as a gain (larger refund) or as a reduced loss (smaller payment required) depending on the amount of taxes withheld during the year.

Further, according to prospect theory, taxpayers' utility functions are likely different for gains versus losses (anecdotal evidence of this is found in the large wagers of contestants on television game shows when they see themselves in a gain situation), and thus different compliance decisions may develop in relation to prior withholding status. The recent findings of Chang et al. [1987] support this perspective; the findings of Jackson and Spicer [1985] do not. Chang et al. used large-city, middle-income executives as subjects; Jackson and Spicer employed jurors of modest income from Colorado Springs.

We felt that further research of this variable among practicing professionals was important. Of practical significance, we believe, is the realization that government has the ability to regulate the year-end over/under payment status of its citizens through regulations related to employer withholdings and individuals' payments of estimated taxes. Relatedly, the tax revision of 1986 requires estimated tax payments equal to 90% of taxes due in order to avoid penalty, whereas previously only 80% was required to avoid penalty.[2] Further, virtually every taxpayer is familiar with the ongoing efforts of the IRS to revise the W-4 withholding form. Recently, it may also be recalled, the government proposed and then withdrew rules requiring financial institutions to withhold taxes related to interest paid to depositors. Given the mixed empirical results to date, the theoretical grounding and the government's ability and willingness to influence this factor, we included this variable in our study. Thus, our third hypothesis is:

H₃: Professional tax preparers will provide more aggressive advice to taxpayer clients when the taxpayer has underpaid estimated taxes and withholdings and faces further payments at year end.

To address these hypotheses, a three factor, fully-crossed between-subjects design was adopted. The statistic envisioned for analysis was Analysis of

Covariance which would also allow for the nonmanipulated, but measured covariates discussed below.

In addition to biases possibly evoked by the client's condition, the advice of the tax professional might also be influenced by characteristics of the tax professionals themselves. This has frequently been found to be the case among auditors in the conduct of their professional responsibilities (see Gibbins [1984], Libby [1985], or Kida [1984] for a related discussion). Among these characteristics might be experience, technical knowledge, age, and perceptions of the equity and fairness of the tax code.

Regarding the first characteristic, experience, three dimensions come to mind in developing an operational measure. They are (1) general experience as measured by the number of years in tax practice, (2) specific experience with the particular type of tax issues engaged in the case scenario provided in the research instrument, and (3) recent experience with the IRS over client disputes, that is, recent won/loss average.

The authors chose to measure and consider all three dimensions. Item (2) was measured in two ways. First, subjects were asked to self-rate their knowledge in the area of real estate tax shelters—the basis of the experimental scenarios in the study. Alternatively, the subjects were asked to indicate the percentage of their tax clients who engage in real estate tax shelters. We expected that subjects with more general experience as well as specific knowledge would recommend more aggressive tax postures given the set of facts provided in the study. This leads to hypotheses 4 and 5:

H_4: Professional tax preparers with more years of tax practice will provide more aggressive advice to taxpayer clients.

H_5: Professional tax preparers with more technical knowledge in the area of real estate tax shelters will provide more aggressive advice to taxpayer clients.

Tax preparers with relatively high rates of successful defense of clients in disputes with the IRS (the third type of experience) were expected to be more aggressive than those with more negative recent experiences. Our sixth hypothesis, thus, was:

H_6: Professional tax preparers with greater recent success with the IRS over client disputes will provide more aggressive advice to taxpayer clients.

Age and perceptions of the equity and fairness of the tax code have been examined in innumerable studies with taxpayers. Findings from these variables are highly mixed (see Lewis [1982] or Jackson and Milliron [1986] for literature review of the topic). Still, as the cost to measure these items was negligible, the authors did so in an attempt to (1) contribute to this aspect of the literature, but more importantly to (2) avoid cloaking an influence of primary interest through unmeasured variables. The direction of the influence of age is difficult to predict, however, given the extant literature; the hypotheses regarding the other items less so. Still, since these factors were not significant in the study, the formal hypotheses development is omitted (related literature of possible interest to the reader may be found in Adams [1965]; Walster, Walster, and Bershield [1978]; Groenland and van Veldhoven [1983]; and Kinsey [1986]).

METHOD

The study examines the recommendations of tax professionals to hypothetical taxpayers in an experimental setting. The subjects were presented with short fact situations and asked to give advice to the taxpayer involved. This approach allowed the authors to control for extraneous variables and to manipulate the variables of interest. The subjects, task, and independent and dependent variables are discussed in order below.

Subjects

The subjects were 133 professionals employed by a "Big-8" accounting firm over a widely dispersed geographical area within the United States. They were tax specialists with three to seven years experience and were attending a professional training seminar organized by the firm.

Task

The task required that the subjects recommend a course of action involving the deduction of depreciation for property which may have been purchased at an inflated price. Bill Nelson, the person for whom the advice was rendered, was described as a client of several years' standing and the president of a major audit client of the firm.

More specifically, Bill Nelson was described as having paid $50,000 down to purchase two condominiums located in Scottsdale, Arizona. The total purchase price was $400,000, with $350,000 of the purchase effected with the execution of a nonrecourse note payable to the developer. This note was secured by the land and buildings, but the taxpayer had no personal liability to pay. The $400,000 purchase price was allocated $100,000 to land and $300,000 to structures. Comparable owner-occupied condominiums (single units) were noted to have sold for about $175,00 per unit ($50,000 allocated to land and $125,000 to structures). On the other hand, sales of similar units by other tax shelter syndicates had reached the $200,000 price paid by Bill Nelson (with the same land and structure allocation). If the $300,000 invested in buildings is accepted as the basis for depreciation, a deduction of $33,000 will result. The case states that "Bill suspects that the IRS may question the valuation of the property, believing it overvalued."

The tax case describes the "Risk Assessment" as follows. "You realize that the IRS may argue that the condos may be overvalued by as much as $25,000 each or $50,000 in total (all related to the structure)."

Each practitioner rendered advice on identical investment situations and a *single set of manipulated variables.* In other words, only one case was presented to each subject and only the three variables described below were altered from respondent to respondent.

Independent Variables

The experiment included eight independent variables—five measured variables and three manipulated variables. The five measured variables included (1) age, (2) years of experience as a tax consultant, (3) percentage of clients in tax sheltered investments, (4) whether recent client audit experience ended favorably or not (percentage of favorable disposition), and (5) the tax preparer's self-assessment of his or her knowledge of tax shelter investments.

The three manipulated variables consisted of (1) the probability that the taxpayer's return would be audited, (2) whether the taxpayer expected to pay additional tax or receive a refund of tax overpayments, and (3) the taxpayer's degree of caution or aggressiveness in tax matters. The result is a 2 x 2 x 2 matrix. The three manipulated variables are described in order below.

Audit Probability

Two levels of audit probability were included in the experiment. The low level was set at 10%, while the higher level was presented as 25%. Under the lower level of audit probability, the case read in part, "From a friend of yours within the local IRS District Director's Office, you know that the Director has decided that tax shelters are a low priority item for audit in the Scottsdale area. There is about a 10% chance of audit for any real estate shelter in this district." In the higher level probability setting, "low priority" and "10%" were replaced by "medium priority" and "25%," with no other changes in wording. Describing the audit probability estimation as information from an "inside" source is felt to improve the effectiveness of the audit probability manipulation.

Overpayment or Underpayment of Estimated Tax

Taxpayers who were expected to receive a refund were described in part as follows. "Bill ... finds that he has *significantly OVERPAID his 1986 estimated tax liability"* (Emphasis in original). This variable was manipulated by substituting *UNDERPAID* for *OVERPAID* in the case materials.

Level of Aggressiveness or Caution

The cases presented taxpayers with two levels of aggressiveness (cautious and very aggressive). In the cautious case the taxpayer was characterized as follows:

> Bill is a very conservative taxpayer but this year he finds that he has significantly [OVERPAID or UNDERPAID] his 1986 estimated tax liability. Bill does not view paying taxes as a profound moral issue and he naturally prefers to pay less than more. Bill genuinely fears the prospect of an IRS audit, however. He was audited six years ago with unfavorable findings. As a result, he generally shies away from anything gray or aggressive.

The more aggressive taxpayer was described as follows:

> Bill could be described as a generally "aggressive," risk-taking taxpayer. This year he finds that he has *significantly* [OVERPAID or UNDERPAID] his 1986 estimated tax liability. Bill does not view paying taxes as a moral issue and he naturally prefers to pay less than more. Furthermore, he believes that it makes good business sense to adopt an aggressive posture in the resolution of gray areas of the tax law. Bill is not particularly afraid of an IRS audit.

Only respondents correctly answering manipulation checks on the above variables were retained in the analyses. Accordingly, twelve subjects were deleted.[3]

Dependent Measure

The subjects were asked to indicate on a scale ranging from 0 to 10 (anchored at the lower end by "Strongly Discourage" and at the higher end by "Strongly Recommend") how they would advise this client. Specifically, the question asked, "How strongly would you recommend that Bill claim the ACRS deduction, as noted above, with an established property basis of $300,000 for the property (and $100,000 for the land)?" Data were analyzed using Analysis of Covariance statistics.

Table 1. Summary Experimental Statistics

1a. ANOVA Statistics: (n = 133)

Source of Variation	Mean Square	F-Score	Tail Probability
SIGNIFICANT COVARIATES			
Recent IRS Success	21.813	4.24	.041
Percentage of Clients in Tax Shelters	32.991	6.41	.012
FACTORS			
Probability of Audit	0.583	0.11	.737
Client Risk Preference	73.750	14.33	.001
Year End Payment Status	18.699	3.63	.059
SIGNIFICANT INTERACTIONS			
None			

1b. Adjusted Cell Means: Scale 0-10; 0 = Strongly discourage, 10 = Strongly encourage

		Audit Probability	
		Low (10%)	High (25%)
RISK SEEKING CLIENT	Overpaid Status	5.3 (n = 15)	5.5 (n = 13)
	Underpaid Status	6.8 (n = 14)	6.6 (n = 15)
ADVERSE RISK CLIENT	Overpaid Status	8.0 (n = 19)	6.9 (n = 20)
	Underpaid Status	7.3 (n = 20)	8.0 (n = 17)

RESULTS

Neither age nor number of years as a tax consultant were found to be significant in this experiment. These variables were measured in response to prior research suggesting that both age and years of experience may be significant determinants of behavior and, although not found to be significant in this context, were not the primary thrust of the research.

By contrast, knowledge, as measured by the percentage of the tax consultant's clients that were reportedly involved in tax shelter investments, was found to be significant at the .05 level (.0126) (see Table 1). As expected, the more actively the subjects were involved in advising tax shelter investors, the more aggressive the positions they adopted.

Similarly, those tax consultants reporting higher percentages of favorable audit experiences over the last two years also adopted more aggressive positions in this experiment. This covariate was significant at the .05 level (.0417).

Interestingly, the change in audit probability (from 10% to 25%) was not significant. This result may be contrasted with that found in other studies (e.g., Chang et al. [1987], Madeo et al. [1987], and Kaplan et al. [1988]) in which audit probability was significantly related to the tax positions that subjects adopted. In those earlier studies, however, audit probabilities were varied at more extreme levels. The lesser, but still 150% increase, in audit probability employed in this work (from 10% to 25%) remains a fairly strong treatment given current personnel and budgetary constraints. But apparently the increase in audit probability at these levels is not strong enough to affect tax recommendations by this group of consultants (subjects indicated in debriefing questions that they concurred that audit rates varied appreciably across districts and that experimental manipulations were not unreasonable).

The client's risk orientation was significantly related (at the .01 level) to the position adopted by the tax consultant but in a surprisingly counterintuitive fashion. The more timid the taxpayer, the more aggressive the consultant, and, the more aggressive the taxpayer, the less strong the position recommended by the tax consultant. If this result is confirmed, it suggests that tax professionals may serve to moderate taxpayer behavior. This may or may not be desirable from a compliance view depending on whether most taxpayers are risk-averse or risk-seeking and on whether these biases systematically vary with avoidance opportunities.

The taxpayer's tax payment status (overpaid, underpaid) was marginally significant (at .059). This result was in the direction predicted, with consultants adopting more aggressive positions if the taxpayer was underpaid and making less aggressive recommendations if the taxpayer expected a refund of taxes paid. A significant result would correspond to the results predicted by prospect theory as discussed in the work of Chang, Nichols, and Schultz [1987].

LIMITATIONS

Interpretation of the findings of this experiment must be tempered by consideration of the limitations endemic to this type of research. Our subjects were not randomly selected from the population of professional tax preparers. Accordingly, generalization of results cannot be made without risks. This danger may be aggravated in this case as all subjects were drawn from one public accounting firm. While the subjects were drawn from a wide geographical base, firm-specific training or philosophy may have influenced their responses. There is no way to assess this possibility short of replication with other subjects drawn from other firms. The authors naturally encourage this effort.

The subjects' responses also may not generalize to cases based upon other tax issues or relating to clients exhibiting different characteristics and needs. For example, within our scenarios, we chose to depict the tax client as also an important audit client of the public accounting firm. We previously discussed our purposes for doing so. Nonetheless, subjects' responses may have been biased by this imposed condition. Again, future research addressing this issue is our only means to evaluate the significance of this limitation.

It may also be worth noting that the tax shelter issues and facts presented in our cases might not display the ambiguity so often present in professional tax preparer deliberations. To the extent that the ambiguity of the facts and the law may themselves serve to reduce the probability of audit by the IRS or the tenacity with which the Service pursues selected items, subjects responses may not generalize to other conditions.

Lastly, we remind the reader that ours was a between-subjects design. The issue of whether to use a within- or between-subjects design is basic to an experiment. Statistically, within-subjects designs gain power as compared to between-subjects designs by having the individual participant serve as the control or "block" effect. The amount of the increase in power in a within-subject design will relate directly to how great differences are among individuals on dimensions not measured (here individual differences in training, aggressiveness, philosophy, and the like). To the extent that individuals differ, the within-subject approach gains strength because it controls for individual differences (see Kirk [1982] Chapter 6 for a detailed, mathematical discussion of the differences in strengths of approaches). A between-subjects approach does not control these differences and considers them as "random error." The result is that significant underlying relationships may not be detected or detected at low levels of confidence.

Several popular statistically-oriented books (e.g., Kirk [1982] and Winer [1971]) have emphasized that this design decision should be made based on factors such as subject availability; within-subjects designs need fewer subjects. The primary cited disadvantage has been restrictive assumptions pertaining to variance-covariance matrices of replies. Typically, the solution suggested for this problem has been to use a conservative measure originally proposed by Geisser and Greenhouse [1958] or Hotelling's T [Hotelling, 1939].

On the other hand, other authors (e.g., Carlsmith, Ellsworth, and Aronson [1976]; Cook and Campbell [1979]; Orne [1962]; Riecken [1962], and Weber and Cook [1972]) have cautioned researchers to be aware of potential "demand characteristics" which are possible in many behavioral experiments, and most probable in within-subject behavioral experiments. Pany and Reckers [1987] conducted an experiment to assess the extent of this danger in behavioral auditing research. They concluded the danger was very real and the influence of demand effects very great. We were swayed by the latter cited proponents of between-subjects designs. While we believe the benefits of between-subjects designs far outweigh the limitations, and we recommend between-subjects design to others, the reader is alerted to the limitations of the method.

DISCUSSION

The failure of tax preparers to respond to changes in audit risk creates an interesting dilemma for Congress. Tax policymakers have generally assumed that the economic model of taxpayer behavior will obtain and that increasing audit probabilities, or taxpayers' perceiving that audit probabilities are increasing, will draw out additional revenue. However, taxpayers frequently exhibit such great uncertainty regarding the likelihood of audit as to prompt them to seek professional assistance. Beck and Jung [1987] have argued that two of the most important services sought from the tax professional are a reduction in the taxpayer's uncertainty regarding the probability of audit and an increase in the taxpayer's probability of successfully defending reporting options. At least with respect to the aggressive ACRS deduction described in this setting, this research suggests that increasing audit probabilities, within realistic constraints, may not significantly affect decision making by tax consultants in advising their clients. If such measures do not motivate tax preparers and large numbers of individuals rely on paid preparers for compliance advice, the effectiveness of this approach by Congress and the IRS is sharply reduced.

Implications regarding preparer sensitivity to recent success/failure with other clients and the IRS are potentially many and likely controversial. Clarification of the likelihood of successful defense of a reporting choice constitutes one of the fundamental services provided by the tax professional to the client. Tax practitioner judgments develop from ongoing interaction with the Service and its local personnel. To the degree that local officers of the IRS vary in the vigor with which they apply or interpret selected sections of law or vary in the disposition of local personnel (as regards confrontational attitudes, tenacity, and the like), tax professionals, in rendering advice, may serve to accentuate these regional, district, or local office differences. Our results are consistent with this speculation.

Our findings relating to the influence of client preferences, considered in the context of prior research findings, allow no clear implications to be drawn at this time. It is not clear to the authors why the tax professionals engaged in Roark's [1985] work provided more aggressive advice to risk-seeking clients but the tax professionals participating in our study apparently sought to mitigate client biases. Different tax issues, different tax professionals, different tax scenarios, and variable manipulations are all possible explanatory factors.

Further research in the area seems necessary if we are to untangle apparently convergent influences.

Finally, our findings provide only limited support for increasing the extent of tax withholding and the requirements for payments of estimated income taxes during the year as a means of increasing tax compliance. However, these results which, are consistent with prospect theory, were only very marginally significant.

NOTES

1. The Reagan administration proposed a fiscal 1989 budget increase of $89.2 million to be devoted to Examinations and Appeals and an additional $17.4 million for Investigations, Collections, and Taxpayer Services. These increases are separate and distinct from salary increases. See Timberlake (February 22, 1988), p. 759.

2. There are other exceptions to the imposition of the penalty, but they are not relevant to the discussion.

3. In experiments of the type reported in this paper, it is appropriate to consider alternative explanations that might explain why subjects' responses to a manipulated variable may be found weak or insignificant. In addition to the obvious possibility that the item being manipulated is simply not important to the subjects when addressing the decision task at hand, it is also possible that the manipulation did not "take" for some of the subjects. That is, the manipulation treatment may have been too subtle or unperceived by the respondents. Accordingly,to aid in the interpretation of insignificant main effects (if they developed), the authors included manipulation checks. Illustratively, pertaining to the case manipulation of audit probability, subjects were asked at the end of the experiment: "Without looking back, what was the likelihood of IRS audit of real estate shelters in the Miami (Washington, D.C., and similar) district?"

REFERENCES

Adams, J., "Inequity in Social Exchange," in L. Berkowitz (ed.), *Advances in Experimental Social Psychology* (Academic Press, 1965).

Allingham, M. G. and A. Sandmo, "Income Tax Evasion: A Theoretical Analysis," *Journal of Public Economics* (November 1972), pp. 323-338.

Beck, Paul J. and W. O. Jung, "Taxpayer Compliance Under Uncertainty," Unpublished working paper (August 1987).

Carlsmith, J. M., P. C. Ellsworth, and E. Aronson, *Methods of Research in Social Psychology* (Addison Wesley, 1976).

Chang, O.H., D.R. Nichols, and J.J. Schultz, "Taxpayer Attitudes Toward Tax Audit Risk," *Journal of Economic Psychology* (December 1987), pp. 299-309.

Cook, T.D. and D.T. Campbell, *Quasi-Experimentation: Design and Analysis Issues for Field Settings* (Rand McNally 1979).

Department of the Treasury, *Statistics of Income Bulletin* (Winter, 1985-1986).

Geisser, S., and S. Greenhouse, "An Extension of Box's Results on the Use of the F-distribution in multivariate analysis," *Annals of Mathematical Statistics* (1958), pp. 885-891.

Gibbins, M., "Propositions About the Psychology of Professional Judgment in Public Accounting," *Journal of Accounting Research* (Spring 1984), pp. 103-125.

106 WILLIAM A. DUNCAN, DAVID LaRUE, and P.M.J. RECKERS

Groenland, E. and G. van Veldhoven, "Tax Evasion Behavior: A Psychological Framework," *Journal of Economic Psychology* (1983), pp. 129-144.

Hotelling, H., "The Generalization of Students Ratio," *Annals of Mathematical Statistics* (1939), pp. 360-378.

Jackson, B., "Stemming Income Tax Evasion," *Journal of Accountancy* (January 1985), pp. 76-80.

Jackson, B. R. and V. C. Milliron, "Tax Compliance Research: Findings, Problems and Prospects," *Journal of Accounting Literature* (1986), pp. 125-165.

Jackson, B. and M. Spicer, "An Investigation of Under or Overwithholding of Taxes on Taxpayer Compliance," Arthur Young Tax Research Grant Report (1985).

Kahneman, D. and A. Tversky, "Prospect Theory: An Analysis of Decision Under Risk," *Econometrica* (1979), pp. 263-291.

Kaplan, S., P. Reckers, J. Boyd and S. West, "An Examination of the Recommendations and Signing Decisions of Professional Tax Preparers," Unpublished working paper (January 1988).

Kida, T., "The Impact of Hypothesis Testing Strategies on Auditors Use of Judgment Data," *Journal of Accounting Research* (Spring 1984), pp. 332-340.

Kinsey, K.A., "Advocacy and Perception: The Structure of Tax Practice," Unpublished working paper (June 1986).

Kirk, R.G., *Experimental Design: Procedures for the Behavioral Sciences*, 2nd ed. (Brooks/Cole, 1982).

Lewis, A., *The Psychology of Taxation* (St. Martin's Press, 1982).

Libby, R., "Availability and the Generation of Hypotheses in Analytical Review," *Journal of Accounting Research* (Autumn 1985), pp. 648-667.

Madeo, S., A. Schepanski, and W. Uecker, "Modeling Judgments of Taxpayer Compliance," *The Accounting Review* (April 1987).

Orne, M., "On the Social Psychology of the Psychological Experiment," *American Psychologist* (1962), pp. 776-783.

Pany, K. and P. Reckers, "Within- vs. Between-Subjects Experimental Designs: A Study of Demand Effects," *Auditing: A Journal of Practice and Theory* (Fall 1987) pp. 39-53.

Riecken, H. W., "A Program for Research in Social Psychology, in *Decision Values and Groups*, N. F. Washburne, (ed.) (Pergamon Press, 1962) pp. 482-496.

Roark, S., *An Examination of the Effect of Client, Subject and Firm Risk on Legal Task Research*, Unpublished Dissertation (Arizona State University, 1985).

Sanders, D. L., *An Empirical Investigation of Tax Practitioners' Decisions Under Uncertainty: A Prospect Theory Approach*, Unpublished Dissertation (Arizona State University, 1986).

Srinivasan, T., "Tax Evasion: A Model," *Journal of Public Economics* (1973), pp. 339-346.

Timberlake, M., "President Submits Budget to Congress," *Tax Notes* (Feb. 22, 1988), pp. 757-758.

Walster, E., G. M. Walster, and E. Bershield, *Equity: Theory and Research* (Allyn and Bacon, 1978).

Weber, S.J., and T.D. Cook, "Subject Effects in Laboratory Research: An Examination of Subject Roles, Demand Characteristics and Valid Inference," *Psychological Bulletin* (1972, Vol. 77), pp. 273-295.

Weiss, L., "The Desirability of Cheating Incentives and Randomness in the Optimal Income Tax," *Journal of Political Economy* (1976), pp. 1343-1352.

Winer, B.J., *Statistical Principles in Experimental Design*, 2nd ed. (McGraw Hill, 1971)

Witte, A. and D. Woodbury, "The Effect of Tax Laws and Tax Administration on Tax Compliance: The Case of the U. S. Individual Income Tax," *National Tax Journal* (March 1985), pp. 1-14.

THE CHARITABLE
CONTRIBUTION DEDUCTION:
NEW EVIDENCE OF A TAX INCENTIVE EFFECT

Richard B. Toolson

ABSTRACT

This study used an experiment to examine the tax incentive effect of the charitable contribution deduction. Specifically, this study tested whether the elasticity of giving has an absolute value greater than or equal to one. The experimental task consisted of asking subjects to make budgeting decisions, including a budgeting decision with respect to charitable contributions, based on an assumed income level. Two factors, marginal tax rate and deductibility, were each manipulated at two levels. A regression model indicated that the absolute value for the elasticity of giving is greater than one, suggesting that the charitable contribution deduction is relatively efficient.

The Revenue Act of 1917 initially allowed charitable contributions to be deducted in computing taxable income [Seidman, 1938]. Legislative discussion prior to the enactment of this act clarified that the purpose of the deduction was to influence taxpayers to make contributions to charity [U.S. Congress, 1917, p. 6728]. The U.S. Supreme Court has reiterated that the intention

Advances in Taxation, Volume 2, pages 107-129.
Copyright © 1989 by JAI Press Inc.
All rights of reproduction in any form reserved.
ISBN: 0-89232-783-9

of Congress in allowing the charitable contribution deduction was to encourage charitable giving [Helvering v. Bliss, 293 US 144 (1934)]. The federal government arguably benefits from encouraging charitable giving in that charitable institutions may be viewed as providing public goods and services that might otherwise have to be provided through government expenditures [Lawrence and Saghafi, 1984, p. 569].

Whenever any tax law is enacted, including the charitable contribution deduction, an implicit assumption exists that the law will achieve its intended behavioral purpose. Prudent tax policy should require periodic reappraisal of whether existing law is, in fact, achieving its intended purpose. In the case of the charitable contribution deduction, empirical evidence may be generated to help assess the assumption that the amount given to charity will increase as a result of favorable tax treatment. If increased giving is not accomplished by the deduction, there may be cause for repeal of this provision of the tax law.

The primary purpose of this study was to determine if the charitable contribution deduction is currently achieving its intended purpose, that is, to act as an incentive to encourage charitable giving. An experiment was performed in which the tax variable was explicitly manipulated in order to assess whether the charitable contribution tax deduction influences the level of charitable contributions. The results of the study do indicate that the deduction influences the level of charitable contributions.

In this paper, the theoretical framework for the charitable contribution deduction is presented. Previous charitable contribution deduction studies are reviewed. The research design and data collection methods employed in this study are explained, and the results of the study are reported. Finally, implications and limitations of the study are noted.

THEORETICAL FRAMEWORK FOR THE CHARITABLE CONTRIBUTION DEDUCTION

Charitable contributions may be viewed as a consumer good which competes for the consumer dollar along with other expenditure categories such as food, housing, clothing, and medical care. The consumer's demand for charitable contributions relative to other consumer purchases is influenced by his net cost of giving or "price" of giving relative to other consumer purchases.

An individual's tax liability is reduced by the amount of his or her marginal tax rate times the amount of tax deductible donations. The complement of the marginal tax rate times the amount of the donation [(1 - marginal tax rate) x donation] would thus determine the taxpayer's price of giving relative to nondeductible consumer purchases. For example, a 30% marginal tax bracket taxpayer, who donates a dollar to charity, would have a price of giving of $.70

[(1-30%) x $1]. An incentive theoretically exists because the tax deductibility of charitable giving lowers its effective price.

The responsiveness of charitable giving to changes in the price of giving may be measured by the price elasticity of demand. Price elasticity of demand, in general, measures the proportionate change in quantity demanded of a commodity as a result of a proportionate change in the price of that commodity. The elasticity of demand for charitable giving measures the proportionate change in the quantity demanded of charitable contributions as a result of a proportionate change in the price of charitable giving. The price elasticity of demand formula for charitable giving might be stated as follows:

$$\frac{\text{Elasticity}}{\text{Coefficient}} = \frac{\text{Percentage Change in Charitable Contributions}}{\text{Percentage Change in the Price of Charitable Giving}}$$

An example illustrates how elasticity of demand is computed. Suppose a taxpayer increases his or her level of giving from $500/year to $600/year as a result of the taxpayer's marginal tax bracket increasing from 20% to 32% and the price of giving decreasing from .80 (1 - .20) to .68 (1 - .32). The elasticity coefficient would be computed as follows:

$$\frac{(\$600 - \$500) \ / \ \$500}{(.68 - .80) \ / \ .80} = -1.33$$

An elasticity of giving with an absolute value[1] in excess of one, as in the above example, implies that the charitable contribution deduction is relatively efficient because this would mean that a $1 loss of revenue to the Treasury has evoked more than $1 in additional charitable contributions. An elasticity of giving with an absolute value of less than one would imply relative inefficiency because this would be interpreted to mean that $1 of tax revenue foregone by the Treasury evokes less than $1 of additional charitable contributions.

PRIOR RESEARCH

Previous empirical studies that have examined the effect of the deduction on charitable giving have not permitted strong tests of causal hypotheses. These studies will be reviewed later in the paper. Strong tests of causal hypotheses have not occurred because these studies have relied on passive-observational data obtained from tax returns and to a lesser extent, surveys.[2] Historical data collected from tax returns and surveys indicate that, in the aggregate, as taxable income increases, charitable donations increase [Internal Revenue Service, 1983]. A basic problem of using this data to determine the tax incentive effect is determining how much of the increase in charitable donations is due to a price (incentive) effect and how much is due to an increase in income. In order to make this determination, the price effect must be statistically separated from the income effect. Since higher taxable income translates to higher marginal tax rates and lower prices, the price effect and income effect are significantly correlated with each other, that is, multicollinearity exists between the two variables. Neter and Wasserman [1974] explain that only imprecise information may be available about the individual true regression coefficients when multicollinearity is present among the independent variables.

Researchers have tried to disentangle the price effect from the income effect by maximizing the amount of independent variation in tax rates. The model to separate the two effects specifies that the demand for charitable contributions is inversely related to the price of the contribution and positively related to the taxpayer's income (for an example of the model, see Feldstein [1975]). The model can be written as follows:

$$\text{Log } C = b_0 + b_1 \text{ Log } Y + b_2 \text{ Log } P$$

where C = Demand for charitable contributions; Y = Income[3]; and P = Price (1 − marginal tax bracket)

The regression coefficients b_1 and b_2 are the income elasticity[4] and price elasticity, respectively, of giving. The coefficient b_2 attempts to measure the tax incentive effect on charitable contributions. The variables of Price and Demand for Charitable Contributions are converted to logarithmic form. As a result, the elasticity model is interpreted to mean (consistent with the definition of constant price elasticity of demand) that a proportionate change in demand for charitable contributions is a constant multiple of the proportionate change in the price of giving. This constancy occurs because a property of logarithms is that equal arithmetic steps of the logarithm represent equal proportionate steps of the variable (see Hirshleifer [1980]).

As measured by the price elasticity of giving, earlier studies that have examined the tax incentive effect have suggested that the deduction is relatively ineffective in encouraging charitable giving. Taussig [1967], using summaries of tax return data obtained from *Statistics of Income, 1962, Individual Income Tax Returns* [Internal Revenue Service, 1983], found the coefficient b_2 (price effect) to not be significantly different from zero. Schwartz [1970], employing the same data source examined data from alternate years, for three income levels. Schwartz's results suggested some incentive effect but a relatively inefficient one since at all income levels price elasticity was less than one.

More contemporary studies have suggested that the incentive effect is relatively efficient. Feldstein [1975], again using summaries of tax returns obtained from *Statistics of Income, Individual Tax Returns* [Internal Revenue Service, 1983] for alternative years, used two definitions of income in the model. For one definition, a price elasticity of -2.044 was obtained. For the other definition, a price elasticity of -1.238 was obtained. Feldstein and Taylor [1976] used special Treasury tax files for 1962 and 1970, which provided samples of individual tax returns, and found a price elasticity of -1.54. Clotfelter [1980], using the same Treasury tax files, obtained a relatively strong incentive effect (elasticity of -1.401) with cross-sectional data but no incentive effect with time series data.

Other studies have used survey data to estimate elasticity. For these studies, the taxpayer's marginal tax rate and taxable income were estimated from information contained in the survey. Feldstein and Clotfelter [1976] estimated elasticity from data obtained from a national survey of the income, assets, and savings of 2,164 households conducted by the Board of Governors of the Federal Reserve System [Projector and Weiss, 1966]. They found a price elasticity of -1.55. Feldstein and Boskin [1977] used survey data collected by the 1974 National Study of Philanthropy, a special household survey conducted by the Survey Research Center of the University of Michigan [Morgan et al., 1979], and obtained a price elasticity of -2.54.

In addition to the collinearity problem between the income and price variables, these researchers have identified other problems and concerns that the use of passive-observational data has presented in their efforts to establish the correlation between the level of giving and the price of giving. First, correlated variables might be omitted from the model, biasing any numerical estimate of the incentive effect (for a discussion of this problem, see Feldstein [1975] and Clotfelter [1980]). Second, an ideal measure of economic income cannot be obtained from tax return data because of such complications as nontaxable income, accrued capital gains, and paper losses. Third, accurate reflection of the price of donated appreciated assets is impossible because the price of appreciated property depends in part on the fraction of the asset's value that is accrued capital gain. Fourth, price itself may be a function of the amount of charitable giving since deductions, including charitable contributions, are subtracted from the taxpayer's income in determining the taxpayer's marginal tax rate.

RESEARCH DESIGN

This study uses an experimental method to test whether the elasticity of giving has an absolute value greater than or equal to one. A causal link between the tax incentive variable and the level of charitable giving was tested by randomly assigning treatments across subjects. Cook and Campbell [1979, p. 84] state that "the unique purpose of experiments is to provide stronger tests of causal hypotheses than is permitted by other forms of research, most of which were developed for other purposes." In contrast to studies that employ the

Table 1. Tax Rate Schedules

If Taxable Income Is:	The Tax Liability Will Be:
Tax Rate Schedule For 22% Level	
$0 - $18,000	17% of taxable income
Over $18,000	$3,060 + (22% x amount over $18,000)
Tax Rate Schedule For 36% Level	
$0 - $9,000	$0
$9,000 - $18,000	28% x amount over $9,000
Over $18,000	$2,520 + (36% x amount over $18,000)

experimental method, correlational studies "by their nature are incapable of determining causal relationships on the effects of treatments" [Hersen and Barlow, 1983, p. 19].

Cook and Campbell [1979] explain that the experimental method is characterized by the presence of control in order to rule out threats to valid causal inference. Control in the context of an experiment is primarily obtained by using random assignment to ensure that every experimental unit has an equal chance to receive any one of the treatments. This random assignment of treatments helps "separate the effects attributable to a treatment from the effects attributable to irrelevancies that are correlated with a treatment" [Cook and Campbell, 1979, p. 8]. For a further discussion of how the experimental method permits tests of causal hypotheses, see Cook and Campbell [1979], Asher [1976], and Abdel-Khalik and Ajinka [1979].

Abdel-Khalik and Ajinka [1979] note that multiplicity of methods or "triangulation" is a desirable feature of research. "The extent to which triangulation produces similar results can be used as a measure of confidence in the findings and the validity of the underlying theory" [Abdel-Khalik, 1979, p. 21]. The use of both the experimental method approach of this study and the correlational approach, employed by previous researchers to address the same research question, is an example of triangulation. If the results between the two methodologies are generally consistent, there is increased confidence that there is, in fact, an incentive effect with respect to the charitable contribution deduction.

The following section discusses the specific experimental task employed to address whether the elasticity of giving has an absolute value greater than or equal to one.

Experimental Task

The experimental task consisted of asking subjects to make certain budgeting decisions based on a salary level of $32,000.[5] The decisions were predicated on the subjects' current marital status and any children they might have. The budgeting exercise included normal categories of expenditures such as housing, taxes, transportation, food, and clothing. Subjects were also asked how much, if any, they would designate for charitable contributions.

It was recognized that creating a budget without access to financial records might be difficult for the subjects. Therefore, to make the derivation of a budget less cumbersome, the budgeting decisions were simplified by providing categorical expenditure choices for most of the budget categories. The category of charitable contributions, however, required an open-ended response.[6] For two categories, amounts were actually provided. One of these categories was a miscellaneous category that was an aggregation of several relatively minor categories. Another category, social security, would not vary among subjects since it is fixed by law. One important category was taxes. Subjects computed a tax liability from the budgetary information.

In order to effectively manipulate the tax variable, four treatments of the research instrument were distributed as follows:

1. Charitable contributions were assumed to be tax deductible, and the maximum marginal tax rate was assumed to be 22%.
2. Charitable contributions were assumed not to be tax deductible, and the maximum marginal tax rate was assumed to be 22%.
3. Charitable contributions were assumed to be tax deductible, and the maximum marginal tax rate was assumed to be 36%.
4. Charitable contributions were assumed not to be tax deductible, and the maximum marginal tax rate was assumed to be 36%.

The 22% and 36% marginal tax rates are reflective of rates imposed on middle-income taxpayers.[7] Middle-income taxpayers were chosen as the targeted subject group since they are responsible for the bulk of charitable donations [Bakal, 1979]. It has been estimated that two-thirds of all charitable donations are made by those with incomes of less than $50,000 [Kowalski, 1985].

In order to manipulate the marginal tax rates at the 22% and 36% levels, two different tax rate schedules were used (see Table 1).

The two tax rate schedules were intended to be "revenue neutral." That is, the two schedules were intended, on balance, to yield approximately the same tax liability. Revenue neutrality across tax rate schedules eliminates the possibility of differences in charitable giving being partially explained by different tax liabilities.

Upon completion of the budgeting exercise, subjects were asked to respond to selected demographic questions. Demographic information elicited from subjects included their age, gender, marital status, income, religion, and frequency of church attendance. In addition, subjects were asked about their

114RICHARD B. TOOLSON

years of tax filing experience, whether they had ever itemized, and the percentage of income they donated to charity last year. The purpose of this information was to obtain a profile of their income and tax filing experience and to permit covariance analysis.

A pilot study was conducted on an afternoon M.B.A. class and an evening undergraduate cost accounting class at Arizona State University (n = 34). The results of the study indicated that the tax variables were being effectively manipulated[8] and revenue neutrality across the two tax rate schedules was being achieved.[9]

Subjects

Appropriate subjects for this study would be taxpayers with tax filing experience as well as an income level sufficient to have resulted in expenditure decisions similar to those contained in the budgeting exercise. Subjects meeting these criteria would find it easier to role play as they complete the budgeting exercise. In as much as the exercise was quantitative in nature, it was also desirable for the subjects to have at least some quantitative aptitude.

A total of 167 subjects participated in the experiment. Subjects chosen for the experiment were obtained from seven evening M.B.A. classes at Arizona State University. Typically, these students have full-time employment during the day and have had a number of years of tax filing experience (see Table 2). Because of restrictive admittance requirements to the M.B.A. program at Arizona State University, these subjects would be expected to have significant quantitative ability.[10]

The four versions (treatments) of the research instrument were preordered by treatment so that equal numbers of each version would be distributed. The research instruments were then distributed at the beginning of each class. Subjects were told that they were to complete a budgeting exercise which might provide them some insight into the relationship between budgeting decisions and taxes. They were assured that their responses would remain anonymous. A calculator was furnished to any subject who needed one. Typically, subjects required 20-30 minutes to complete the research instrument. Few subjects completed the exercise in a period of less than 20 minutes.

Variables and Hypotheses

Consistent with the definition of constant elasticity, the independent variable was the logarithm of the price of giving. To derive the values for the price of giving, two factors were each manipulated at two levels. The two factors were marginal tax rate and deductibility, each of which were each manipulated at two levels: 22% versus 36% and deductible versus not deductible. Since the complement of the assumed marginal tax rate determines the price of giving,

Table 2. Subject Demographic Data

Category	Frequency	Percentage
Income Level (including that of spouse, if married)		
Less than $15,000	25	15
$15,000 to $25,000	21	13
$25,000 to $35,000	45	28
$35,000 to $45,000	27	17
More than $45,000	43	27
Total	161	100
Years Filed a Tax Return		
Less than 5 years	26	16
5 to 9 years	59	37
10 to 14 years	38	24
More than 14 years	38	23
Total	161	100
Ever Itemized?		
Yes	126	78
No	36	22
Total	162	100

the independent variable of price had three possible values: .78 (1.00 − .22), .64 (1.00 − .36), and 1.00 (1.00 − 0). (Regardless of one's marginal tax bracket, the marginal tax rate, with respect to charitable giving, is 0% for those subjects for whom charitable contributions were assumed not to be deductible.)

The dependent variable was the logarithm of charitable contributions. The hypothesis, stated in the null form, is as follows:

H_0:   The charitable contribution deduction will not result in an absolute value greater than or equal to one.

Comparison of Charitable Contribution Observations

A comparison was made of the distribution of charitable contribution observations generated from the experiment with the distribution of charitable contribution observations obtained from filed tax returns. Charitable contribution observations from filed tax returns were obtained from the Arthur

Table 3. Comparison of Data Sets

Statistic	Observations of Contributions From Experiment	Observations of Contributions From Data Base
Mean	$508	$469
Standard Deviation	$847	$762
Standard Error of Mean	65.5	59.0
Minimum Value	0	0
Maximum Value	$4,660	$4,703

Young Research Tax Database (University of Michigan). The purpose of the comparison was to verify whether the distribution of observations, obtained in an experimental setting, was similar to the distribution of observations from filed tax returns.

One hundred sixty-seven cash charitable contribution observations, the same sample size as the experimental data, were obtained from the data base for taxpayers with reported incomes approximating $32,000 per year. The $32,000 income level was selected to correspond with the assumed level of income in the budgeting exercise.[11] The observations were obtained from returns filed in 1983 for taxpayers living throughout the United States.

Table 3 presents several descriptive statistics comparing the distribution of these two sets of data.

In addition to comparing the two sets of data by means of descriptive statistics, the Student's t test was utilized to determine if there was a significant difference between the means of the two data sets. A p-value for the t test of .66 (t = .44) indicated no significant difference between the means of the two data sets.

Thus, both the descriptive statistics and the t test support the conclusion that the experimental observations display a distribution similar to the tax return data. This similarity between the two data sets strengthens the case that the budgeting exercise elicited realistic responses.

DATA ANALYSIS

Prior to testing the hypothesis, an analysis was made to identify appropriate variables, if any, to be included as covariates in the model. Covariance analysis uses the correlation between the response variable and an independent variable to reduce the experimental error and make the experiment more powerful for studying treatment effects. Neter and Wasserman [1974] state two criteria for including a variable as a covariate in the model: (1) the variable has a relation

Table 4. Parameter Estimates of Regression Model

Variables	DF	Parameter Estimate	Standard Error	T for H₀: Parameter = 0	P-Value
Intercept	1	1.836	.070	25.904	.0001*
Log Price	1	-1.909	.585	-3.265	.0013*
Contributions last year	1	.147	.018	8.100	.0001*

Note: * Significant at .01

to the dependent variable; (2) the variable does not interact with the treatment variables.

To identify variables that had a relation to the dependent variable, a correlational analysis was made of charitable contributions to the following variables: age, gender, marital status, income, number of children, religion, frequency of church attendance, years filed a tax return, whether the taxpayer had ever itemized, and the amount of charitable contributions in the prior year as a percent of income. Three variables were significantly correlated with charitable contributions (level of significance = .05): marital status ($p = .0331$), church attendance ($p = .0001$), and contributions last year ($p = .0001$).

A test for parallel slopes was then made to determine if a significant interaction existed between these variables and the treatments. An interaction makes inclusion of a variable as a covariate in the model inappropriate.[12] Marital status and contributions last year fell outside the region for rejecting the no interaction conclusion, and church attendance fell within the rejection region.[13] Thus, church attendance significantly interacted with the treatments, requiring elimination of this variable as a covariate.

Marital status and contributions last year were jointly included in the ANCOVA model. Although contributions last year was still highly significant in the model ($F = 186.83$, $p = .0001$), marital status ($F = .71$, $p = .4020$) was not significant. Thus, marital status also was eliminated as a covariate, leaving contributions last year as the only covariate in the model.[14]

Analysis of the Hypothesis

To test this hypothesis, the following regression model was used to estimate the elasticity of giving:[15]

$$Log\ C = b_0 + b_1\ Log\ P + b_3 X$$

where C = Demand for Charitable Giving; P = Price of Giving; and X = Contributions Last Year.

Table 4 presents the parameter estimates of the independent variables and their corresponding test statistics (t) for the null hypothesis that the parameter estimates equal zero.

According to Table 4 p-values, all the parameter estimates, including the estimate for the logarithm of price variable, are significantly different from zero at a level of significance of .01.

The parameter estimate for the variable logarithm of price is −1.909. This means that $1.909 of additional charitable contributions are induced by the deduction for every dollar of tax revenue foregone. The test statistic (t) (to test whether the elasticity of giving is greater than one) is computed from the parameter estimate and the standard error as follows:

$$t = \frac{1.909 \text{ (parameter estimate)} - 1}{.585 \text{ (standard error)}} = 1.55$$

The p-value for this test statistic is .061. The conclusion is that the null hypothesis, elasticity of giving is not greater than or equal to the absolute value of one, is rejected at a level of significance of .10.

IMPLICATIONS

The elasticity estimate of this study (−1.909) provides support for the more contemporary elasticity estimates obtained using a correlational approach. The general consistency of the results between the two methodologies adds confidence to the conclusion that there is an incentive effect with respect to the charitable contribution deduction. As noted earlier, triangulation is a desirable feature of research.

The results of this study indicate that the charitable contribution deduction is efficient, that is, the absolute value of elasticity of giving is greater than or equal to one. The principal policy implication of these results is that the legislative objective of the deduction, to encourage charitable giving, is being achieved. The attainment of the deduction's intended objective lends support for the continuation of the deduction.

Under the Tax Reform Act of 1986, the price of giving increases for two reasons. First, fewer taxpayers find it advantageous to itemize and the charitable contribution deduction is limited to taxpayers who itemize. Second, there is an across-the-board reduction in marginal tax rates (see U.S. Congress, [1986]). Because of the limitations of this study, particularly with respect to external validity (see last section for a discussion of these limitations), it is problematic whether this study can be generalized beyond this study's sample. Results from this sample, however, do suggest that, "all other things being equal," the tax act would negatively affect the level of revenue obtained by charitable organizations. Any revenue loss should be of concern to government because some of the revenue shortfall may have to be assumed by them.

LIMITATIONS

This study has several limitations with respect to its research design and its generalizability beyond the participants in this study.

Because the budgeting exercise was completed in the absence of supporting financial records, it was necessary to provide categorical expenditure choices for several major budget categories. The categorical choices may have biased the subjects' responses to the open-ended charitable contributions category. However, a comparison of the distribution of the charitable contribution observations from this experiment with charitable contributions from filed tax returns reduces this concern. Moreover, randomization across treatments minimizes the likelihood that any response bias would effect the results.

Hypothesis-guessing is always of concern in any experiment, including this one.[16] In order to minimize this concern for this experiment, a between-subjects design was used and the charitable contribution category was not presented to the subjects differently than the other budget exercise categories.

Discrete marginal tax rate levels were adopted in the research design. Caution should be exercised in generalizing these results to other tax rate levels, particularly to tax rate levels considerably different than those chosen for this experiment. The rates, however, that are effective for 1988 and thereafter (0%, 15%, 28%, and 33%), reasonably parallel the rates introduced in this experiment.

The targeted population of interest in this study was U.S. middle-income taxpayers. Caution needs to be exercised in generalizing this study to the targeted population of interest. Subjects selected in this study were well-educated (all subjects had at least an undergraduate degree) and therefore probably had a higher level of tax sophistication than the targeted population of interest. If subjects possessed a higher level of tax sophistication, this may have influenced the results.

Finally, the distribution of the research instrument was restricted to subjects located in the Phoenix, Arizona metropolitan area. It is problematic, therefore, whether the study can be generalized to taxpayers located throughout the United States.

SAMPLE RESEARCH INSTRUMENT

Dear Participant:

The purpose of this study is to gain insight into the way in which tax laws impact personal budgeting decisions.

As you respond to the exercise, please keep in mind the following:

1. The exercise involves role-playing; the financial information given may not actually fit your situation.

2. There are no right or wrong responses.

3. Your responses are anonymous.

The results of this study will be available upon request. Thank you for your help.

Sincerely,

Directions

The following exercise involves making some basic budget decisions and requires the calculation of a personal income tax liability.

You are to assume that you currently earn $32,000 per year in salary, before any amount is taken out for income or social security taxes. This is the only source of compensation for you (and your family, if applicable).

It is the beginning of the year and your task is to make certain budget decisions based on this salary level of $32,000.

The budget decisions that you make should be predicated on your current marital status. If you are currently single, your decisions should be based on this status. If you are currently married, with or without children, your decisions should be based on this status. IN MAKING YOUR DECISIONS, YOU MAY WISH TO CONSIDER THE TAX EFFECTS OF SUCH DEDUCTIBLE ITEMS AS HOME MORTGAGE INTEREST AND AUTO LOAN INTEREST.

The budget decisions generally involve making categorical expenditure choices. Because of this limitation, the budget decisions may not be those you would make under unconstrained conditions. However, please select the option that comes the closest to what you would choose under unconstrained conditions.

Please use the information under the heading "Budget Information" to complete the budget ("Calculation of Annual Budget"). After completing the budget, please answer the brief questionnaire.

Budget Information

In deriving your budget, you are to assume that you currently have $20,000 in accessible savings in the bank (including $10,000 from the recent sale of your townhouse). Medical and dental needs are adequately taken care of by an employer-paid health insurance policy.

In making your budget decisions, you are to assume your taxable income is subject to the following rates:

If taxable income is:	The tax liability will be:
$0-$18,000	17% of taxable income
Over $18,000	$3,060 + (22% x amount over $18,000)

ACCORDING TO THIS TAX RATE SCHEDULE, YOU ARE TO ASSUME THAT YOUR MARGINAL RATE IS 22%.

1. *Housing*: You have recently sold your small townhouse, netting $10,000, and are in the process of looking for a detached single family house to purchase. You have narrowed your choice down to three possible options. For each of the three options, you are to assume that you can obtain a conventional mortgage financed over 30 years at a 10% interest rate. The downpayments will vary with the cost of the house. All three options are in equally desirable locations, that is, they are all reasonably close to schools, work, shopping, and churches.

The monthly payments would include not only principal and interest payments but also payments for property taxes and insurance. BASED ON THE ASSUMPTION THAT INTEREST AND PROPERTY TAXES BUT NOT PRINCIPAL AND INSURANCE WOULD BE DEDUCTIBLE, 90% OF THE MONTHLY HOUSE PAYMENT WOULD BE DEDUCTIBLE.

1. $70,000 purchase price, $5,000 down, 1,200 square feet, 3 bedrooms, 2 baths, carport; $638/month ($7,656/yr.)
2. $80,000 purchase price, $10,000 down, 1,600 square feet, 3 bedrooms, 2 baths, den or 4th bedroom, carport; $690/month ($8,280/yr.)
3. $90,000 purchase price, $15,000 down, 1,900 square feet, 3 bedrooms, 2 baths, den or 4th bedroom, double garage; $742/month ($8,904/yr.)

2. *Transportation:* Your present and only vehicle is quite old and has lately been experiencing considerable mechanical difficulties. You are to choose between either retaining your present vehicle or replacing it with a new one. If you retain your present vehicle you estimate that your repair bills for the year will be $1,000 whereas they will be negligible for the new car.

a. *Car Purchase:* In the event a new car is purchased, the old car and funds from savings will be used as the down payment. The amount of the down payment will increase as the purchase price increases. The remaining balance will be paid over 5 years at an annualized interest rate of 12%. YOU ARE TO ASSUME THAT 50% OF THE PAYMENT IS INTEREST AND TAX DEDUCTIBLE.

The new car will be chosen among the following options:

Purchase Price	Down Payment	Monthly Payment	Annual Payment
1. $8,000	$1,000	$154	$1,848
2. $10,000	$2,000	$177	$2,124
3. $12,000	$3,000	$199	$2,388
4. $15,000	$5,000	$221	$2,652

    b.   *Repairs:* $1,000 if retain old car, $0 if purchase a new car
    c.   *Fuel:*Please select one of the following options:

        1. $500/year
        2. $1000/year
        3. $1500/year

Conditions that might warrant selection of a lower amount might include one driver and/or a conservative number of miles driven. Conditions that might warrant selection of a higher amount might be multiple drivers and/or liberal usage of the automobile.

    d.   *Car insurance:*   Please select one of the following options:

        1. $500/yr.
        2. $1000/yr.
        3. $1500/yr.

Conditions that might warrant selection of a lower amount might include a single driver, a good driving record, and/or retention of the old car. Conditions that might warrant selection of a higher amount include multiple drivers, a blemished driving record, and/or purchases of a relatively expensive car.

    3.   *Charitable Contributions:*   Please select an annual expenditure level for charitable contributions.

IN DECIDING HOW MUCH YOU WOULD GIVE TO CHARITY, PLEASE ASSUME THAT CONTRIBUTIONS TO CHARITABLE INSTITUTIONS ARE NOT TAX DEDUCTIBLE.

    4.   *Income Tax Liability:*   The income tax liability is to be computed by subtracting from income ($32,000), interest and property taxes on the home and any interest on a car loan in order to derive taxable income. The tax liability is then derived by multiplying taxable income by the appropriate tax rates. Please use the tax rates and Schedule A (see "Calculation of Annual Budget") to make this computation:

To compute tax liability:

If taxable income is:	The tax liability will be:
$0-$18,000	17% of taxable income
Over $18,000	$3,060 + (22% x amount over $18,000)

5. *Utilities:* Please select one of the following options:

   a. $75/month ($900/yr.)
   b. $125/month ($1,500/yr.)
   c. $175/month ($2,100/yr.)

Conditions that might warrant selection of a lower amount include conservative usage and/or the selection of a housing option with fewer square feet. Conditions that might warrant selection of a larger amount include liberal usage and/or the selection of a house with relatively more square feet.

6. *Food and Beverages:* The amount allocated to this category would include the cost of the food eaten at home, the cost of meals eaten away from home, and any liquor purchases.

   a. $75/week ($3,900/yr.)
   b. $125/week ($6,500/yr.)
   c. $175/week ($9,100/yr.)

Conditions the might warrant selection at the lower end might include a small family, frugality when grocery shopping ("coupon clipping"), and/or rarely eating out. Conditions that might warrant selection of a larger amount might include a large family and/or frequently eating out at restaurants.

7. *Clothing:* Please allocate an amount to this category. Include any jewelry purchases.

8. *Entertainment and Vacations:* Please allocate an amount to this category. In addition to vacations, this category would include such items as reading materials, sporting goods, toys and hobbies, and admission fees to entertainment events.

9. *Other:* An amount, $2,000, has been allocated to this category to cover such miscellaneous items as personal care items (cosmetics, toiletries), personal care services (barber shop, beauty salon), furniture purchases, household operations (cleaning supplies, repairs, maintenance), and life insurance.

10. *Social Security Tax:* It will be assumed that the payment of social security tax is mandatory and is a flat 7% of gross salary. Based on a salary of $32,000, social security tax would be $2,450. This amount has already been entered into the budget.

CALCULATION OF ANNUAL BUDGET

ANNUAL BUDGET $32,000

1. Housing .... _____
   (Options: $7,656, $8,280, $8,904

2. Transportation
   a. Purchase of new car .... _____
       (Options: $1,848, $2,124, $2,388, $2,652)

   b. Repairs .... _____
       ($1000 if retain old car, $0 otherwise)

   c. Fuel .... _____
       (Options: $500, $1000, $1500)

   d. Insurance .... _____
       (Options: $500, $1000, $1500)

3. Charitable Contributions .... _____

4. Tax Liability (see schedule A below) .... _____

5. Utilities .... _____
    (Options: $900, $1500, $2100)

6. Food and Beverages .... _____
    (Options: $3,900, $6,500, $9,100)

7. Clothing .... _____

8. Entertainment and Vacations .... _____

9. Other $2,000

10. Social Security Tax $2,345

Total Outlays (add lines 1-10)   _____

Savings or (Dissavings) = $32,000 − Total Outlays   _____

Schedule A-Computation of Tax Liability

Gross Income $32,000
Deduct:

a. Housing (Deduct Interest and Taxes on Housing)   _____
    1.   Interest and Taxes = $6,890 (total payments = $7,656)
    2.   Interest and Taxes = $7,461 (total payments = $8,290)
    3.   Interest and Taxes = $8,014 (total payments = $8,904)

b. Car Loan (Deduct Interest on Car Loan)   _____
   1. Interest = $924 (total payments = $1,848)
   2. Interest = $1,062 (total payments = $2,124)
   3. Interest = $1,194 (total payments = $2,388)
   4. Interest = $1,326 (total payments = $2,652)

Total Deductions (lines a + b)   _____

Taxable Income ($32,000 − Total Deductions)   _____

Tax Liability (see tax rate schedule)   _____

PLEASE DO THIS PART AFTER DOING THE BUDGET EXERCISE

GENERAL INFORMATION

1. Please refer to the amount of the budget you have allocated to charitable contributions and estimate how much of this amount you would allocate to religious organizations (churches) and how much to nonreligious organizations (such as educational institutions, health organizations, social services). Please continue to assume that charitable contributions are not tax deductible.

     _____ Religious organizations

     _____ Nonreligious organizations

     _____ Total

2. What is your age? _____ Years

3. What is your gender? Female _____ Male _____

4. Are you married? Yes _____ No _____

5. No. of children? _____

6. What is the highest academic degree you hold?

    B.S./B.A. _____   M.S. _____

    Other, please specify _____

7. What is your approximate annual level of income (include income of spouse if married)?

     _____ less than $15,000

     _____ $15,000 to $25,000

_____ $25,000 to $35,000

_____ $35,000 to $45,000

_____   More than $45,000

8. For approximately how many years have you filed a personal income tax return (including this year)? _____

9. Have you ever itemized your deductions? _____ Yes _____ No

10. What is your religion?

         Protestant _____

         Catholic _____

         L.D.S. _____

         Jewish _____

         None _____

         Other _____

11. About how often do you attend religious services?

         _____ Once a week or more often

         _____ 2-3 Times a Month

         _____ Once a Month

         _____ A Few Times a Year

         _____ Never

12. To what extent do you think that whether charitable contributions are tax deductible influences the level of contributions you give to charity?

Not at all   _____   To a Great Extent

                1   2   3   4   5   6   7

13. Which of the following options most closely reflects how much you (and your spouse, if married) gave to charity last year? (For example, if you gave $200 last year to charity and your income was $25,000, the option to choose would be ".61% to .8% of income" since $200 is .8% of $25,000.)

_____ 0% of income	_____	4.01% to 4.5% of income
_____ .01% to .2% of income	_____	4.51% to 5.0% of income
_____ .21% to .4% of income	_____	5.91% to 5.5% of income
_____ .41% to .6% of income	_____	5.51% to 6.0% of income
_____ .61% to .8% of income	_____	6.01% to 6.5% of income
_____ .81% to 1.0% of income	_____	6.51% to 7.0% of income
_____ 1.01% to 1.5% of income	_____	7.01% to 7.5% of income
_____ 1.51% to 2.0% of income	_____	7.51% to 8.0% of income

_____	2.01% to 2.5% of income	_____	8.01% to 8.5% of income
_____	2.51% to 3.0% of income	_____	8.51% to 9.0% of income
_____	3.01% to 3.5% of income	_____	9.01% to 9.5% of income
_____	3.51% to 4.0% of income	_____	9.51% to 10.0% of income

ACKNOWLEDGMENTS

This paper is adapted from a Ph.D. dissertation written at Arizona State University. The author wishes to acknowledge the aid received from members of his committee: Charles Christian, Steven Kaplan, Philip Reckers, Keith Shriver, and Robert Wyndelts. Financial support for this study was provided by the Deloitte Haskins and Sells Foundation.

NOTES

1. The elasticity of demand for a consumer good is normally a negative expression since a decrease in the price of a commodity would be expected to evoke a corresponding increase in the quantity demanded of the commodity. An alternative, more understandable, way of stating elasticity is to use absolute value to express elasticity as a positive value.

2. The survey data contained demographic information on individuals, including information on their income, expenditures and personal characteristics. This information was used to estimate a taxpayer's taxable income and marginal tax bracket.

3. Income is not defined more precisely in the model because the definition of income varied across researchers.

4. Income elasticity of demand for charitable contributions is the proportionate change in charitable contributions demanded as a result of a proportionate change in income.

5. The $32,000 salary was selected in order to provide enough income to support an intermediate budget for a family of four as estimated by the Department of Labor.

6. It was desirable for the categorical choices to be reasonable in light of the assumed income level of $32,000. In order to assure the reasonableness of the amounts, sources were consulted which provided information on average amounts of family expenditures for a number of categories (see *Monthly Labor Review* [1982], p. 44; Bureau of Business and Economic Research, Arizona State University [1985]).

7. For 1985, for married taxpayers filing jointly, taxable income over $21,020, but not over $25,600, was taxed at a 22% rate. Taxable income over $36,630, but not over $47,670, was taxed at a 33% tax rate. For 1985, for single taxpayers, taxable income over $16,190, but not over $19,640, was taxed at a 23% rate. Taxable income over $31,080, but not over $36,800, was taxed at a 34% rate (Internal Revenue Code [1985]).

8. After completion of the budgeting exercise, subjects were to indicate their marginal tax rate and whether their version assumed charitable contributions to be deductible or not deductible. Ninety-four percent of the subjects (32 out of 34) were able to respond correctly to both questions.

9. There was only a 5% ($215) difference in the mean tax liabilities between the 22% maximum marginal tax rate schedule group and the 36% maximum marginal tax rate schedule group. A Student's t-test indicated that there was not a significant difference between the means ($t = .81$, $p = .42$).

10.   According to an estimate provided by the Graduate Programs Office in the College of Business at Arizona State University, those admitted to the M.B.A. program for Fall 1985, ranked, on average, in the top 15% of those taking the Graduate Management Admission Test.

11.   To derive "income" from the tax returns, the long-term capital gain exclusion was added to adjusted gross income, line 32, Form 1040, 1985.

12.   The test for parallel slopes consists of examining whether the interaction variables (treatment(s) x covariates(s)) significantly reduce the error sums of squares. See Neter and Wasserman [1974, pp. 702-703] for a detailed explanation of this test.

13.   The test statistics for the three prospective covariates were as follows: marital status, $F = .84$; contributions last year, $F = 2.29$; church attendance, $F = 4.20$. At a level of significance of .05, the region for rejecting the no interaction conclusion is 3.07.

14.   The variable marital status was probably not significant in the model even though it was significantly correlated with the response variable because marital status is slightly more correlated with contributions last year ($r = -.1716$) than with the response variable, charitable contributions ($r = -.1665$). Neter and Wasserman [1974, p. 341] explain that when multicollinearity is present, that is, independent variables are correlated among themselves, "estimated regression coefficients individually may be statistically not significant even though a definite statistical relation exists between the dependent variable and the set of independent variables."

15.   Of the 167 charitable contributions observations included in the model, 32 consisted of a zero. It is not possible to express a zero as a logarithm (for a discussion of logarithms, see Kenner, Small, and Williams [1965]). In order to include the zero response in the model, a transformation of the data was required. Ten dollars was added to all charitable contribution observations. This same transformation was adopted by Clotfelter [1980] and Feldstein and Boskin [1977]. These researchers justify adding ten dollars to all observations by observing that most people who report no giving actually did give a small amount that has since been forgotten or was regarded as too small to mention.

16.   Hypothesis-guessing involves the subjects' guessing what the experimenter is trying to find out and altering their responses as a result (see Cook and Campbell, [1979], p. 66).

REFERENCES

Abdel-Khalik, R. and B. Ajinka, *Empirical Research in Accounting A Methodological Viewpoint* (American Accounting Association, 1979).

Asher, H., *Casual Modeling* (Sage, 1976).

Bakal, C., *Charity U.S.A.* (Times Books, 1979).

Bureau of Business and Economic Research, Arizona State University, "Metropolitan Phoenix Consumer Price Index," (November 1985).

Clotfelter, C.T., "Tax Incentives and Charitable Giving: Evidence from a Panel of Taxpayers," *Journal of Public Economics* (January 1980), pp. 319-340.

Cook, T. and D. Campbell, *Quasi-Experimentation* (Houghton Mifflin, 1979).

Feldstein, M., "The Income Tax and Charitable Contributions: Part I—Aggregate and Distributional Effects," *National Tax Journal* (March 1975), pp. 81-100.

Feldstein, M. and M. Boskin, "Effects of the Charitable Deduction on Contributions by Low Income and Middle Income Households: Evidence from the National Survey of Philanthropy," *Review of Economics and Statistics* (August 1977), pp. 351-354.

Feldstein, M. and C. Clotfelter, "Tax Incentives and Charitable Contributions in the United States: A Microeconomic Analysis," *Journal of Public Economics* (January 1976), pp. 1-26.

Feldstein, M. and A. Taylor, "The Income Tax and Charitable Contributions," *Econometrica* (November 1976), pp. 1201-22.

Hersen, M. and D. Barlow, *Single Case Experimental Designs* (Pergamon, 1983).

Hirshleifer, J., *Price Theory and Applications* (Prentice-Hall, 1980).

Internal Revenue Code of 1954 (Prentice-Hall, 1985).

Internal Revenue Service, *Statistics of Income, Individual Income Tax Returns* (U.S. Government Printing Office, 1929-1966, 1983).

Kenner, M.R., D.E. Small, and G.N. Williams, *Concepts of Modern Mathematics* (American Book Company, 1965).

Kowalski, J., "Tax Reform Could Leave Arts Less to Bank On," *Arizona Republic* (July 14, 1985), p. f1.

Lawrence, D. and M. Saghafi, "The Flat-Rate Income Tax, Tax Burden, and Charitable Contributions," *National Tax Journal* (December 1984), pp. 569-574.

Monthly Labor Review, "Family Budgets," (July 1982), p. 44.

Morgan, J. et al., *Results from Two National Surveys of Philanthropic Activity* (University of Michigan, 1979).

Neter, J. and W. Wasserman, *Applied Linear and Statistical Models* (Richard D. Irwin, Inc., 1974).

Projector, D.S. and G.S. Weiss, "Survey of Financial Characteristics of Consumers," (Board of Governors and the Federal Reserve System, 1966).

Schwartz, R.A., "Personal Philanthropic Contributions," *Journal of Political Economy* (Nov./Dec. 1970), pp. 1264-91.

Seidman, J.S., *Legislative History of Federal Income Tax Laws* (Prentice-Hall, 1938).

Taussig, M., "Economic Aspects of the Personal Income Tax Treatment of Charitable Contributions," *National Tax Journal* (March 1967), pp. 1-19.

U.S. Congress, *Congressional Record*, 65th Congress, 1st Session, (U.S. Government Printing Office, 1917).

U.S. Congress, *Joint Conference Committee Rep. No. 99-841*, 99th Congress, 2nd Session (1986).

INFLUENCING TAXPAYER COMPLIANCE THROUGH SANCTION THREAT OR APPEALS TO CONSCIENCE

Betty R. Jackson and Pauline R. Jaouen

ABSTRACT

Two psychological theories, deterrence theory and reward theory, suggest that appeals to conscience may influence taxpayer attitude. Deterrence theory would describe the effect of appeals to conscience as causing psychological pain associated with guilt feelings. Reward theory would describe the effect as making people feel good because they value alignment with a worthy cause. This article explored the relative influence of incremental sanction threats versus appeals to conscience on the tax resistance attitude of subjects selected from a pool of potential jurors. This research did not demonstrate significant differences between the sanction, appeals, or control groups, but did reveal a significant gender difference by treatment group.

Compliance with the U.S. income tax laws has apparently diminished dramatically in recent years [IRS, 1988], but we do not have adequate measures by which to determine trends in the intentional and unintentional components of noncompliance. The Internal Revenue Service's (IRS) traditional response

Advances in Taxation, Volume 2, pages 131-147.
Copyright © 1989 by JAI Press Inc.
All rights of reproduction in any form reserved.
ISBN: 0-89232-783-9

to perceived compliance problems has been to assume intentionality and to alter the expected value of tax evasion by increasing the penalties associated with an underpayment determination and by increasing the probability of detection. However, the former Commissioner of Internal Revenue, Lawrence Gibbs, has taken the initiative of deemphasizing that focus in favor of a focus on a facilitative attitude on the part of the IRS. This change is consistent with some academic research that questions the validity of the traditional approach of emphasizing threats and punishments as the most effective way to encourage compliance. One avenue of investigation has begun to explore appeals to conscience as an alternative to threatening taxpayers with sanctions [Schwartz and Orleans, 1967; Grasmick and Scott, 1982].

This article reports the results of a study designed to build upon previous research comparing differential effects of increasing sanction threats versus making appeals to conscience on taxpayers' attitudes toward taxes and tax evasion. The two approaches are not mutually exclusive, and any prospective changes would be incremental to the existing system. However, in this study we are interested in determining as a first step the relative strength of the methods as independent incremental influences on taxpayers to provide a foundation for future research exploring interaction effects of the two approaches.

The rest of this paper is organized as follows. Previous research on two psychological theories relating to sanction threat and appeals to conscience is reviewed. Then the research questions and experimental design are discussed. Results, limitations, and conclusions follow.

PREVIOUS RESEARCH

The question of interest in this study is whether stressing the powers of the IRS in imposing sanction threats currently in place would be as effective in deterring evasion as an appeal to the taxpayer's conscience. The question was examined within a deterrence theory framework by Grasmick and Scott [1982]. Deterrence theory encompasses three factors that inhibit deviant behavior: (1) fear of legal sanctions, (2) fear of interpersonal sanctions, and (3) moral commitment to a norm [Grasmick and Scott, 1982, p. 213]. Certain crimes may be more effectively deterred by one factor than another. There is some evidence that tax evasion may be more susceptible to interpersonal sanctions and moral commitment than to legal sanctions [Grasmick and Scott, 1982] although the evidence is not consistent [Tittle, 1980].

Schwartz and Orleans [1967] provided early evidence that taxpayers reduced evasion more in response to appeals to conscience than to sanction threat. Grasmick and Scott [1982] found threat of guilt feelings to be a stronger deterrent than penalty threats in a survey of taxpayers. However, research in neutralization theory by Thurman, St. John, and Riggs [1984] urges caution in rushing to deter deviant behavior through the introduction of guilt feelings. This study demonstrated the ability of subjects to neutralize their guilt feelings by developing justifications of their intended behavior.

The deterrence theory framework views the issue of deterrence as one of imposing penalties. The psychological pain felt as a result of the guilt feelings associated with deviation from a valued norm may, on the one hand, be a penalty. On the other hand, an appeal to conscience may not cause pangs of guilt but may, instead, be a reaffirmation that the moral commitment to a valued norm is valid. Thus, the appeal to conscience may be a form of a reward.

Extensive research in behavior modification in other contexts demonstrates the superiority of rewards over punishment [Skinner, 1953]. The ultimate question of interest to policymakers will be that of why the strategy of appeals to conscience has the effect it has because there are different possible extensions of each theory. We do not attempt to differentiate the two psychological theories here. Both frameworks provide a basis for the hypothesis that taxpayers' responses to appeals to conscience will be stronger than their responses to legal sanctions. This hypothesis is constrained by assumptions as to the level of penalty and detection risk. For example, in the extreme case, if the probability of detection is 100%, it is obvious that legal sanctions will loom as a critical variable.

RESEARCH QUESTIONS

The first question is whether taxpayer compliance can be directly modified either by appeals to conscience or threats of punishment. Actual tax compliance behavior cannot be directly observed in a controlled environment. Therefore, this research adopted a measure of tax resistance, the Tax Resistance Scale developed by Spicer and Lundstedt [1976], as an indicator of taxpayer attitude. We examine attitude because, while it is not always consistent with behavior, it may be a component of the behavior decision [Fishbein and Ajzen, 1975] and provides preliminary evidence of expected behavior, although a recent study questions this conclusion for taxpayer self-reports.[1]

Consequently, the first null hypothesis is

H_1: Taxpayer attitudes toward tax compliance are not affected by appeals to conscience and threat of punishment.

If attitudes can be modified by external actions, the relative strength of appeals to conscience versus punishment threat is an important question. Deterrence and reward theories provide some evidence that appeals to conscience may be a more effective behavior modifier than sanction threat within certain boundaries. Therefore, the second null hypothesis is:

H₂: There is no difference between the effects of an appeal to conscience or a threat of punishment on taxpayers' attitudes toward tax compliance.

The relationship between demographic variables and tax evasion behavior has long been of interest [Tittle, 1980; Spicer and Lundstedt, 1976]. Four personal characteristics for which there is evidence of a relationship are age, gender, education, and knowledge of peer noncompliance [Jackson and Milliron, 1986]. In particular, taxpayers appear to become more compliant as they grow older [see e.g., Tittle, 1980; Aitken and Bonneville, 1980], although other studies have found no relationship [e.g., Yankelovich et al., 1984].

Studies that have examined the relationship between gender and compliance are about equally divided between those that have reported that men are more likely to evade [e.g., Tittle, 1980] and those that have found no relationship [e.g., Westat, 1980; Yankelovich et al., 1984]. It is interesting to note that more recent studies tend to be the ones in which no relationship is found. Grasmick et al. [1984] provided evidence that "nontraditional" women entering the taxpaying population in growing numbers may behave more like men and narrow this gap. This finding highlights the need to look beyond the gender variable itself to identify the relevant underlying variables.

Education has been less frequently investigated than the other variables discussed. When a relationship has been found, it has generally been that more educated taxpayers are more compliant. The final variable, knowledge of others who evade, has been shown consistently to be related to evasion in survey studies, although two experimental studies [Chang, 1984, and Spicer and Hero, 1985] reported no relationship. The variables of age, gender, and the number of evaders personally known by the subject were included as covariates in the analysis.

EXPERIMENTAL DESIGN

Tax compliance research has commonly used students as subjects. This approach is troublesome when we compare the relative financial and quantitative sophistication of those subjects with that of the general population. There is also a significant experiential difference relevant to tax compliance studies. In an attempt to overcome the problems related to the nonrepresentativeness of student subjects, we used potential jurors awaiting jury selection in Golden, Colorado as subjects for this study. The jurors had been selected randomly from a list compiled by the district on the basis of city directories, vehicle registrations, and

Table 1. Demographic Data

	Appeals	*Penalties*	*Control*
Total Number of Subjects	21	21	24
Gender			
Male	9	11	13
Female	12	10	11
Age			
Under 30	4	5	4
30-39	4	5	7
40-49	7	4	6
50 and over	6	7	7
Education			
High School-Some College	13	14	16
College Graduate	8	7	8

voter registrations. While this group is not a random selection from the population of taxpayers in the district, (i.e., all persons in the district are not on the juror selection list, nor are all persons on the juror selection list taxpayers), it is a particularly appropriate group because of the scope and independence of the selection process. Further, in this district there is a policy of excusing very few jurors from making an initial appearance. The demographic characteristics of the subjects who participated are shown in Table 1.

The subjects were assigned randomly to one of three groups. The packets given to the subjects were identical except for the content of an introductory essay that comprised the first two pages in the packet. Group 1 was given the instrument introduced with an essay strongly emphasizing tax penalties and the IRS recourse possible against noncomplying taxpayers (Exhibit 1). Group 2's packet was introduced with an essay emphasizing the obligation of citizens to support the government and explaining how tax dollars are used (Exhibit 2). Group 3, the untreated group, was given a neutral essay describing the legislative process followed in enactment of tax provisions (Exhibit 3). Written stimuli have been used to test changes in attitudes in a variety of psychological studies and have been found to affect attitudes in such diverse contexts as the effects of smoking [Maddux and Rodgers, 1983] and gay rights [Maass and Clark, 1983]. This approach was adopted because of its ease of administration and because it could be adopted by the government at relatively low cost in conjunction with the tax return packets mailed to taxpayers each year.

Following the essay, the subjects were asked to complete a questionnaire (Exhibit 4) in which they were first queried about their agreement or disagreement with 23 attitudinal statements. The questionnaire included 15 items from Spicer and Lundstedt's [1976] tax resistance scale, four questions concerning flat-tax and value-added tax proposals, and four additional questions concerning general attitudes about evasion. The additional questions were included because we anticipated using them for other purposes. They are not analyzed in this study. Then subjects were asked to indicate their knowledge of evaders and whether they had ever taken unjustified deductions or failed to report income. Finally the subjects were asked certain demographic information (Exhibit 5).

Of the 81 persons asked to complete the questionnaire, 75 agreed. Of those 75, 66 completed usable questionnaires. The composition of each group is shown in Table 1. The subjects were asked individually to participate in the study and were told that the questionnaires were for research purposes only. Anonymity of the subjects was assured.

RESULTS

The dependent variable in this study was the sum of responses on the 15 questions reflecting tax resistance. The reported means in Table 3 have been deflated by 15 to reflect the measure on the 5-point scale with one as least resistant and 5 as most resistant. This variable is taken as the surrogate for the subjects' propensity to evade. The tax resistance scale is intended to reflect a single underlying variable. The reliability of the scale in representing the same underlying variable was assessed by calculating a reliability coefficient (Cronbach's alpha) of .87395. This coefficient indicates that the scale is reasonably reliable. In Spicer and Lundstedt's [1976] original work with this scale, a reliability coefficient of 84% was calculated on their data.

The demographic variables of age, gender, education, and number of evaders known to the subject were examined for correlation with the dependent variable. Age and gender were significantly ($r = .32$ and .31, respectively) correlated with the tax resistance measure while education and the number of evaders known were not. All four variables have been linked to tax resistance and/or tax evasion in previous research [Jackson and Milliron, 1986]. The variables age, gender, education, and number of evaders personally known were used as covariates in the analysis. The "number of evaders personally known" question was not answered by 3 of our 66 subjects and was not a significant covariate. Therefore, we eliminated that covariate in order to retain the subjects who did not answer the question. The variables age, gender, and education were used as classification variables because there was no reason a priori to hypothesize a linear relationship between these variables and the tax resistance measure.

Table 2. Analysis of Variance

Source	D.F.	Sum Squares	Mean Square	F	p	R^2
Model	7	1543.146	308.629	4.38	.002	.27
Error	58	4223.884	70.398			
Total	65	5767.030				
Group	2	215.085		1.53	.225	
Gender	1	510.442		7.25	.009	
Age	1	626.663		8.90	.004	
Education	1	103.186		1.46	.231	

The effects of group assignment, age, gender, and education were analyzed simultaneously using Analysis of Variance (ANOVA). The results of the analysis are presented in Table 2. No significant differences were found between groups. Therefore, we were unable to reject the null hypotheses. There were no significant interactions in this analysis. The variables of gender and age were significant (.009 and .004, respectively). Responses of subjects by gender were analyzed to determine treatment effects by gender. The gender effect has frequently been found to be significant. However, the finding of a gender effect has been of limited use because no theory has been advanced to explain it. Thus, it tells us nothing about the relevant underlying variables represented by the variable "gender." From a policy perspective, it would be impossible to use that variable as an audit criterion, despite its frequently documented relationship to evasion. We examined the relationship between the two treatments and gender in an attempt to gain insights to help guide future research attempts to uncover relevant underlying variables.

Table 3 presents the means and ANOVA results for the between-group analysis on males and females. The appeals treatment had a marginally significant (p = .088) effect on females but not on males, suggesting that women responded more to appeals to conscience than to sanction threat. It is also interesting to note that the direction of the means suggests that the penalty essay induced greater resistance, although that effect was not significant in this study. Within the appeals group, women's resistance to taxpaying was significantly lower than men's (p = .012); but in the penalties and control groups, there were no significant differences between the resistance scores of men and women.

The implication from our research is that some people approach tax situations in a more economically rational fashion than others. In our society, men are more likely to be more highly trained and experienced in risky economic choices and, as a result, are more likely to evaluate decisions from this framework. Therefore, the gender variable may, in part, be a proxy for this combination of a particular type of experience and training. Future

Table 3.   Means by Group and Gender

Group Means	All Subjects	Males	Females
Appeals	1.99	2.42	1.67
Penalties	2.32	2.44	2.19
Control	2.23	2.30	2.16
F	1.587	.220	2.638
p	.213	.804	.088

Note: The group means have been deflated by 15.

research can specifically explore this and other dimensions of gender differences in the necessary step of eliminating the use of a gender variable in tax compliance research.

LIMITATIONS AND CONCLUSIONS

This research examined the relative influence on juror subjects' "tax resistance" responses of using appeals to conscience or sanction threats as incremental approaches to current administrative procedures. The magnitude of the noncompliance problem demands that nontraditional approaches to addressing the problem be investigated. Former Commissioner Gibbs initiated such a process. It is likely that these efforts would be more efficient if research could provide a predictive foundation.

The hypothesis that the two approaches tested herein might have different effects on taxpayer attitudes is supported by research in different contexts. Psychological research in general [Skinner, 1953] supports the notion that rewards are more effective behavior modifiers than punishment. It seems reasonable to assume that appeals to conscience result in a "reward" to a taxpayer because the taxpayer feels good doing what he or she views as the "right" thing to do. An equally valid interpretation is that if a person does not do what he or she perceives as "right," the punishment is guilt feelings. Researchers have used both interpretations without explicitly addressing the issue of whether the appeal results in a reward or an alternative form of a penalty. This research was not concerned with the resolution of that issue, but with exploring alternatives to penalties and sanctions as approaches to the tax compliance problem.

Our study does not support differential effects of the two behavior modification strategies overall. This study does confirm the relationship between age and gender demonstrated in other studies. This finding is important because our subjects are more nearly representative of the general taxpaying population than the subjects in many other studies. Further, we find that women are more responsive to appeals to conscience than to sanction threat and that within the appeals group, they are significantly less resistant than men. However, because gender is an inappropriate criterion for administrative policymaking, we offered one explanation for the difference found and recommend additional research effort on the gender variable.

There are several possible explanations for our finding of no overall treatment effect. First, taxpayers may not respond to direct manipulations of the type used in these experiments because the indirect influences (e.g., previous sanction threat messages, peer influence, perceptions of unfairness in taxation) are so much stronger. For example, the past sanction threat message may be so strong that it overwhelms an appeal message which is perhaps viewed as only meaningless rhetoric. A determination that indirect influences are difficult to overcome has important implications for the government's ability to counterbalance those influences and is worthy of further research effort.

It is also possible that the hypotheses of this paper are valid but that the treatments in this experiment were not salient operationalizations of the concepts, at least in a hypothetical setting. Written stimuli may not be as influential in the tax setting as it has been shown to be in others because of differences in experiential effects or psychological constructs of the issues.

Taxpayer compliance is a problem both in absolute magnitude and in terms of the distributional effects on taxpayers. Nontraditional approaches of influencing compliance have the potential for improving the efficient administration of our tax laws and, therefore, deserve increased research attention.

NOTE

1. Hessing et al. [1988] compares self-reported past evasion behavior with "official data" and reports no correlation between the two measures. The authors conclude, on the basis of this study, that we cannot believe what taxpayers say. However, because they have not validated the "official data" measure as being a reliable objective measure of "true compliance," the only conclusion that can be drawn from the study is that the measures are different. Because taxpayers are in control of the facts and the government officials, in most cases, have the better understanding of the law, it is likely that "true compliance" is somewhere between the two measures. The criticisms of this study are excellently articulated in Kinsey [1988].

REFERENCES

Aitken, S. and L. Bonneville, "A General Taxpayer Opinion Survey," IRS Office of Planning and Research (CSR Incorporated, March 1980).

Chang, O., "Tax Avoidance: A Prospect Theory Perspective," Unpublished Ph.D. Dissertation, University of Illinois (1984).

Fishbein, M. and I. Ajzen, *Belief, Attitude, Intention and Behavior* (Addison-Wesley, 1975).

Grasmick, H., N. Finley, and D. Glaser, "Labor Force Participation, Sex-Role Attitudes, and Female Crime: Evidence from a Survey of Adults," *Social Science Quarterly* (1984), pp. 703-18.

Grasmick, H. and W. Scott, "Tax Cheating and Mechanisms of Social Control: A Comparison with Grand and Petty Theft," *Journal of Economic Psychology* (1982), pp. 213-230.

Hessing, D., H. Elffers, and R. Weigel, "Exploring the Limits of Self-Reports and Reasoned Action: An Investigation of the Psychology of Tax Evasion Behavior," *Journal of Personality and Social Psychology* (March 1988), pp. 405-413.

Internal Revenue Service, "Income Tax Compliance Research: Gross Tax Gap Estimates and Projections for 1973-1992," Publication 7285 (March 1988).

Jackson, B. and V. Milliron, "Tax Compliance Research: Findings, Problems, and Prospects," *Journal of Accounting Literature* (1986), pp. 125-165.

Kinsey, K., "So What's the 'Real' Compliance Measure: New Data on Taxpayer/Auditor Disagreements," Presentation at the First European Conference on Law and Psychology, Maastricht, The Netherlands (June 1988).

Maass, A. and R. Clark, "Internalization Versus Compliance: Differential Processes Underlying Minority Influence and Conformity," *European Journal of Social Psychology* (July-Sept. 1983), pp. 197-215.

Maddux, J. and R. Rogers, "Protection Motivations and Self-Efficacy: A Revised Theory of Fear Appeals and Attitude Change," *Journal of Experimental Social Psychology* (Sept. 1983), pp. 469-479.

Schwartz, R. and S. Orleans, "On Legal Sanctions," *University of Chicago Law Review* (1967), pp. 274-300.

Skinner, B. *Science and Human Behavior* (MacMillan, 1953).

Spicer, M. and R. Hero, "Tax Evasion and Heuristics: A Research Note," *Journal of Public Economics* (Feb. 1985), pp. 263-67.

Spicer, M. and S. Lundstedt, "Understanding Tax Evasion," *Public Finance* (1976), pp. 295-305.

Thurman, Q., C. St. John, and L. Riggs, "Neutralization and Tax Cheating: How Effective Would Moral Appeal Be in Improving Compliance to Tax Laws?" *Law and Policy* (1984), pp. 309-27.

Tittle, C., *Sanctions and Social Deviance: The Question of Deterrence* (Praeger, 1980).

Westat, Inc., "Self-Reported Tax Compliance: A Pilot Survey Report," prepared for the Internal Revenue Service (March 1980).

Yankelovich, Skelly, and White, Inc. "Taxpayer Attitudes Study: Final Report," prepared for the Internal Revenue Service (1984).

EXHIBIT 1

As taxpayers, we all report our own income, deductions, and calculate our own tax. Recently, because some taxpayers do not comply with tax laws, Congress has placed in force numerous penalties. There are basically two types of penalties assessed: (1) penalties added to and assessed as part of our tax; and (2) criminal penalties enforceable by suit or prosecution.

Penalties added to our tax include a penalty for failure to file of up to 25% of our tax due; penalty for failure to pay on time of up to 25% of tax due plus an interest which is currently 11% (now the rate may be increased by 120% if a lack of tax paid resulted from a tax-motivated transaction). This interest is compounded daily meaning that interest is paid on interest. There are also penalties for a substantial understatement of tax liability as well as a $500 penalty for filing a "frivolous return" which was instituted to stop so-called "tax protestors" from filing returns with inadequate information.

Criminal penalties can involve fines and/or imprisonment. Some of the major fines include the following: (1) willful attempt to evade or defeat any tax: $100,000; (2) willful failure to keep records, report information, or pay any tax or estimated tax: $25,000; (3) willful filing of a false declaration under penalty of perjury, aiding or abetting in the preparation of false or fraudulent documents, execution of a false document, or concealment of goods to evade or defeat any tax: $100,000; and (4) willful delivery of a false or fraudulent document to the IRS: $10,000.

Assessment of these penalties are the result of examinations of tax returns and/ or prosecution. All business and individual tax returns are now processed by an electronic automatic data system. This involves checking for mathematical accuracy and checking for completeness by observing income reported to the IRS by employers (salaries), corporations (dividends), and/or banks (interest), and matching these with the income reported by us as individuals. Returns are also selected for examination because the returns report income at a certain level, the returns have unusual dependency exemptions, the returns report substantial income not reported on W-2s or the returns are selected through the Discriminant Function (DIF) system. DIF gives each return a score related to items reported or lacking items on a return. If the score is outside a set range, the return is picked up for examination. Once picked, taxpayers are notified or summonsed and returns are assessed penalties or processed through our court system.

EXHIBIT 2

Nations have declined because they were defeated in war, lost their economic advantage, or suffered a failure of leadership. The United States may become the first great power in history to falter because it has lost the ability to collect taxes. Politically and economically, few matters are as important as the taxes people pay to their government. Supreme Court Justice Holmes once described taxes as a mark of the *privilege* of citizenship in civilized society. Because our tax system is based largely on voluntary compliance in which we as taxpayers report and calculate our own tax, our government must depend on its citizens to pay their taxes.

Although all of us grumble and complain, we must never forget that we have built one of the most complex and powerful nations in the world. With our taxes, our government pays directly to individuals 42% of every dollar. Our government spends for our national defense 29% or every dollar, for grants to states and localities 11%, for interest to meet our budget 12%, and for other operations 6%. The programs supported by our tax dollars are many and reflect the national needs which can only be fulfilled by our government.

Our government does provide for the defense of the American people, its institutions, its lands, and must preserve a balance of power to promote peace and security. Our government directs foreign policy in order to achieve world peace and promote the respect for human rights. Our government seeks to ensure long-term scientific and technological strength through support of our space programs and the funding of research. Our government promotes programs designed to ensure responsible management and conservation of natural resources; to ensure returns to farmers based on competition, costs and improved technology; to support state and local governments in providing safe, efficient movement of people and distribution of goods and services; and to promote economic and social growth of communities. Our government provides assistance to education in order to promote equal access for all Americans and to help those of special needs. Our government also provides a number of programs to help in the training for long-term employment and provides social services for the needy. Our government seeks to assure to quality health care services through programs such as Medicare and Medicaid, and also encourages reductions in costs, and supports research and training. Of prime importance to us and our government is income security. Our government pays to the aged, disabled, and unemployed approximately 33% of the total federal government budget to insure that its citizens have income security.

Although our system of government is not perfect, with widespread concern and continued support of America's citizens, we will not be a nation that falters because of the loss of the ability to collect taxes. It is imperative that all of us pay our taxes in support of the programs and the democratic way of life.

EXHIBIT 3

Since 1939, Congress has codified all Federal Tax law. The present Internal Revenue Code was codified in 1954. Amendments to the tax law are brought about by legislative process.

Generally, tax legislation originates in the House of Representatives where it is first considered by the House Ways and Means Committee. Once accepted by the House Ways and Means Committee, the proposed bill is referred to the whole House of Representatives. Approved bills are then sent to the Senate Finance Committee. From the Finance Committee, bills that are accepted are sent to the Senate. If there were no changes made between the House and Senate bills, the bill is forwarded to the President for approval. If approved by the President or if the President's veto is overridden, the bill is incorporated into the code.

However, whenever the Senate version of the bill differs from that passed by the House, the Joint Committee, which includes members of both the House Ways and Means Committee and the Senate Finance Committee, meets to resolve differences. The compromise bill is then sent to both the House and the Senate. If accepted by the House and Senate, the bill is sent to the President for approval.

When a bill is incorporated into the code, the code authorizes and instructs the Secretary of the Treasury or his delegates to issue regulations interpreting the tax law. The Internal Revenue Service is a subdivision of the Treasury Department and does issue rulings dealing with the administration and interpretation of tax laws.

A Typical Legislative Process

House Ways and Means Committee

Consideration by the House of
Representatives

Senate Finance Committee

Consideration by the Senate   Joint Conference Committee
                                               (if House and Senate bills
                                               differ)

                                               Consideration by House and
                                               Senate

Approval or Veto by President

Incorporation into Code

EXHIBIT 4

There are a number of statements that reflect what some people think about certain
aspects of taxation, especially federal income taxes. Please circle the appropriate score
as to how you feel about taxes.

> a = Strongly agree
> b = Agree
> c = Uncertain
> d = Disagree
> e = Strongly disagree

1. Given present tax burdens, one can hardly
   blame tax evaders.   a   b   c   d   e
2. The new flat-rate proposals would make peo-
   ple less likely to evade taxes.   a   b   c   d   e

3. Given the easy availability of opportunities to evade taxes, one can hardly blame tax evaders.   a   b   c   d   e

4. If in doubt about whether or not to report a certain source of income, I would not report it.   a   b   c   d   e

5. Since the government gets enough taxes, it does not matter that some people evade taxes.   a   b   c   d   e

6. Taxes are so heavy that tax evasion is an economic necessity for many to survive.   a   b   c   d   e

7. Flat taxes would ensure that the rich pay their fair share.   a   b   c   d   e

8. If I received $2,000 in cash for services rendered, which is not included on a W-2, I would not report it.   a   b   c   d   e

9. Cheating on taxes is justifiable in light of the unfairness of the tax system.   a   b   c   d   e

10. I would never pad my deductions.   a   b   c   d   e

11. Taxes are something which are taken away from me.   a   b   c   d   e

12. Since everybody evades taxes, one can hardly be blamed for doing it.   a   b   c   d   e

13. I would never evade taxes.   a   b   c   d   e

14. The new flat tax proposals would make taxes more equitable.   a   b   c   d   e

15. When it comes to paying taxes, I say take the IRS for what you can get.   a   b   c   d   e

16. There is nothing bad about underreporting taxable income on one's tax return.   a   b   c   d   e

17. If a man intentionally lists less income on his tax return than legally required, more power to him.   a   b   c   d   e

18. A value added tax (a national sales tax) would make taxes more equitable.   a   b   c   d   e

19. I would feel no qualms at all about not reporting all my income to the Internal Revenue Service.   a   b   c   d   e

20. Since tax evasion hurts no one but the government, it is not a serious offense.   a   b   c   d   e

21. Considering the high cost of living today, one should be fined but not jailed for padding a few income tax deductions.   a   b   c   d   e

22. In dealing with the IRS, the main thing is not
    to get caught.   a   b   c   d   e

23. There are so many "loopholes" favoring the
    rich that the average taxpayer should not be
    expected to obey all his tax obligations.   a   b   c   d   e

Thank you. I would like to ask you just a few more questions about your experiences
and reactions to income taxes.

24. How many people do you know personally who do not report all their income
    and/or pad their deductions?

    a. none _____

    b. 1-5 _____

    c. 5-10 _____

    d. 10-15 _____

    e. over 15 _____

25. Which of the following statements best sums up your behavior with respect
    to taking tax deductions?

    a. I never take a deduction I don't believe is
    justified. _____

    b. I will occasionally take deductions that I don't
    believe are justified. _____

    c. I often take deductions I know are not justified.

    _____

26. Which of the following statements best sums up your behavior with respect
    to reporting taxable income?

    a. I always report every cent that I know I have
    earned. _____

    b. I will occasionally not report some income that I
    have earned. _____

    c. I often do not report parts of my income. _____

EXHIBIT 5

General Background Questions

1. Please circle your sex: Male   Female

2. Do you usually prepare your own tax return?   Yes   No

Do you usually file a long (1040) form?   Yes   No

3. What is your occupation?   self   spouse
                                                                (if applicable)

     a. self-employed   _____   _____

     b. not self-employed   _____   _____

4. Please indicate your age.

     a. Under 21 _____

     b. 21-29 _____

     c. 30-39 _____

     d. 40-49 _____

     e. 50-59 _____

     f. 60 or over _____

5. What was the last grade you completed.

     a. some high school _____

     b. high school graduate _____

     c. some college _____

     d. college graduate _____

     e. postgraduate or professional education _____

6. Please indicate your (and your spouse, if applicable) total average annual
     income from salaries and self-employment.

                                                 self   spouse

     a. under $10,000   _____   _____

     b. $10,000 to $14,999   _____   _____

     c. $15,000 to $19,999   _____   _____

     d. $20,000 to $29,999   _____   _____

     e. $30,000 to $39,999   _____   _____

     f. $40,000 and over   _____   _____

7. Please indicate your (and your spouse, if applicable) total average annual income from sources *other than* salaries or self-employment income.

	self	spouse
a. under $2,000	_____	_____
b. $2,000 to $9,999	_____	_____
c. $10,000 to $19,999	_____	_____
d. $20,000 and over	_____	_____

INVESTMENT RETURNS AND INFLATION NEUTRALITY UNDER ALTERNATE TAX STRUCTURES:
INVESTMENT AND PUBLIC POLICY IMPLICATIONS

William R. Reichenstein and William A. Raabe

ABSTRACT

This paper discusses important differences in the investment and public policy implications of five tax structures. The expected real wealth position from an investment in each structure is influenced by the inflation indexation of the cost basis of an investment, the deferral of tax liability on any related investment appreciation and yield until distribution occurs, the proportion of return in unrealized capital gains, and the exclusion of the investment amount from gross income. The importance of the length of the investment horizon, the prevailing real rate of interest, the expected rate of inflation, and the effective tax rate also varies greatly among the tax structures. The expected real wealth from some tax structures is found to be independent of the level of expected inflation (i.e., it is inflation-neutral), while other tax structures inappropriately tax the inflation premium that is imbedded in nominal rates of investment return. The government effectively subsidizes an investment in the Individual Retirement Account (IRA)

Advances in Taxation, Volume 2, pages 149-163.
Copyright © 1989 by JAI Press Inc.
All rights of reproduction in any form reserved.
ISBN: 0-89232-783-9

structure with deductible contribution, when the tax rate in the year of withdrawal is less than the rate in the year of deposit.

This paper discusses investment and public policy implications of five alternate tax structures. The tax structures have been chosen to highlight the importance of specific tax features. Although the structures are not intended to be complete models of specific tax systems, the key features of each system do correspond to important features of prevailing or recently proposed tax structures.

The expected real wealth position from an investment in each structure is heavily influenced by the combination of such key features as inflation indexation of the cost base of an investment, the deferral of tax liability on any related investment appreciation and yield until distribution occurs, the exclusion or deduction of the investment amount from gross income and the proportion of return in unrealized capital gains. After considering such factors as the length of the investment horizon, the real rate of interest, the expected rate of inflation, and the effective tax rate that applies to the investor, it becomes apparent that the expected real wealth from some of the structures is inflation-neutral, while other tax structures inappropriately tax the market-derived inflation premium.

The tax structure models are described in the next section of the paper. The expected real wealth positions of the tax structures are modeled for a world of inflation-certainty. The models illustrate key differences in the investment and public policy implications of the tax structures. The final section presents a brief summary of the major conclusions of this paper.

TAX STRUCTURE MODELS

In this section, we present models of five alternative tax structures: (a) a model characteristic of the prevailing tax structure for debt, in which investment returns (including original issue discount) are taxed as ordinary income; (b) a model characteristic of the prevailing tax structure for many equity portfolios, where taxes on capital gains are deferred until realization; (c) a model with inflation indexation of the cost basis of an investment; (d) a model of the IRA tax structure with deductible contribution; this structure closely parallels an expenditure tax system; and (e) a model of the IRA structure without deductible contribution. The models represent the expected real wealth for an investment subject to each tax structure.

Model 1:   The Prevailing General Tax System

Model 1 is characterized by (1) Fisher neutrality, that is, the assumption that interest rates vary one-to-one with expected inflation [Fisher, 1930]; (2)

investment media that do not generate income tax deductions upon investor selection; (3) the annual realization of returns; (4) the inclusion in gross income of the entire nominal yield on an investment; and (5) the lack of inflation indexation of the cost base of an investment.

The Fisher hypothesis [1896] asserted that

$$i = p + I \qquad (1)$$

where i is the investor's expected nominal yield, p is the expected real, before-tax return on the investment, I is expected inflation rate, and all rates are continuously compounded. The inflation premium (I) represents a market repayment of the expected loss of purchasing power of principal. Thus, under the Fisher hypothesis, I represents a return *of* the original purchasing power, rather than a return *on* the investment, and is not an appropriate element of the income tax base.

Fisher neutrality is commonly assumed in scholarly analyses of interest rates [Modigliani and Shiller, 1973; Feldstein and Chamberlain, 1973; Fama, 1981; Fama and Gibbons, 1982]. In fact, it is the cornerstone of virtually all interest rate models [Elliott and Baier, 1979]. Moreover, studies that directly examine the relationship of nominal interest rates and expected inflation such as Wilcox [1983], Brown and Santoni [1983], and Kelly and Miles [1984] maintain that Fisher neutrality adequately describes the prevailing economy.

In a tax structure that includes in gross income the entire nominal yield on an investment, given marginal tax rate (t), the investor's annual expected real, after-tax return p_a can be stated as

$$p_a = i \, (1 - t) - I. \qquad (2)$$

The tax falls fully on i, but the investor's real return excludes the fictional effect of receiving I. Inserting the Fisher neutrality hypothesis (1) yields

$$p_a = p \, (1 - t) - It, \qquad (3)$$

which, after accumulation for n periods and expressed as a future value, generates for the investor the following measure of inflation-adjusted wealth,

$$M1 = e^{[p \, (1 - t) - It]n} \qquad (4)$$

where e is the common exponential function.

Equation (4) treats all nominal returns, including the return of principal in the form of I, as ordinary income and subjects them fully to taxation at rate t. A key feature of the model is the taxation of the inflation premium (It), which represents the taxation of principal from an economic perspective.

Model 2:   Tax System with Preferential Treatment of Capital Gains

In the second model, we assume (1) Fisher neutrality; (2) investment media that do not generate income tax deductions upon investor selection; (3) g percent of annual nominal return in the form of capital gains; (4) an annual portfolio turnover rate of v percent; and, (5) the lack of inflation indexation of the investment's cost basis.

Setting $g = 0.60$ and $v = 0.40$ makes this model indicative of the common stock return prospects for individuals practicing a relatively inactive portfolio strategy; a portfolio turnover rate of 0.40 implies that 40% of capital gains are realized annually. Model 1 is indicative of return prospects both for debt investments and for actively managed equity portfolios, that is, $v \simeq 1.0$.

Doyle [1984] developed a model of the after-tax value of an investment where g percent of annual returns is in the form of capital gains, and v is the portfolio turnover rate. The nominal amount of the investment after n-years is:

$$e^{rn} - t_n (1 - v) \, gi \, [e^{rn} - 1)/r] \qquad (5)$$

where $r = (1 - tv) \, gi + (1 - t) (1 - g)i$. The product $(1 - g)i$ represents the income (i.e., interest and dividends) proportion of the security's nominal return. The product gi represents the proportion of return in the form of capital gains, and giv represents the portion of realized capital gains. Thus, r is the annual return before the funds are withdrawn in year n, and e^{rn} is the extent of the funds withdrawn in n years. The amount to the right of the minus sign gives the tax on capital gains realized upon withdrawal in n years, where t_n is the applicable tax rate for year n.

Inserting the Fisher neutrality hypothesis (1) produces

$$e^{rn} - t_n (1 - v) \, g \, (p + I) \, [e^{rn} - 1)/r]. \qquad (6)$$

Adjusting this nominal amount for expected inflation produces the expected real wealth,

$$M2 = e^{(r - I)n} - t_n (1 - v) \, g \, (p + I) \, [e^{rn} - 1)/r]_e^{In}]. \qquad (7)$$

Thus, the deferral of taxes on unrealized capital gains does not eliminate the taxation of principal. Further derivational notes relative to Eqs. (4)-(7) are included in the Appendix.

Model 3:   Inflation Indexation

Model 3 is characterized by (1) Fisher neutrality; (2) investment media that do not generate income tax deductions upon investor selection; (3) the annual realization of all returns; and, (4) inflation indexation of the cost base of an investment.

The 1984 Treasury Department report "Tax Reform for Fairness, Simplicity and Economic Growth" (Treasury I) contained a feature that allowed for an adjustment of the cost basis of many investments to reflect applicable inflation (but not deflation). Although the details of specific inflation indexation proposals therein were concerned with such factors as the minimum holding period of the investment and price indices, the stated intention of the proposals was the elimination of the inappropriate taxation of the inflation premium. For our purposes, the importance of inflation indexation can best be analyzed by ignoring specific proposal details and assuming complete asset-by-asset inflation indexation.

Model 3 completely eliminates the inflation premium from the tax base. Thus,

$$p_a = p(1 - t).$$

After n periods, the investor has the following measure of expected real wealth:

$$M3 = e^{[p(1-t)]n} \tag{8}$$

Brinner [1973, p. 570] describes Model 3 as theoretically "the 'perfect' reform," and he uses the after-tax real wealth on an investment subject to this structure as a fairness benchmark.

Brinner [1973, p. 566] proposed a tax procedure that "is equivalent to one in which the government charges interest equal to the real appreciation rate on unpaid, accrued tax liabilities" to eliminate the advantage of deferring taxes on unrealized capital gains. Under this tax structure, the Model 3 values could also apply to investments held longer than one year. Thus the assumption that all returns are realized annually is not critical to the assessment of M3's theoretical merits.

There are practical problems in applying Brinner's procedure. Folsom [1978] shows that Brinner's suggestion for estimating the interest rate seldom will prove optimal. Folsom suggests that the government set the interest rate, and discusses the merits of this proposal. Other practical problems exist when taxes are not assessed annually on the investment's full return.[1]

Model 4: IRA With Tax Deferral of Contribution

Another means by which to remove the inflation premium from the income tax base has been a part of the prevailing tax system for more than 10 years, but only with respect to most Individual Retirement Accounts (IRAs), Simplified Employee Pensions (SEPs), retirement plans for self-employed individuals ("Keogh" or "H.R. 10" plans), and other statutorily qualified pension and profit-sharing arrangements. For simplicity, we refer to such a structure herein as the IRA model with tax deferral of contribution. However, the model also represents other qualified retirement plans whereunder the investment amount is deductible in the year of contribution by the payor.

The major characteristics of Model 4 include: (1) Fisher neutrality; (2) a deduction in computing Adjusted Gross Income of the investment amount itself; (3) a deferral of any tax liability on the related investment appreciation and yield until an investor-directed distribution occurs; (4) inclusion in gross income of the full nominal amount of withdrawal upon investor-directed distribution; and, (5) the lack of inflation indexation of the cost basis of an investment.

A distribution from a prevailing qualified retirement plan generally is available without an "early withdrawal" penalty only after the investor reaches age 59 1/2, or upon the investor's early retirement, death, or disability. Aside from these conditions, a 10% early withdrawal penalty is imposed which may severely limit the liquidity of such investments subject to this tax structure. In the interest of generality, no such liquidity barriers are assumed herein with the Model 4 tax structure.[2] Other statutory restrictions to full contribution-year deductions also are ignored, so as to facilitate our comparison of the posited tax computation models.

Using alternative terminology, the investor is subject to an expenditure tax in Model 4: Amounts that are earned but not spent, and any related appreciation thereon, are not included in gross income until they are withdrawn from the investment medium and spent.

Equation (9) reflects the expected nominal wealth at time n for a taxpayer who is subject to the foregoing conditions. The taxpayer invests "pre-tax dollars" in the instrument, (so called because of the related income tax deduction in year 0), and the entire nominal proceeds upon withdrawal in year n are included in gross income. The model is:

$$M4 = \frac{1}{(1 - t_0)} \, e^{[(p + I)n]} (1 - t_n) \qquad (9)$$

where t_0 and t_n are the marginal tax rates in years 0 and n, respectively. The nominal wealth can be converted to real wealth by dividing by expected inflation e^{In}. Rearranging terms produces:

$$M4 = \frac{1 - t_n}{1 - t_0} \, e^{pn} \qquad (10)$$

Throughout the present analysis, the ratio term of equation 10 will be referred to as the tax-rates scale. The taxation of the inflation premium disappears altogether under Model 4 assumptions, despite the lack of specific inflation indexation, and the tax falls solely upon the investor's increase in real wealth where $t_n = t_0$, that is, where the tax-rates scale equals one. This result is attributable to the deferral of both the investment amount and the returns on the investment.

In fact, the combination of the two deferral features eliminates the taxation of principal (It) and the taxation of the real return (pt) in the M1 tax structure.[3] Accordingly, specific inflation indexation may be inappropriate for investments that are subject to a deferred-income tax structure.

Model 5: IRA Without Tax Deferral of Contribution

The final model presents an IRA tax structure in which the contribution is not deductible. The major characteristics of Model 5 include (1) Fisher neutrality; (2) deferral of any tax liability on the related investment appreciation and yield until an investor-directed distribution occurs; (3) inclusion in gross income of the amount of withdrawal, less the original contribution, upon an investor-directed distribution; and, (4) the lack of inflation indexation of the cost basis of the investment.

The original contribution grows at $p + I$ for n years. Upon withdrawal in year n, all but the original \$1 investment, $e^{[p + I]n} - 1$, is taxed at the marginal tax rate in year n, t_n. The original \$1 basis in the investment is withdrawn tax-free. Dividing the after-tax amount of the withdrawal by the n-year expected inflation rate produces the expected after-tax real wealth:

$$[(e^{[p + I] n} - 1) (1 - t_n) + 1] / e^{In}$$

which, after rearranging terms, can be expressed:

$$e^{pn} (1 - t_n) + t_n e^{-In}. \tag{11}$$

INVESTMENT AND PUBLIC POLICY IMPLICATIONS

We begin this part of our analysis with the commonly cited policy objective that an income tax system should fall upon the return on investment, but not the return of the original investment [*Doyle v. Mitchell Bros.*, 1918]. If substantial inflation had existed at the time of the drafting of the income tax provisions of the first Revenue Act, perhaps that law would have included provisions to adjust for inflation. An adjustment of the cost basis of investment to reflect inflation is a key feature of most modern proposals for comprehensive income tax reform.

Table 1.   Expected Real Wealth from $1 After-Tax Investment
in Various Tax Structures

Tax Model	Investment Horizon (years)					
	1	*5*	*10*	*15*	*25*	*35*
M1 (I = .03)	1.016	1.081	1.168	1.262	1.473	1.720
M1 (I = .10)	0.991	0.956	0.914	0.874	0.799	0.730
M2 (I = .03)	1.016	1.08569	1.18854	1.30991	1.61522	2.01893
M2 (I = .10)	0.991	0.97309	0.97295	0.98976	1.05291	1.13830
M3	1.0263	1.139	1.297	1.477	1.916	2.484

Assumptions: p = .04; t = .35; I = .03 or .10; g = .6; v = .4

Inflation Neutrality

We have shown that Model 3 is inflation-neutral, meaning expected real purchasing power is not affected by the level of expected inflation. Model 4 is inflation-neutral, such that no tax falls on I, only when the tax-rates scale equals one, that is, where the applicable contribution- and withdrawal-year tax rates are identical. Model 5 has relatively little inflation sensitivity, especially for long-term investments. For a positive I and a large n, M5 approaches $e^{pn} (1 - t_n)$.

Models 1 and 2 are not inflation-neutral. This is illustrated in Table 1. For illustrative purposes, the real return on investment is assumed to be 4%,[4] the marginal income tax rate to be 35%, the portfolio turnover rate to be 40%, and the capital gain portion of the annual portfolio return to be 60%,. The difference between inflation-neutral real wealth position M3 and M1 is due to the taxation of principal It. The M3 expected wealth position exceeds the M1 position, with the magnitude increasing with expected inflation (I), the tax rate (t), and the length of the investment horizon (n).

M2 is only slightly less inflation-sensitive than is M1 for the values in Table 1. Comparing expected wealth from M2 with 3% inflation [M2 (I = 0.03)] and 10% inflation [M2 (I = 0.10)], shows the model's sensitivity to inflation. For sufficiently high expected inflation, the expected return on an investment subject to M1 and M2 is negative.

In general, M2's inflation sensitivity decreases with an increase in g and with a decrease in v. For g = 1 and v = 0, M2 reduces to M5, which has virtually no inflation sensitivity.

It is difficult to imagine a diversified portfolio of securities with no current income and no portfolio turnover. However, if we ignore property taxes, an investment in undeveloped real estate has these characteristics. This implies that real estate is a good hedge against unanticipated inflation.

Under tax structure M1 and structure M2 (with values of v and g common to securities portfolios), the government can effectively expropriate private property without due recourse if it purposely produces inflation. If, as some currently believe, the primary engine of persistent inflation is monetary policy [Burger, 1978], and that is under the dominant influence of the executive and legislative branches [Weintraub, 1978; Auerbach, 1985; Brenner, 1981; and Hetzel, 1985a, 1985b], then the present tax structure gives the government the ability to expropriate private property.

In practical terms, this may be justified by the government's need to recoup its own purchasing power losses. Nonetheless, to the extent that such appropriations occur by the "bracket creep" effect, in which increasing marginal rates are applied to stable real income, major policy goals are frustrated [Fellingham and Wolfson, 1978].

Tax Deferral

A key investment distinction between the tax structure M1 and the IRA structure with nondeductible contribution M5 is the latter's deferral of taxes on investment return. Two additional important distinctions between M5 and M4 are the deferral of the recognition of gross income due to the related investment deduction, and the effect of different tax rates on the tax-rates scale, $(1 - t_n)/(1 - t_0)$. The importance of each factor is illustrated in Table 2.

The deferral of taxes on investment return produces a substantial long-term benefit, as shown by comparing the long-term values of M1 and M5. Another important distinction between these models is the investor's opportunity to time his or her withdrawals from M5 to occur in low-tax-rate years.

Comparing values of M5 and M4, where the tax-rates scale (s) equals one, illustrates the advantage of the tax deferral of the contribution. This advantage allows substantially higher returns for all investment horizons. For example, the one-year expected return on M4 (s = 1) in Table 2 is over six times the M5 return. Although the M5 return is quite small in absolute terms, M4 (s = 1) provides an immediate reward for the investor, due chiefly to the contribution-year deduction.

Differences in levels of expected wealth become substantial for longer investment horizons. For high values of the product (In), M4 is approximately the product of M5 times $1/(1 - t_0)$. This long-term advantage is substantial. For example, the 35-year expected wealth for M4 (s = 1) in Table 2 exceeds M5 by 51%.

Table 2. Expected Real Wealth from $1 After-Tax Investment
in Various Tax Structures

	Investment Horizon (years)					
Tax Model	1	5	10	15	25	35
M3	1.026	1.139	1.297	1.477	1.916	2.484
M1	1,005	1.025	1.051	1.078	1.133	1.191
M5	1.006	1.053	1.162	1.327	1.845	2.679
M4 (s = 1)	1.041	1.221	1.492	1.822	2.718	4.055
M4 (s = 1.269)	1.321	1.550	1.893	2.312	3.450	5.146

Assumptions: $p = .04$; $t = .35$; $I = .06$

$$s = \frac{(1 - t_n)}{(1 - t_0)}$$

$s = 1.269$ when $t_n = .15$ and $t_0 = .33$.

Finally, the values of M4 ($s = 1$) and M4 ($s = 1.269$) illustrate the investor's advantage when he/she is subject to a lower tax rate upon withdrawal, that is, $t_n < t_0$. The expected wealth of M4 ($s = 1.269$) exceeds M4 ($s = 1$) by 26.9% for all investment horizons. The tax rates scale is sensitive only to the rates t_0 and t_n; it is not sensitive to n, p, or I.

It is entirely possible for an investment subject to the M4 tax structure, even with a 10% early withdrawal penalty, to substantially outperform the same investment under other tax structures, given a sufficiently large s. In fact, the M4 structure with an early withdrawal penalty can be the preferred tax structure for even a 48-hour investment, as long as the investment period spans two tax years. For example, $1 deposited on December 31 and withdrawn on January 1 is worth 26.9% more (before penalty) if the tax rates in the year of deposit and withdrawal are 33% and 15%.

Table 2 shows that the tax rates scale is clearly the most important variable for short investment horizons. However, the tax deferral of the contribution usually produces a larger long-term benefit. This long-term benefit approaches $1/(1 - t_0)$ as the product In approaches infinity. Accordingly, M4 ($s = 1$) is 151% of M5 when the investment horizon is 35 years. This is twice the benefit of the tax rates scale in Table 2.

Initial analyses of the Tax Reform Act of 1986 often suggest that the elimination of the tax deferral of the IRA contribution for most upper-income investors represents the elimination of IRAs as an effective investment tax structure. M5 clearly is less advantageous than M4, especially when s exceeds one. However, the M5 structure continues to promise substantial long-term benefits, compared to tax structure M1. For example, the 35-year expected wealth from M5 is 225% of the expected M1 wealth in Table 2. In fact, this

225% amount far exceeds the further marginal advantages of conversions to models employing the tax deferral of contribution [M4 (s = 1)] and the tax-rates scale [M4 (s = 1.269)]. Investors who have exhausted savings opportunities under deferred contribution plans similar to structure M4 would be well-advised to consider the remaining benefits of an IRA, even without a deductible contribution.

Another investment implication of the IRA models is the relative importance of the real rate (p). A higher or lower real rate has the most pronounced impact, ceteris paribus, on these investments. The impact of a higher or lower p is shared with the government in the other tax structures. This feature is especially important for long-term investment horizons. Reichenstein [1986, 1987] argues that the expected long-term benefits of investing in higher risk securities may be obtained without significantly increasing long-term risk.[5]

From a public policy perspective, the government taxes neither an M4 investment's principal amount, nor the inflation premium, when the tax-rates scale is one. When the scale exceeds one, the investor's expected real return exceeds the real return on the investment. For a one-year investment, the expected real return is $(s - 1)(1 + p)$ greater than the investment's real return. In such situations, real taxes are negative, resulting in a government subsidy of the investor's decision. If the tax rates scale is sufficiently *below* one, the resulting expected real wealth is negative. Rational investors will avoid the deferred tax structure when such circumstances are present, for example, when tax rates that apply to the investor are expected (statutorily or circumstantially) to increase.

For the M5 tax structure, one can expect to pay taxes of approximately t_n times the accumulated real return. Since the investor has the option to time withdrawals, t_n will often be low. The tax rate could be zero, (perhaps in a year in which the taxpayer incurred catastrophic medical expenses), in which case none of the real return is taxed. A zero rate of taxation could be prevented by imposing a minimum tax on withdrawals. The 10% early withdrawal penalty is a partial step in this direction.

The imposition of a minimum tax on withdrawals from the M4 tax structure would not eliminate the possibility of a federal government subsidy, unless the minimum tax rate itself were set at the maximum federal marginal tax rate. Investments may have been made in a M4 tax structure since before 1981, which means that such a minimum tax rate could be as high as 70%. Assuming such a rate to be politically and economically unreasonable, the federal government continues to subsidize some investments in the M4 tax structure. The imposition of a 33 percent tax on withdrawals would eliminate the possibility of a subsidy on additional investments in a M4 tax structure (assuming that 33% remains the maximum federal marginal tax rate).

CONCLUSIONS

This paper examines the public policy and investment implications of five tax models. The models generally reflect the prevailing general tax structure, an inflation-indexed structure, an IRA structure with tax deferral of contribution, and an IRA structure without tax deferral of contribution.

In general, the expected after-tax, real purchasing power of investments subject to the general tax structure exhibit (M1) and similar models with preferential treatment of capital gains exhibit a strong, negative relationship with expected inflation. For sufficiently high inflation, the investor can expect to lose purchasing power. This occurs because the tax structures inappropriately tax the inflation premium imbedded in nominal rates of investment return. These structures discourage investments and enable the federal government to expropriate wealth by producing inflation.

The expected wealth from the inflation-indexed tax structure (M3) is inflation-neutral. The IRA structure with deductible contributions (M4) is inflation-neutral only when marginal tax rates are equal in the year of contribution and withdrawal. The expected wealth for the IRA structure without deductible contributions (M5) is relatively insensitive to expected inflation.

The M4 structure presents the best tax structure for most investors, especially if a lower tax rate is expected upon withdrawal from the investment vehicle. However, the lower tax rate upon withdrawal can imply a subsidy with the return to the investor that exceeds the return on the underlying investment.

Although the M5 structure is less favorable to the investor than the M4 structure, it presents substantial long-term benefits, especially compared with tax structure M1. However, unlike the IRA structure without deductible contributions, this feature does not imply a subsidy for the investor.

APPENDIX

Derivation of Eqs. (4)-(7)

Derivation of Eq. (4)

The value of \$1 continuously compounded at the annual rate x for n years is e^{xn}, where e is the exponential function (e = 2.71828 ...). Substituting Eq. (1) into (2) yields the annual after-tax growth rate,

$$pa = p(1 - t) - It. \qquad (3)$$

The after-tax value of this investment after n years is therefore,

$$e^{[p(1-t)-It]n} \qquad (4)$$

Derivation of Eqs. (5)-(7)

The product $(1 - g)i$ represents the current income (interest or dividends) of a security's i percent annual return. Thus $(1 - t)(1 - g)i$ is the after-tax return from current income. The product (gi) represents annual capital gains, of which v percent is realized annually. Tax on realized gains is thus $tvgi$, and the annual after-tax return from capital gains is $gi - tvgi$ or $(1 - tv)gi$. The annual after-tax return (r) is the sum of the annual after-tax returns from current income and capital gains.

The product to the right of the minus sign gives the tax on capital gains realized upon withdrawal in n years, where t_n is the applicable tax rate in year n. Since gi represents capital gain income, the unrealized annual return in the form of capital gains is $(1 - v)gi$. The dollar amount of the gain increases with the beginning-of-year investment amount. The unrealized gain is $\$(1 - v)gi$ in the first year, and it grows with the beginning-of-year investment amount at r percent annually. Thus,

$$\sum_{j=0}^{n-1} (1 - v)\, gi\, erj = (1 - v)\, gi \sum_{j=0}^{n-1} erj \tag{1A}$$

is the accumulated unrealized gain after n years. From the future value of an annuity formula we know the reduced form of the last summation in (1A) is $[e^{rn} - 1]/r$. Making the substitution and multiplying by the tax rate t_n gives the tax liability upon withdrawal on accumulated capital gains, Eq. (5).

Equation (6) makes the substitution $i = p + I$. Dividing the expected nominal wealth in (6) by expected n year inflation e^{In} produces Eq. (7).

NOTES

1. For example, a large capital gain may force an investor's other income into a higher marginal tax rate. Brinner and Munnell [1974] suggest averaging capital gains and losses separately from ordinary income.

2. Other, less frequently encountered, exceptions to the IRC §72(t) 10% early withdrawal penalty also are available. The lack of a withdrawal penalty has several antecedents in the prevailing tax law, for example, with respect to certain withdrawals from employer fringe benefit plans, or from annuity vehicles that are provided by tax-exempt employers.

3. The reason for this effect can best be seen by considering a one-year investment horizon with constant tax rates, for example $t_0 = t_n$ and $s = 1$.

A $1 after-tax investment in the M1 tax structure must be compared with a $1/(1 - t)$ before-tax investment in the M4 structure. The $1/(1 - t)$ investment can be thought of as a $1 investment plus a $t/(1 - t)$ investment due to tax savings. The real, after-tax return on the $1 is $p(1 - t)$ $- I$. The tax savings $t/(1 - t)$ earn the nominal rate, $p + I$. After adjusting for taxes (i.e. multiplying by $(1 - t)$, thereby eliminating the $(1 - t)$ denominator), the real return increases by $pt + pI$.

4.   The 4% real rate represents the approximate 1925-1984 real rate of return on a balanced bond-equity fund, before management fees and transaction costs, and thus is a reasonable real rate assumption for many investors. See Reichenstein [1986, 1987].

5.   Reichenstein [1986] argues that the long-term probability distribution of a high risk (p) portfolio may dominate the long-term distribution of a low risk portfolio. In such circumstances, it is difficult to call the high p portfolio riskier than the low p portfolio, since it is virtually certain to produce a better long-term return.

REFERENCES

Auerbach, R.D. (1985), "Politics and the Federal Reserve," *Contemporary Policy Issues* (Fall 1985), pp. 43-58.

Brenner, K. (1981), "Policymaking, Accountability, and the Social Responsibility of the Fed," in *Shadow Open Market Committee*, University of Rochester Graduate School of Management (March 1981), pp. 69-83.

Brinner, R. (1973), "Inflation, Deferral and the Neutral Taxation of Capital Gains," *National Tax Review* (December 1973), pp. 565-573.

Brinner, R. and A. Munnell (1974), "Taxation of Capital Gains: Inflation and Other Problems," *New England Economic Review* (September-October 1974), pp. 3-21.

Brown, W.W., and G.J. Santoni, "Monetary Growth and the Timing of Interest Rate Movements," *Federal Reserve Bank of St. Louis Review* (August/September 1983), pp. 16-25.

Burger, A.E., "Is Inflation All Due to Money?" *Federal Reserve Bank of St. Louis Review* (December 1978), pp. 8-12.

Doyle, R.J., Jr., "IRAs and the Capital-Gains Tax Effect," *Financial Analysts Journal* (May-June 1984), pp. 60-66.

Doyle v. Mitchell Bros. Co., 247 US 179 (1918).

Elliott, J.W., and J.R. Baier, "Econometric Models and Current Interest Rates: How Well Do They Predict Future Rates?" *The Journal of Finance* (September 1979), pp. 975-986.

Fama, E.F., "Stock Returns, Real Activity, Inflation, and Money," *American Economic Review* (September 1981), pp. 545-565.

Fama, E.F., and M.R. Gibbons, "Inflation, Real Returns, and Capital Investments," *The Journal of Monetary Economics* (1982), pp. 297-323.

Feldstein, M., and G. Chamberlain, "Multimarket Expectations and the Rate of Interest," *The Journal of Money, Credit, and Banking* (November 1973).

Fellingham and Wolfson, "The Effects of Alternative Income Tax Structures on Risk Taking in Capital Markets," *National Tax Journal* (December 1978), pp. 339-347.

Fisher, I., *Appreciation and Interest* (New York 1896).

Fisher, I., *The Theory of Interest* (Macmillan Press, 1930).

Folsom, R.N., "Neutral Capital Gains Taxation Under Inflation and Tax Deferral," *National Tax Review* (December 1978), pp. 401-405.

Hetzel, R.L., "A Congressional Mandate for Monetary Policy," *The Cato Journal* (Fall 1985a).

————, "A Mandate of Price Stability for the Federal Reserve System," *Contemporary Policy Issues* (Fall 1985b), pp. 59-67.

Kelly, W.A., Jr., and J.A. Miles, "Derby and Fisher: Resolution of a Paradox," *The Financial Review* (March 1984), pp. 103-110.

Modigliani, F., and R.J. Shiller, "Inflation, Rational Expectations and the Rate of Interest," *The Journal of Money, Credit, and Banking* (November 1973).

Reichenstein, W.R., "When Stock is Less Risky Than Treasury Bills," *Financial Analysts Journal* (November-December 1986), pp. 71-75.

————, "On Standard Deviation and Risk," *Journal of Portfolio Management* (Winter 1987), pp. 39-40.

Weintraub, R., "Congressional Supervision of Monetary Policy," *Journal of Monetary Economics* (April 1978), pp. 341-362.

Wilcox, J.A., "Why Real Interest Rates Were So Low in the 1970s," *American Economic Review* (March 1983), pp. 44-53.

THE QUALITY OF
PRACTICIONERS' JUDGMENTS
REGARDING SUBSTANTIAL AUTHORITY:
AN EXPLORATORY EMPIRICAL INVESTIGATION

Chee W. Chow, Michael D. Shields, and
Gerald E. Whittenburg

ABSTRACT

A major challenge facing tax practioners is evaluating the level of available substantial authority for alternate tax treatments. Since many sources of authority exist, and these sources frequently conflict, different tax practioners may disagree regarding the level of authority in support of a particular tax treatment. The resultant divergence of evaluations can significantly affect the welfare of both tax clients and tax practitioners. This paper reports on an exploratory empirical investigation of the judgment consistency and consensus of 53 experienced tax practitioners regarding substantial tax authority. The findings indicated that while these practitioners had a high level of judgment consistency, they only had a low level of judgement consensus. These findings are used as the basis for identifying potential directions for future research.

Advances in Taxation, Volume 2, pages 165-180.
Copyright © 1989 by JAI Press Inc.
All rights of reproduction in any form reserved.
ISBN: 0-89232-783-9

The proper evaluation of authority for a tax position has long been a challenge to tax practitioners [Norwood et al., 1979; Raby, 1982; Parker and Marshall, 1987]. In evaluating alternate tax treatments, tax practitioners are required to recommend positions for which they have authority [Quattrochi, 1982; Raabe, Whittenburg, and Bost, 1987]. However, because multiple sources of authority exist (e.g., the judicial, statutory, and administrative systems) and these often conflict, the level of authority is frequently a matter of subjective judgment [Sommerfeld and Streuling, 1975; Quattrochi, 1982]. Given this ambiguity, tax practitioners may disagree on whether the IRS will interpret that authoritative support exists for a given tax position [Gaffney et al., 1986; Sommerfeld et al., 1982]. Since such evaluations are an important input into the advice given to clients [Ayres et al., 1986], the advice offered may also diverge across tax practitioners as well.

Prior to the enactment of Internal Revenue Code Section 6661 in 1982, taxpayers found to have taken aggressive tax positions without substantial authoritative support (absent negligence or tax fraud) were only assessed the tax and any interest due on the underpayment. However, Section 6661(a) imposes a 25% penalty for a substantial understatement of a tax liability, where a "substantial understatement" is defined under Section 6661(b)(2)(A) as the greater of 10% of the tax required to be shown, or $5,000 ($10,000 for a regular corporation). Section 6661(b)(2)(B) further provides that the amount of the understatement to which the penalty applies is reduced (except for "tax shelters") by that portion of the understatement which is attributable to the tax treatment of any item by the taxpayer if there is, or was, substantial authority for such tax treatment, or the facts relevant to the item were adequately disclosed.[1]

Thus, Section 6661 has increased the costs to taxpayers of inaccurately assessing the available authority for a given tax treatment. As a result, it has also become more important for the management of a tax practice to ensure that the tax staff make accurate evaluations of authoritative support. If the tax staff consistently support overly conservative tax positions, then clients may switch to more aggressive advisors. On the other hand, frequent support of overly aggressive tax treatments may expose the practice to penalties and sanctions from the regulatory agencies [Johnson, 1984; Merritt, 1983]. If clients face understatement penalties due to relying on the professionals' advice, then the tax practice may lose client goodwill, suffer damages to its reputation, or face damage claims from clients [Raby, 1982].

This paper reports on an exploratory empirical investigation into tax practitioners' judgment consistency and consensus regarding substantial authority. The results indicate that these practitioners have a high level of judgment consistency and a low level of judgment consensus concerning substantial authority for a particular tax situation. These results provide a starting point for a discussion of potential directions for further research into the quality of tax practitioners' judgments.

The rest of this paper is organized as follows. The next section briefly discusses the background of the "substantial authority" standard. This is followed by an overview of alternate approaches to assessing the quality of subjective judgments. The research method and results are then described. The final section provides a summary and discussion of potential directions for future research.

BACKGROUND

The Substantial Authority Standard

The substantial authority standard is one of the latest attempts by Congress and the IRS to provide guidance in interpreting conflicting tax authority. An earlier attempt was the AICPA's 1977 Statement on Responsibility in Tax Practice No. 10, which provides that:

> In preparing a tax return a CPA may take a position contrary to Treasury Department or Internal Revenue Service interpretation of the Code, ... (or) a specific section of the Internal Revenue Code where there is *reasonable support* for the position.

Since the 1970s, there has been a substantial increase in concern about the fairness of, and lack of compliance with, the tax system [AICPA, 1983; Jackson, 1985; Egger, 1986]. In response, Congress enacted new tax compliance penalty provisions in 1982, of which Section 6661 was one. According to the committee reports related to this Section, the "substantial authority" standard is meant to be less stringent than a "more likely than not" standard but more stringent than a "reasonable basis" standard [Bradley, 1986]. The courts have not yet had time to rule as to the clear operational meanings of the above phrases. Hopefully in the near future a consensus will evolve from the courts. The Conference Committee report indicates that the conferees were unaware of any judicial or administrative decision interpreting the phrase "substantial authority" [Raby, 1982; Bradley, 1986], even though the final Regulations made it clear that substantial authority is an objective criterion which requires consideration of both adverse and supporting authorities. Final determination of whether substantial authority exists in a given situation was left up to the judicial and administrative authorities.

Recently the IRS has proposed major changes involving substantial authority in Circular 230. Under the proposal a tax practitioner could face suspension or disbarment for recommending any position that results in a taxpayer penalty for substantial understatement of tax [Podolin, 1988].

Although this change has not been enacted, it would cause an increase in the impact of Section 6661 because the penalty could directly affect the tax practitioner as well as the taxpayer.

Given the recency of the substantial authority standard, a large base of decisions by the applicable authorities has not yet been accumulated. The absence of such guidance implies that subjective judgment is necessary in evaluating the level of substantial authority for many tax treatments. Since these judgments are subjective, tax practitioners may disagree on the level of available authoritative support for a given tax treatment, or a tax practitioner may be inconsistent in his or her evaluations of substantial authority over time and/or cases.

Alternate Approaches to Assessing
The Quality of Subjective Judgments

To our knowledge, the quality of tax practitioners' judgments regarding authority has not yet been subject to systematic empirical research, though studies of judgment quality have been performed using experts in other areas of accounting. (For reviews, see Ashton [1982]; Libby [1981]; and Libby and Lewis [1977, 1982].) In assessing judgment quality, some prior accounting research has used a criterion of judgment accuracy. For example, experiments have had individuals use accounting information to predict stock price changes or insolvency/bankruptcy. However, in many decision contexts of interest to accounting researchers, an accuracy measure cannot be used because it requires an objective criterion (realized event), which either does not exist (e.g., the quality of internal control) or is too costly to obtain. In such cases, researchers have typically employed consensus and consistency measures as surrogates for accuracy.

Consensus is the level of agreement across individuals' judgments and consistency is the level of agreement when one individual makes the same judgment in repeated trials with the same set of information. While consensus and consistency are necessary for accurate judgments over individuals and over time, they are not sufficient to ensure accuracy.[2] Lack of complete consistency is prima facie evidence that the individual has made at least one inaccurate judgment, but complete consistency does not necessarily imply accuracy because all of the judgments may have been inaccurate. Similarly, lack of complete consensus is prima facie evidence that either some or all of the individual judgments are inaccurate, but complete consensus does not necessarily imply accuracy, since all of the individuals may have made the same inaccurate judgment.[3]

Consensus by itself, however, is an important indicator of judgment quality. As Libby [1981] has observed, a major objective of CPA firms' professional training programs is to increase consensus, so that if several employees were

Table 1.   Distribution of Respondents' Professional Characteristics
(Numbers of respondents are in parentheses)

1. Number of seasons of tax experience	
2	7
3	10
4	14
≥5	22
Total	53
2. Degrees held:	
BS/BA	43
NBA	3
MS/MA (Tax)	4
MS/MA (Accounting)	2
JD/LLB	1
Total	53
3. Present job position:	
Staff	6
Senior	29
Manager	7
Partner	9
Other	2
Total	53
4. Type of CPA firm worked for:	
Regional	16
Local	37
Total	53

assigned to the same task they would make the same judgment independently. Many large CPA firms have responded to the voluminous findings on auditors' lack of judgment consensus by increasing the amount of training provided to their auditors and by employing decision aids which increase the structure of audit decision processes [Libby, 1981; Joyce and Libby, 1982]. If research finds that tax practitioners have low consensus or consistency, CPA firms may desire to implement similar training programs and decision aids.

EMPIRICAL METHOD

A questionnaire was administered to 53 tax professionals attending a segment of the AICPA's National Tax Training Program. Summary statistics on selected demographic variables are presented below, followed by a discussion of the survey instrument.

Sample

Table 1 presents descriptive statistics on the subjects' work experience, type of CPA firm, position, and degrees held. These data indicate that the sample is comprised of experienced tax professionals. A total of 23 states were represented, with no more than five subjects from any one state. Hence, the results are unlikely to be affected by factors specific to a particular region (e.g., industries, regulatory climate).[4]

Instrument

Each respondent was asked to rate the degree to which particular sources[5] provided authoritative support for a tax treatment. To avoid confounding by differences in the subjects' experience with particular types of tax issues, a context free evaluation was sought: "For each of the sources below, please indicate how much authoritative support you believe it provides for a particular tax position taken by a taxpayer." The response scale ranged from zero to 100, with endpoints of "absolutely no authority" (0) and "absolute authority" (100).

The sources of authority were those listed in Reg. Sec. 1.6661-3(b)(2) as constituting acceptable substantial authority:

1.   Code and other statutory provisions,
2.   Temporary and final Regulations,
3.   Court cases,
4.   Administrative pronouncements (including revenue rulings and procedures),
5.   Tax treaties, and
6.   Congressional intent (e.g., committee reports).

Of the sources listed, court cases constitute the judicial hierarchy, while the remainder are part of the statutory/ administrative hierarchy. To permit a more detailed analysis of substantial authority judgments, we disaggregated some of the categories (e.g., court cases were divided into U. S. Claims Court, District Court, Tax Court, Court of Appeals, and Supreme Court), thus obtaining a total of 12 individual sources of authority (Table 2). Because the difficult cases in evaluating substantial authority are likely to involve conflicting sources within and between the two hierarchies, we constructed all possible pairings of the 12 sources by alternately assigning to each member of a pair positive and negative signs to denote positive and negative support for the taxpayer's position. Four tax partners from three Big Eight firms[6] were asked to indicate which of these pairs were likely to be encountered in practice. Based on their input, 44 paired sources were selected for inclusion. Thus, including the 12 individual listings, each subject evaluated 56 alternate sources (Table 3). In

Table 2.   Sources of Authority Included in this Study

Administrative/Statutory Hierarchy

Committe Reports
Internal Revenue Code
IRS Booklets
Letter Rulings
Regulations
Revenue Rulings
Tax Treaties

Judicial Hierarchy

Court of Appeals
District Courts
Tax Court
Supreme Court
U.S. Claims Court

addition, two sources (Revenue Rulings (+) and Tax Court (−), and Revenue Rulings (+) and District Court (+)) were repeated in the instrument as part of the test for judgment consistency.[7] Finally, order effects were controlled by presenting the sources to the subjects in eight different orders.

RESULTS

Table 3 lists the 56 sources in descending order by mean level of rated support for the taxpayer's position. The highest mean is 95.2 for Supreme Court (+), and the lowest mean is 36.2 for District Court (−) and Tax Court (−), the latter being the only double-negative combination in the set.[8] As might be expected, positive sources (both individual items or pairs) tend to be rated higher than those involving conflicts. The 22 highest-rated sources are all positive (out of a total of 26 positive sources in the set). More detailed analyses of these ratings are presented below.

Judgment Consistency

Two tests of judgment consistency were performed. The first involved computing Pearson correlations for the subjects' repeat ratings of the two sources that were included twice in the instrument. The values of these correlations (0.82 and 0.76, both $p < 0.001$) are comparable to those reported in auditor judgment studies, and indicate a high—though not perfect—level of consistency in the subjects' evaluation of substantial authority.[9]

Table 3.   Subjects' Ratings of the Authoritative Support Provided
(by Sources of Authority)

Rank	Sources of Authority	Mean Rating	Standard Deviation
1	Supreme Court (+)	95.2	10.8
2	Regulations (+) & Tax Court (+)	88.8	9.8
3	Regulations (+) & Court of Appeals (+)	88.3	10.9
4	Regulations (+) & District Court (+)	87.9	10.6
5	Internal Revenue Code (+)	87.3	16.1
6	Tax Court (+) & District Court (+)	85.9	12.3
7	Revenue Rulings (+) & Court of Appeals (+)	85.8	14.7
8	Revenue Rulings (+) & Tax Court (+)	84.7	14.1
9	Tax Court (+) & U.S. Claims Court (+)	84.1	14.1
10	Revenue Rulings (+) & District Court (+)	82.3	13.8
11	Committee Reports (+) & Revenue Rulings (+)	81.0	15.5
12	Regulations (+) & Revenue Rulings (+)	81.0	17.7
13	Committee Reports (+) & Regulations (+)	81.0	17.3
14	Regulations (+)	79.6	17.3
15	IRS Booklets (+) & Tax Court (+)	78.1	17.4
16	IRS Booklets (+) & District Court (+)	77.7	17.0
17	Revenue Rulings (+)	76.5	16.2
18	IRS Booklets (+) & Court of Appeals (+)	75.8	18.3
19	Tax Court (+)	74.5	16.8
20	District Court (+)	73.9	15.7
21	Committee Reports (+) & Letter Rulings (+)	71.5	19.6
22	Court of Appeals (+)	71.5	19.7
23	IRS Booklets (−) & Tax Court (+)	71.1	17.7
24	U.S. Claims Court (+)	70.8	16.6
25	IRS Booklets (−) & Court of Appeals (+)	69.8	17.3
26	IRS Booklets (−) & District Court (+)	68.8	16.2
27	Tax Treaties (+)	68.5	25.4
28	Revenue Rulings (−) & Tax Court (+)	65.5	15.6
29	Tax Court (+) & U.S. Claims Court (−)	64.5	16.8
30	Committee Reports (−) & Regulations (+)	62.8	19.5
31	Revenue Rulings (+) & Court of Appeals (−)	61.3	19.7
32	Regulations (−) & Tax Court (+)	61.1	19.9
33	Committee Reports (−) & Revenue Rulings (+)	61.0	19.1
34	Revenue Rulings (−) & District Court (+)	60.5	15.1
35	Committee Reports (+)	58.3	25.5
36	Revenue Rulings (−) & Court of Appeals (+)	58.2	20.3
37	Regulations (−) & Court of Appeals (+)	58.1	21.6
38	Tax Court (+) & District Court (−)	57.8	20.3
39	Letter Rulings (+)	57.3	26.2
40	Revenue Rulings (+) & Tax Court (−)	56.9	18.9
41	Regulations (−) & Revenue Rulings (+)	56.7	20.4
42	Regulations (+) & District Court (−)	55.5	19.2
43	Regulations (−) & District Court (+)	55.5	16.8

(continued)

Table 3.   (continued)

Rank	Sources of Authority	Mean Rating	Standard Deviation
44	Regulations (+) & Revenue Rulings (−)	54.6	19.8
45	Tax Court (−) & U.S. Claims Court (+)	53.8	21.1
46	Tax Court (−) & District Court (+)	53.0	17.9
47	Regulations (+) & Court of Appeals (−)	52.8	20.9
48	Regulations (+) & Tax Court (−)	51.6	22.4
49	Committee Reports (−) & Letter Rulings (+)	49.2	25.5
50	Committee Reports (+) & Letter Rulings (−)	47.6	23.0
51	IRS Booklets (PUB. 17, ETC.) (+)	47.5	26.6
52	Committee Reports (+) & Regulations (−)	46.3	20.3
53	Committee Reports (+)& Revenue Rulings (−)	45.5	20.2
54	IRS Booklets (+) & Court of Appeals (−)	40.3	24.4
55	IRS Booklets (+) & District Court (−)	39.1	25.1
56	District Court (−) & Tax Court (−)	36.2	35.4

The second test compared the subjects' relative ratings of 24 couplets of paired sources. Both pairs of a couplet contained the same two sources of authority, with one pair of the couplet having positive signs for both sources and the other having a negative sign for one of the sources (e.g., Tax Court (+) and Revenue Rulings (+) versus Tax Court (+) and Revenue Rulings (−)). Since a negative sign denotes negative support for the taxpayer's position, the latter pair should be rated lower than the former.

Table 4 shows that the number of subjects (out of 53) who violated this relative ordering for a given couplet ranged from zero to nine, with a mean (median) of 3.29 (3.0). The total number of violations (79) was 6.21% of the total of 1272 cases (53 subjects times 24 couplets each). While this proportion of inconsistent judgments may seem small, a proportions test [Winkler and Hays, 1975] indicated that it was significantly greater than zero ($Z = 9.18$, $p < 0.01$). The result remained significant even when the five subjects with the most violations were excluded.[10] Inspection of Table 4 also reveals that the nonzero proportion of inconsistent judgments was not specific to the hierarchy of authority involved. Significant departures from zero also were indicated in separate tests using couplets involving only the judicial hierarchy, the statutory/administrative hierarchy, and both the judicial and statutory/administrative hierarchies.[11]

Taken as a whole, these tests indicate that although the subjects were highly consistent in their judgments, there remained a statistically significant, though proportionally small, degree of inconsistency. Whether the latter is cause for concern depends on the costs and benefits of judgment errors.

Table 4.   Consistency Results

Couplets of Paired Sources	Number of Inconsistent Orderings
Panel A:—Judicial Hierarchy	
District Court (+) & Tax Court (+)	
District Court (+) & Tax Court (−)	1
U.S. Claims Court (+) & Tax Court (+)	
U.S. Claims Court (+) & Tax Court (−)	3
Total	4
Panel B:—Administrative/Statutory Hierarchy	
Committee Reports (+) & Regulations (+)	
Committee Reports (+) & Regulations (−)	2
Committee Reports (+) & Revenue Rulings (+)	
Committee Reports (+) & Revenue Rulings (−)	2
Committee Reports (+) & Letter Rulings (+)	
Committee Reports (+) & Letter Rulings (−)	4
Regulations (+) & Committee Reports (+)	
Regulations (+) & Committee Reports (−)	6
Revenue Rulings (+) & Committee Reports (+)	
Revenue Rulings (+) & Committee Reports (−)	6
Letter Rulings (+) & Committee Reports (+)	
Letter Rulings (+) & Committee Reports (−)	5
Regulations (+) & Revenue Rulings (+)	
Regulations (+) & Revenue Rulings (−)	5
Revenue Rulings (+) & Regulations (+)	
Revenue Rulings (+) & Regulations (−)	8
Total	38
Panel C:—Between the Judicial and Statutory/Adminstrative Hierarchies	
Regulations (+) & Court of Appeals (+)	
Regulations (+) & Court of Appeals (−)	0
Regulations (+) & Tax Court (+)	
Regulations (+) & Tax Court (−)	0
Regulations (+) & District Court (+)	
Regulations (+) & District Court (−)	0
Court of Appeals (+) & Regulations (+)	
Court of Appeals (+) & Regulations (−)	1
Revenue Rulings (+) & Court of Appeals (+)	
Revenue Rulings (+) & Court of Appeals (−)	5
Revenue Rulings (+) & Tax Court (+)	
Revenue Rulings (+) & Tax Court (−)	2

Table 4. (*continued*)

Couplets of Paired Sources	Number of Inconsistent Orderings
Court of Appeals (+) & Revenue Rulings (+) Court of Appeals (+) & Revenue Rulings (−)	2
Tax Court (+) & Revenue Rulings (+) Tax Court (+) & Revenue Rulings (−)	4
District Courts(+) & Revenue Rulings (+) District Courts (+) & Revenue Rulings (−)	5
Revenue Rulings (+) & Tax Court (+) Revenue Rulings (+) & Tax Court (−)	3
IRS Booklets (+) & Court of Appeals (+) IRS Booklets (+) & Court of Appeals (−)	3
IRS Booklets (+) & District Courts (+) IRS Booklets (+) & District Courts (−)	1
Tax Court(+) & IRS Booklets (+) Tax Court (+) & IRS Booklets (−)	2
District Courts (+) & IRS Booklets (+) District Courts (+) & IRS Booklets (−)	9
Total	37

Judgment Consensus

Following the research on auditor judgment, between-subjects consensus was assessed by forming all possible pairings of the 53 subjects ($N = 1378$) and for each pair computing the Pearson correlations for the 56 authority evaluations. The mean (median) value of this distribution of 1378 correlations was 0.451 (0.479), with a standard deviation of 0.189 and a range of -0.226 to 0.839.

Only 20 (1.4 %) of the correlations were negative. While the mean of the distribution was significantly greater than zero ($t = 45.1$, $p < .001$), its value was relatively low compared with studies on auditor judgment.[12] This result suggests that the subjects had a low level of judgment consensus.

Another indication of judgment consensus is the dispersion of individual judgments around the group mean. To investigate whether the level of consensus is a function of agreement or conflict among alternate sources, we tested whether the mean of the standard deviations of the 15 pairs in which both members had positive signs ($\overline{X} = 14.87$) was significantly different from that of the 26 pairs in which the members had conflicting signs ($\overline{X} = 19.79$). The t-statistic of 5.29 was highly significant ($p < 0.001$).[13] This result indicates that consensus was significantly higher when alternate sources are in agreement rather than in conflict.

Cross-sectional Analysis

To test whether the selected demographic variables affected the judgments, we dichotomized the sample along the experience, position, and firm type dimensions as follows:

- experience: ≤ 4 years = low [$N = 31$] and ≤ 5 years = high [$N = 22$];
- position: staff and senior = low [$N = 35$] and manager and partner = high [$N = 16$]; and
- firm type: regional [$N = 16$] and local [$N = 37$].

A multivariate analysis of variance was conducted using these three dichotomized independent variables, and the subjects' evaluations of each of the 56 authority sources as the dependent variables. The results indicated that none of the demographic variables was significant:

- experience, $F = 1.93$ ($p < 0.52$);
- position, $F = 2.28$ ($p < 0.21$);   and
- firm type, $F = 1.09$ ($p < 0.65$).

Separate tests on each of the 56 sources also supported this conclusion.

For each of the three dichotomized demographic variables, t tests were conducted between the two subgroups' mean ratings for each of the sources. The experience dimension produced no significant t-statistics at the 0.05 level, while position and firm type each had two significant t-statistics out of the 56 computed. Hence, the cross-sectional tests as a whole indicated that for tax practitioners with at least two years of experience, judgments regarding substantial authority did not vary significantly with experience, position, or firm type.[14]

SUMMARY AND DISCUSSION OF POTENTIAL DIRECTIONS FOR FUTURE REFERENCE

This exploratory study of tax practitioners' judgments regarding substantial authority has found such judgments to have high, though not perfect, consistency. However, the level of consensus was low, particularly when conflicting authority sources were involved. These results were not a function of experience, position, or firm type.

An important limitation of this exploratory research is that the subjects were presented with a restricted set of information (i.e., the judgment setting was context free and there was a maximum of two sources of authoritative support provided). We believe that this restricted set of information reduced the realism or richness present in most actual tax engagements. However, benefits obtained from using a restricted information set include both presenting subjects with a series of parsimonious situations which allowed examining the level of consensus over a variety of information conditions and isolating the effects of variation in authoritative support on judgments without the confounding effects of other information. Future research should expand the information set provided to subjects.

Another potential limitation of this exploratory research is the interpretation to be given to the dependent variable. The questionnaire asked the subjects to indicate how much authoritative support they believe a source(s) provides for a particular tax position, on a 0 (absolutely no authority) to 100 (absolute authority) scale. Because the source(s) of support were either negative or positive, there is ambiguity whether subjects interpreted a response of zero as providing no authority or negative authority. Future research should use a more unambiguous response scale.

Judgments regarding substantial authority are an important input into the advice that tax practitioners give to clients. Hence, the findings of this exploratory research may indicate the desirability for managements of tax practices—like managements of audit practices—to develop ways of improving the quality of the judgments by their staffs. However, before making such generalizations to practice, extensive replications and refinements of this exploratory study are necessary. Below, we suggest three potentially fruitful directions for future research.

First, the results' external validity can be enhanced by developing experimental materials from court cases and CPA firms' client files. By selecting cases for which the final resolution is known (i.e., acceptance or challenge by the IRS and, if applicable, final court decisions), a direct test of practitioners' judgment accuracy would become feasible. For each case, tax practitioners can be asked to assess the probability that the taxpayer's position is accepted or upheld, and judgment accuracy can be appraised by comparing these assessments to the known outcomes.

A second desirable extension is to analyze the extent to which the specific tax issue and the mix of applicable authority may interactively affect judgment quality. Future research might use a systematic survey of seasoned tax professionals to identify the mixes of authority most frequently encountered and the types of tax issues to which they pertain. The survey responses can be combined with the findings of archival research to develop representative case scenarios involving a broad spectrum of tax treatments.

Finally, note that the preceding discussion has assumed a setting in which the set of information on authoritative support is prespecified. In such a setting, the tax professional's role is limited to evaluating the information provided. While this scenario may be descriptive of part of most tax professionals' work, it is more likely for a given tax professional to be charged with both researching the available authority and interpreting the evidence obtained. This implies that the nature of a tax practitioner's information search (e.g., thoroughness and competence) also may affect the quality of his or her judgments regarding substantial authority.

A number of individual-, firm-, and engagement-specific characteristics are likely to affect the marginal costs and benefits of various degrees and types of information search, thereby influencing a tax professional's choice of information search behavior. Potentially relevant individual-specific characteristics include tax expertise, risk and effort preferences, and the marginal utility of pay. Firm-specific factors may encompass the availability of technical assistance and data bases (such as LEXIS and Westlaw), and the performance evaluation and reward system (e.g., whether individuals are evaluated on time spent on engagements and/or the total amount of client billings). Finally, the nature of the engagement (e.g., client size, type of tax issue, long-term versus one-time engagement) also may influence the cost/benefit tradeoff of different degrees of information search. Future research might explore how these factors independently and interactively affect tax practitioners' information search and judgments.

NOTES

1.   While decisions regarding tax treatments involve both choice of treatment and disclosure, this study only deals with the former. It is likely that the two choices would be related (e.g., treatments that have substantial authority may be more likely to be disclosed), and that the disclosure judgment may be affected by other factors. Examining such issues is a potentially fruitful area for future research.

2.   Einhorn [1974] provides a more detailed discussion of why consensus and consistency are necessary, but not sufficient, conditions for accurate judgments.

3.   Only limited empirical evidence is available on the relationship between consensus and accuracy. A. Ashton [1985] reports that in two accounting decision contexts (budgeting decisions by managers and going-concern predictions by auditors), a high level of association ($r = 0.84$ and 0.82, respectively) was found between consensus and accuracy.

4.   One limitation of the sample is that all of the subjects worked for either local or regional firms. Since national and Big Eight firms were not represented, our results are not generalizable to them. It might be expected that since these firms tend to have more intensive and uniform in-house training programs, their tax practitioners may have higher levels of judgment consistency and consensus. Extending the analysis to these firms is a fruitful area for future research.

5.   To avoid clutter, the term "source" is used to denote both single and multiple sources of authority.

6. One was a National Tax Partner, one was a Regional Tax Partner, and the other two were partners in local offices. This was a convenience panel of tax experts.

7. These two sources were chosen at random from the sources that, a priori, seemed unlikely to be at either extreme of the authority continuum. Having less extreme sources provides a more powerful assessment of judgment consistency because the answers tend to be less obvious.

8. It would seem that the Supreme Court, being the highest court, should be rated at the top of the authority scale (i.e., 100). In the case where both sources are negative, there is little support for the taxpayer's position. Hence, the mean of 95.2 for Supreme Court (+) and 36.2 for the double-negative combination—which is statistically greater than zero ($t = 7.46, p < 0.01$)—pose somewhat of a puzzle. A plausible explanation is some people's aversion to using the endpoints of the zero to 100 scale. The survey instrument did not ask for the probability that the taxpayer's position would be challenged or found faulty. Perhaps if the question had been posed this way, the ratings for the two sources in question would have been much closer to the two endpoints. While the data that were collected precluded further analysis of this issue, note that the statistical tests that we performed primarily focused on the *relative ordering* of authority sources. As such, they should only be minimally affected by the preceding factors.

9. Libby's [1981] review of auditor judgment studies reports that the mean values of correlations among repeat cases range between 0.81 and 0.91.

10. The number of subjects making a given number of inconsistent orderings (in parentheses) are as follows: 1 (8); 2 (7); 2 (5); 3 (4); 6 (3); 3 (2); 11 (1); and 25 (0). Excluding the five subjects with the most inconsistent orderings reduced the total number of violations to 47, which was 4.08% of the 1152 cases applicable (48 subjects times 24 couplets each). This proportion was still significantly greater than zero ($Z = 7.00, p < 0.01$).

11. The results were as follows: within the judicial hierarchy: $Z = 2.04$ ($p < 0.05$); within the statutory/administrative hierarchy: $Z = 6.46$ ($p < 0.01$); and the judicial-statutory/administrative mix: $Z = 6.24$ ($p < 0.01$). We also compared the proportions of inconsistent orderings across these three categories. The only significant difference was between statutory/administrative (X = 0.0896) and the judicial-statutory/administrative mix (X = 0.0499) ($Z = 2.67, p < 0.01$).

12. Libby's [1981] review of auditor judgment studies classified nine studies as having low consensus. The means of these studies' correlations ranged from 0.12 to 0.54. He also classified seven studies as having high consensus. These had mean correlations in the 0.66 to 0.80 range. Our mean value of 0.451 falls in the lower range.

13. The nonparametric Mann-Whitney U-test also yielded a similar result ($Z = 4.09, p < 0.001$).

14. It is important to recall that our sample only included local and regional firms, and it would be inappropriate to generalize our results to other types of firms (e.g., national or Big 8).

REFERENCES

AICPA, *Underreported Taxable Income: The Problem and Possible Solutions* (AICPA, 1983).

Ashton, A. H., "Does Consensus Imply Accuracy in Accounting Studies of Decision Making?" *The Accounting Review* (April 1985), pp. 173-85.

Ashton, R. H., *Human Information Processing in Accounting*, Studies in Accounting Research v17 (American Accounting Association, 1982).

Ayres, F., B. Jackson, and P. Hite, "An Empirical Analysis of Factors Related to Tax Return Positions Taken by Professional Tax Preparers," Unpublished manuscript (April 1986).

Bergherm, D. E., "The IRS and Business," *Journal of Accountancy* (August 1982), p. 64.

Bradley, J. A., "How Taxpayers Can Avoid Imposition of the Substantial Understatement Penalty," *Taxation for Accountants* (October 1986), p. 222.

Egger, R. L. (ed.), *The Price Waterhouse Guide to the New Tax Law* (Bantam Books, 1986).

Einhorn, H., "Expert Judgment: Some Necessary Conditions and an Example," *Journal of Applied Psychology* (October 1974), pp.562-71.

Gaffney, D. J., D. Skadden, J. Wheeler, B. Laverty, E. Outslay, and K. Skadden, *Federal Income Taxation* Wiley , 1986).

Jackson, B. R., "Stemming Income Tax Evasion," *Journal of Accountancy* (January 1985), p.76.

Johnson, J. M., "Current Compliance Rules Need Not Interfere with Effective Tax Return Preparation," *Taxation for Accountants* (January 1984), pp. 14-18.

Joyce, E. J. and R. Libby, "Behavioral Studies of Audit Decision Making," *Journal of Accounting Literature* (1982), pp. 103- 123.

Libby, R., *Accounting and Human Information Processing: Theory and Applications* (Prentice-Hall, 1981).

Libby, R., and B. L. Lewis, "Human Information Processing Research in Accounting: The State of the Art," *Accounting, Organizations and Society* (December 1977), pp. 245-268.

————, "Human Information Processing Research in Accounting: The State of the Art in 1982," *Accounting, Organizations and Society* (December 1982), pp. 231-85.

Merritt, J. E., "T.E.F.R.A. Tightens Compliance," *American Bar Association Journal* (April 1983), pp.456-461.

Norwood, F. W., S. W. Chisolm, F. R. Burke, and D. M. Vaughan, *Federal Taxation Research, Planning, and Procedures* (Prentice-Hall, 1979).

Parker, J. E. and D. C. Marshall, *Programmed Guide to Tax Research* (Kent Publishing Co., 1987).

Podolin, L., "Treasury Raises the Stakes in Circular 230 Proposal," *Journal of Accountancy* (April 1988), pp. 60-68.

Quattrochi, J. A., *Federal Tax Research* (Harcourt Brace Jovanovich, 1982).

Raabe, W. A., G. E. Whittenburg, and J. C. Bost, *West's Federal Tax Research* (West Publishing Co., 1987).

Raby, W. L., "TEFRA: Impact on Taxpayer Compliance," *Journal of Accountancy* (November 1982), p. 64.

————, "Advocacy in Tax Practice," *Journal of Accountancy* (March 1983), p. 70.

Sommerfeld, R. M. et al., *An Introduction to Taxation: Advanced Topics* (Harcourt Brace Jovanovich, 1982).

Sommerfeld, R. M. and G. F. Streuling, *Tax Study No. 5, Tax Research Techniques* (AICPA, 1975).

Winkler, R. L. and W. L. Hays, *Statistics: Problems Inferences and Decisions* 2nd ed. (Holt Rinehart and Winston, 1975).

MULTISTATE APPORTIONMENT OF INCOME:
AN EMPIRICAL ANALYSIS

Kevin T. Stevens

ABSTRACT

A three-factor formula, based on equal weighting of sales, property, and payroll, is widely used to allocate interstate corporate income among the various states. However, several recent studies have shown that this formula does not apportion income as accurately as a number of other competing formulas. This paper evaluates the statistical relationship among three factors used in the formulas and income.

It uses ridge regression to go beyond prediction of the dependent variable to explanation of the independent variables, even when multicollinearity is present in the data. The results indicate that, for nonindustrial firms, sales and property have an approximately equal positive effect on accounting income. The effect of payroll on accounting income is shown to be negative. However, for industrial firms, sales and property do not have an equal effect on accounting income. Moreover, the effect of payroll on income is shown to be postive.

Advances in Taxation, Volume 2, pages 181-200.
Copyright © 1989 by JAI Press Inc.
All rights of reproduction in any form reserved.
ISBN: 0-89232-783-9

INTRODUCTION

Under current law, a multistate corporation can allocate its taxable income among the states in which it earns that income by one of three general methods: (1) separate accounting, (2) specific allocation, and (3) formulary apportionment [Schmidt, 1986, p. 19]. Of these three methods, McLure [1986, p. 29] notes that the "vast majority of corporate income is divided among states through the use of formulary apportionment." The Supreme Court has consistently held that there must be "some minimum connection (nexus) between the state and the person, property or transaction it seeks to tax" [*Miller Bros. Co. v. Maryland,* 347 U.S. 340, 1953]. Furthermore, there must be "a rational relationship between the income attributed to the State and the intrastate values of the enterprise" [*Exxon Corp. v. Wisconsin Dept. of Revenue,* 447 U.S. 207, 1980]. The Supreme Court in *Container Corporation of America v. Franchise Tax Board* [103 S.Ct 2933, 1983] held that when apportionment formulas are used that not only must there exist the aforementioned "rational relationship," but also that the "factors used in the apportionment formula must actually reflect a reasonable sense of how income is generated."

There has been much discussion about whether the three-factor formula used in some form by 38 states and the District of Columbia [Raabe, 1986] does "reasonably and fairly" allocate income. The most commonly used version of that formula [McLure, 1986, p. 29] allocates income by multiplying total taxable income by a fraction composed of three equally-weighted parts: the ratios of in-state sales to total sales, in-state property to total property, and in-state payroll to total payroll [National Tax Association, 1939]. As in many other areas of taxation, the exact meaning of such nebulous terms as "reasonably" and "fairly" is unspecified. One possible criterion for determining the fairness of a given apportionment formula is the correlation between the income allocated by the formula to the states and the actual income earned in those states. Thus, a perfectly "fair" formula would be one that allocated income to each state exactly as the income was actually earned in each state. Interestingly, much of current state tax planning is based on utilization of the *lack* of correlation between how formulas allocate income and how such income is actually earned in those states.

Because of the difficulty of obtaining the necessary data on foreign (non-U.S.) income, property, sales, and payroll, this study focuses on multistate allocation of income, rather than multijurisdictional allocation of income. Therefore, both the numerator and the denominator of the apportionment formula examined exclude foreign sales, property, and payroll.

Research Objectives

When statistically examining the fairness or propriety of using an apportionment formula to allocate corporate income, the researcher is confronted with two problems: the validity of pooling data over time and/or cross-sectionally, and the presence of severe multicollinearity in the data, which makes difficult the *explanation* of the independent variables (sales, property, and payroll). The purpose of this study is correspondingly twofold. First, the study employs ordinary least squares regression (OLS) to assess the validity of pooling of time series and/or cross-sectional data. Second, the study examines the propriety of the current apportionment formula through use of a statistical technique, ridge regression. Ridge regression should prove useful for three reasons:

1. It allows the researcher to determine which variables are causing the multicollinearity.
2. It produces stable, albeit biased, estimates of the coefficients of the correlated variables.
3. It allows the researcher to go beyond prediction of the dependent variable to explanation of the effects of the independent variables.

Related Research

Hreha and Silhan [1986], relying on predictive ability, found that the equally-weighted three-factor apportionment formula may not allocate income fairly among the states. They addressed the issue of allocative fairness by investigating the effects of alternative factor weightings on income allocations. Their results suggest that the payroll factor tends to distort income allocations and that several simpler models provide more accurate allocations.

Hreha and Silhan [1986] compared the current three-factor formula to 10 other formulas in terms of allocative accuracy which was measured by comparing apportioned income with income determined under separate accounting for a sample of 180 COMPUSTAT firms. Four of the ten formulas used restricted least squares (RLS) regression coefficients as factor weightings, three used equal weightings on two factors, and three used single factors. RLS was used in order to force the sum of the coefficients to equal one. The RLS coefficients were based on a separate estimation sample of 102 COMPUSTAT firms. Seven formulas outperformed the current three-factor formula. The four RLS formulas were included in this group.

Hreha and Silhan [1986] concluded that the payroll factor tends to distort income allocations because the four worst performing formulas each contained a positively weighted payroll factor. In addition, the RLS coefficients for the payroll factor were consistently negative over the 12-year estimation period. They recommended that perhaps states should consider an equally-weighted sales-property formula.

Schmidt [1986] also addressed the issue of apportionment formula fairness in a study similar in design to that of Hreha and Silhan. He focused on industry effects and factor substitutions. Schmidt examined the equally-weighted three-factor formula plus 10 alternate apportionment formulas. These formulas included various combinations of the gross and net measures of the property factor, double-weighting of the sales factor, and the use of employees as a measure of payroll.

Using ordinary least squares (OLS) regression, he found that the beta coefficient (i.e., standardized regression coefficient) for payroll was consistently negative. He regressed property, payroll, and sales on income for a sample of 252 corporations. He found that together property, payroll, and sales significantly reflected the income-generating processes of businesses as shown in high coefficients of determination.

Similar to Hreha and Silhan [1986], Schmidt [1986] used allocative accuracy to assess the validity of the current formula. He demonstrated that alternate two- and three-factor formulas perform as well as the standard formula. However, he did not use the beta coefficients to allocate income in the predictive tests which followed.

Schmidt [1986] also examined the question of stability of factors and concluded that the factors were stable across time, but not across industries. He addressed the stability issue by performing separate regressions on each of the industries and over each of the time periods (1977-1981), and then by examining the stability of beta coefficients and sign. The current study extends Hreha and Silhan [1986] and Schmidt [1986] by using ridge regression to statistically examine the relationship of the factors in the formula to income. It also reexamines model stability over time and across industry.

RESEARCH METHODOLOGY

The model examined in this study is a reiteration of the three-factor formula and is similar to the one presented in the Schmidt study [1986, p. 25]. It is described as follows:

$$Y_k = b_0 + b_1 x_{1k} + b_2 x_{2k} + b_3 x_{3k} + e_k$$

where: Y_k = accounting income associated with firm k; x_{1k} = sales associated with firm k; x_{2k} = property associated with firm k; x_{3k} = payroll associated with firm k; b_i = factor coefficients; and, e_k = error term.

In this model the sales variable is defined as sales net of returns and allowances. The property variable is defined as net property plant and equipment, and the payroll variable is defined as sales and administration expense plus direct and indirect wages.

The Sample

An initial random sample (based on Standard Industrial Classification (SIC) codes) of 300 firms was taken for this study. Of these, 50 firms were included in the final sample. Thus, the sample used in this study is not as large as the sample used in the Hreha and Silhan [1986] or the Schmidt [1986] study for two reasons. First, data for the firms sampled were gathered from microfiches of 10K forms. Consequently, the size of n was limited by resource and processing constraints. Second, not all manufacturing firms disclose sufficient information on payroll expenditures in their 10K reports. Instead, the cost of labor is often buried in the cost of goods sold section [Schmidt, 1986, p. 24]. Ten years of data (1977-1986) on income from operations, sales, property, and payroll were gathered from 10K reports for 25 industrial firms and 25 mercantile firms. Entities such as financial institutions and regulated firms were excluded from the study because the three-factor formula typically is not used in the allocation of the income of firms such as banks, life insurance companies, and utilities [Hreha and Silhan, 1986, p. 11].

Ordinary Least Squares

The first step in this study was to perform an ordinary least squares regression (OLS) on the model described above. Dillon and Goldstein [1984, p. 209] note that regression analysis is primarily concerned with the estimation/prediction of the mean value of a criterion (Y) on the basis of the known values of one or more predictor variables (X). Because similar matrix notation will be used to describe ridge regression, the model can be written as:

$$Y = XB + e;$$

where: $Y = n$ x 1 column vector of observations on the dependent variable Y; $X = n$ x p matrix that results from n observations on p − 1 independent variables X2 ... Xp, where the first column of X consists of 1s, to represent the intercept term B1; $B = p$ x 1 column vector of unknown parameters B1, B2 ... Bp, where B1 is the intercept term, and B2 ... Bp are the partial regression coefficients; and $e = n$ x 1 column vector of n errors.

To solve for the estimates of B, the unknown population parameters, the following well-known equation is used:

$$b = \{x'x\}^{-1} x'y$$

Ridge Regression

One important issue concerning the OLS regression analysis is whether multicollinearity is present in the data. Ridge regression is a procedure designed to mitigate the problems associated with such multicollinearity [Dillon and Goldstein, 1984]. In essence, ridge regression "invents" extra data and produces (through an interative procedure) parameter estimates that are closer to the true population parameters than are OLS estimates [*SUGI Supplemental Library Users' Guide* Version 5, 1986]. Ridge regression first performs an OLS regression and then derives extra data until the coefficients of the independent variables become stable. Inventing the additional data is done by adding a small biasing constant to the diagonal of a matrix. Briefly, the ith diagonal element of the x'x (variance-covariance) matrix is augmented by the addition of a postive "biasing constant, k $(0 \leq k \leq \infty)$" before the matrix is inverted for least squares estimation [Vinod and Ullah, 1981, pp. 169, 171-172]. The ridge estimates of the parameters are biased because of the errors introduced by the added data points.

While the estimators generated by OLS are solved for by the familiar equation:

$$b = \{ x'x \}^{-1} x'y,$$

ridge regression [Dillon and Goldstein, 1984, p. 284] solves for the estimators by the equation:

$$b^* = [x'x + kI]^{-1} x'y,$$

where k = a dimensionless scalar which can be thought of as being proportional to the number of (invented extra) observations added to drive the parameters toward zero (away from the original OLS estimators); and

I = the identity matrix.

Hoerl and Kennard [1970a] provided the primary justification for ridge regression by proving that a positive k exists such that the mean square error (MSE) of b* is less than the MSE of b from OLS or RLS. (Much of the controversy that exists concerning ridge regression is based on determining that k value and will be discussed below.) There are two advantages of using ridge regression rather than RLS or OLS. First, because the the estimators of the variables are stable and have minimum MSE [Wannacott and Wannacott, 1979, p. 354], the relative importance of the independent variables can be accurately determined. Second, the sign of the independent variables can also be determined. The estimators determined by ridge regression are more stable than the OLS or RLS estimators and therefore less likely to change signs over different regressions on samples drawn from the same population.

A disadvantage of using ridge regression is that it produces biased estimators. However, the bias of the estimators need not be of undue concern for several reasons. First, Vinod and Ullah [1981, p. 169] express the degree of bias as follows:

$$\text{Bias } (b_k) = Eb_k - B = -k (X'X) + kI)^{-1} B$$

Thus, the amount of bias depends on the unknown B (the population parameter). However, note "that as k approaches infinity, b approaches zero" (p. 169). In other words, ridge regression "shrinks the estimates towards zero" (p. 170). Vinod and Ullah [1981] argue that this shrinkage provides conservative estimates and reflects the true spirit of scientific research that assumes, absent contrary information, that a given independent variable has no effect on the dependent variable. Second, Thiel [1971, p. 91] states that while unbiasedness is desirable, "it is good not to attach too much importance" to that criterion. Third, and most important, the purpose of this study is to determine the relative, rather than the absolute, magnitude of the weights of the independent variables. That is, the issue at hand is not to determine *exactly* how sales, property, and payroll affect income, but, rather, to determine the relative importance of those variables. Thus, the fact that the ridge estimators are biased, that is, the estimators are not absolutely precise, is not important. What is of crucial importance is that the estimators are *stable* and have minimum variance.

Debate still continues over the validity of ridge regression. Of particular concern is whether it is possible to choose correctly the k values needed to derive the ridge estimators. Hoerl and Kennard [1970b] suggest using the ridge trace and such criteria as reasonableness of signs and stability of coefficients to determine k values. Brown and Beattie [1975] advocate selecting the k value at which the ridge estimator reaches its maximum absolute sign. Marquardt and Snee [1975] propose visual inspection of the ridge trace to determine when the coefficients have stabilized at the appropriate k value. However, Judge et al. [1985, p. 915] assert that inspection of the ridge trace is "an art form" and not a scientific approach to decision making. Further, Judge et al. [1985, p. 916] state that when the "parameter k is a function of the sample data and thus stochastic, [the ridge estimators] do not have the same properties [in particular, ridge estimators no longer guarantee lower MSE than OLS estimators]." Kmenta [1971, p. 41] criticized ridge regression because of the arbitrary manner in which k was derived from the data. (But see below for a change in Kmenta's view). Draper and Smith [1981, pp. 319, 324] state that ridge regression is "absolutely the correct way to proceed" in only two restrictive circumstances: (1) the distribution of the parameter is stipulated in advance, "by imagining a multivariate normal distribution of prior belief on the values of B_i; or (2) "a spherical restriction [is placed] on the parameter space."

Lin and Kmenta [1982] and Vinod and Ullah [1981] have addressed some of the criticisms noted above. Lin and Kmenta [1982, p. 491] acknowledge that in most cases the value of k is not given a priori but "is determined on the basis of sample observations." When this is the case, "the ridge estimator is no longer linear and its properties are unknown." Lin and Kmenta performed a Monte Carlo simulation to compare the loss of accuracy (as measured by the distribution of the square error loss of OLS) of using ridge regression vesus OLS. They incorporated both restrictions noted by Draper and Smith [[1981, pp. 319, 324] (the assumption of a prior distribution and the restriction of parameter space) by varying the relative centrality of the parameters and the parameter shapes.

Based on this research, Lin and Kmenta [1982] made a number of observations. First ridge regression estimators never perform significantly worse than OLS, and they often perform very much better in many regressions. Second, the advantage of ridge regressions estimators over the OLS estimators is greater (1) the higher the degree of multicollinearity, (2) the lower the value of the noncentrality parameter (the closer to the origin), and (3) the higher the number of explanatory variables. Finally, the shape of the regression coefficients affects the performance of the ridge estimators. Other things unchanged, the improvement the ridge estimators can achieve is smaller when all the coefficients are equal.

Lin and Kmenta [1982, p. 493] conclude that even when k is derived from the sample data, the "ordinary ridge regression estimators do out-perform (as measured by a loss criterion even other than MSE) the OLS estimator very substantially when multicollinearity is medium or high" and that the estimators "can compete with the OLS estimators on equal terms with the same prior information." Further, while the shape of the parameter space and the distance from the origin of the parameters affect the performance of the ridge estimators, those estimators generally still outperform the OLS estimators.

Vinod and Ullah [1981, p. 190] state that "computational shortcuts" to derive k values such as "the usual computer program for multiple regression can be used to obtain ridge solutions correctly." (As will be discussed, the ridge solutions in this study were obtained through such a "shortcut.") Vinod and Ullah [1981, p. 187] also note that the prior assumption some Bayesians believe is necessary for RR is not a problem for two reasons. First, the assumption that the distribution of B_k is centered around the null vector is realistic because "in the absence of specific prior knowledge it is often scientifically conservative [and appropriate] to shrink toward the zero vector." Second, the existence of such minimax ridge estimators as Euclidean, Mahalanobis, and Strawderman distances "shows that ordinary ridge estimates can reduce the MSE of OLS everywhere. This avoids unscientific discussions of the 'realism' of priors."

The Pooling Issue

In studies that pool data, it is assumed that the structure of the relationship hypothesized remains constant. In other words, the observations on the independent variables must be considered fixed in repeated samples. If the form of the relationship differs across time and/or types of firms, the OLS estimates of the parameters will be biased and interpretation of those estimates questionable [Green, 1978, p. 92].

Hreha and Silhan [1986] performed separate RLS regressions on 12 separate years to determine if the coefficients tended to be stable over time. Schmidt [1986] ran separate OLS regressions on five separate years and on 27 separate industries. Schmidt also used a "dummy variable" model which allowed for the specification of differences over industry groups as well as any differences over time. His results indicated that the factors explained a significant portion of the variation. Similar to Hreha and Silhan [1986], Schmidt [1986] also visually inspected the coefficients and noted that, despite multicollinearity, the coefficients appeared to be stable over time. However, they were not stable across industries.

The current study uses a different approach to address the pooling issue. One overall OLS regression is performed on the pooled data and separate OLS regressions are performed on the data divided into different time periods or across different sections (e.g., industrial versus mercantile firms). A large difference between the pooled error sum of squares (SSE) and the SSE from the separate OLS regressions would indicate that the relationships are not constant. A Chow test can then be performed to determine if that difference is statistically significant by computing

$$F*1 = \frac{(s_2 = s_1/g)}{s_1/(n_1 + n_2 - 2g)}$$

where $s_1 =$ error sum of squares (SSE) from the separate OLS regressions on time period 1 (1982-1986) and time period 2 (1977-1981);

$s_2 =$ SSE for the pooled regression;

$n_1 =$ number of observations from time period 1;
$n_2 =$ number of observations form time period 2;
$g =$ number of parameters including the intercept term; and

$$F*2 = \frac{(s_2 = s_3/g)}{s_3/(n + n - 2g)}$$

where $s_3 =$ SSE from the separate OLS regressions on mercantile firms and industrial firms;

$s_2 =$ SSE for the pooled regression;

$n_1 =$ number of observations from mercantile firms;

$n_2 =$ number of observations form industrial firms;

$g =$ number of parameters including the intercept term.

Both F*1 and F*2 are distributed as F statistics and can be compared to a critical F with g degrees of freedom (d.f.) in the numerator and $(n_1 + n_2 - 2g)$ d.f. in the denominator. If F*1 or F*2 is significantly greater than critical F (at the prespecified alpha of .05), then the two regressions are not the same.

RESULTS

OLS regressions and the pooled regressions indicate that F*1 = 1.38 and that F*2 = 3.32. The critical F1 (with alpha = .05) with 4 d.f. in the numerator and $[25 + 25 - 2(4)]$ d.f. in the denominator is appoximately 2.49 as is the critical F2. Consequently, because the F*1 of 1.38 is not significantly greater than the F1 of 2.49, the regressions are similar over the different time periods, and, thus, the data can be pooled over time. However, since the F*2 of 3.32 is significantly greater than F2 of 2.49, the regressions on industrial versus mercantile firms are not similar. Hence, data from industrial and nonindustrial firms should not be pooled. These conclusions agree with those of Schmidt [1986].

Validity of the Model

The overall validity of the model was tested using the F statistic. Because the Chow test indicated that data should not be pooled across firms, separate regressions were performed on data from nonindustrial firms and data form industrial firms. The achieved probability that income is not a function of sales, property and payroll was less than 0.001 for both types of firms, confirming the results of Schmidt [1986].

Table 1 presents the coefficients for sales, property, and payroll for nonindustrial firms. Note that all three coefficients are statistically significant at the .05 alpha level. Further, the sign of the payroll factor is negative, confirming the previous findings of Hreha and Silhan [1986] and Schmidt [1986]. Moreover, the coefficient for sales is nearly twice as large as the coefficient for property (0.100 to 0.063), which would be interpretable were it not for the presence of multicollinearity, as indicating that sales is relatively twice as important in causing a change in income as property.

Table 1 also presents the coefficients for sales, property, and payroll for industrial firms. Note that the coefficient for sales is not significant at the .05 alpha level, indicating that sales does not have a statistically significant effect on income. Further, the sign of the payroll factor for industrial firms is *positive*,

Table 1. Ordinary Least Squares Parameter Estimates

Variable	DF	Parameter Estimate	Standard Error	T for Ho: Parameter = 0	prob > | T |
		A. Data from Nonindustrial Firms			
Intercept	1	49.246071	8.2164	5.994	0.0001
Sales	1	0.100437	0.0109	9.216	0.0001
Property	1	0.062973	0.0225	2.798	0.0056
Payroll	1	-0.242697	0.0234	-10.437	0.0001

$R^2 = 50\%$; F Value $= 9.495$; Prob $> F\ 0.0001$

		B. Data from Industrial Firms			
Intercept	1	-7.550550	13.5817	-0.556	0.5788
Sales	1	0.013012	0..0083	1.556	0.1187
Property	1	0.036618	0.0121	3.018	0.0028
Payroll	1	0.406739	0.0516	7.881	0.0001

$R^2 = 51\%$; F Value $= 18.164$; Prob $> F\ 0.0001$

not negative as it was for nonindustrial firms. Again, however, the presence of multicollinearity makes interpretation of the sizes or signs of the independent variables questionable.

Factors such as sales, property, and payroll seem likely to be correlated. Indeed, examination of the correlation matrix presented in Table 2 indicates the presence of bivariate multicollinearity, particularly between sales and property (79%) and sales and payroll (63%).

Whether such correlations are harmful, however, is an empirical issue. The results from the ridge regression can be used to determine which of the parameters are unstable due to the multicollinearity.

Ridge Regression Results

Dillon and Goldstein [1984, p. 287] note that coefficients that are unstable will rapidly decrease in absolute value as extra data points are derived. This decrease can be viewed as evidence that multicollinearity in the data is causing the coefficients to be unstable. Kelejian and Oates [1981, p. 199] observe that one approach to resolving the problem of multicollinearity is to increase the number of observations.

The ridge trace plots the effect on the coefficients of adding data. Evidence of multicollinearity is present when the coefficients change appreciably. Figures 1-6 present ridge traces for each of the independent variables for data pooled across time but not across firms. The traditional default values (provided by many statistical software packages) of .005 and .25 were used to obtain the ridge traces.

Table 2. Correlation Matrix of the Pearson Coefficients

	Sales	Property	Payroll
Sales	—	.7894	.62937
Property	.7894	—	.49174
Payroll	.62937	.49174	—
Income	.58091	.51639	.30671

For both industrial and nonindustrial firms, the ridge traces of sales and property indicate that the coefficients of those two variables are unstable and affected by multicollinearity. Moving away from the k = 0.00 value toward larger values of k causes the value of the coefficients of sales and property to change rapidly. However, the ridge traces of property for both types of firms move relatively little as the values of k increase, indicating that the coefficient for property remains *stable* as the k values change. Thus, for both industrial and nonindustrial firms, the sales and payroll variables are highly correlated with each other and are, therefore, unstable, while property does not correlate as highly with any other independent variable.

Ridge regression does more than diagnose which coefficients are unstable. It also produces stable and efficient estimators that explain the relative effect of the independent variables on the dependent variable. The decision rule to be used in determining when the coefficients have stabilized is to select the value of k where the ridge traces stabilize. Inspection of the ridge traces for the nonindustrial firms (and examination of the values of the independent variables and k values in tables available from the author but not presented here due to space limitation) appears to indicate that the coefficient for sales stabilizes at a k value of approximately 0.20 with a coefficient of appoximately 0.044 and the coefficient for property at a k value of approximately 0.17 with a coefficient of approximately 0.050. (The coefficients and the traces for all the variables are averages for the 10 year period.) Thus, the coefficients for sales and property stabilize at nearly equal values, indicating that these factors contribute equally to the explanation of accounting income. Also, the ridge trace of the payroll factor is negative, indicating that payroll has a negative effect on income for nonindustrial firms.

Inspection of the ridge traces (and the data not presented) indicate that much different conclusions can be drawn about the effect of the independent variables on accounting income for industrial firms. The sales factor appears to stabilize at a coefficient of approximately 0.018 while the property variable appears to stabilize at a coefficient of approximately 0.033. Thus, sales and property do not appear to have an equal effect on accounting income. Further, the ridge regression values for the payroll variable are consistently positive. This indicates that payroll has a positive effect on accounting income for industrial firms.

(*Text continued on page 199*)

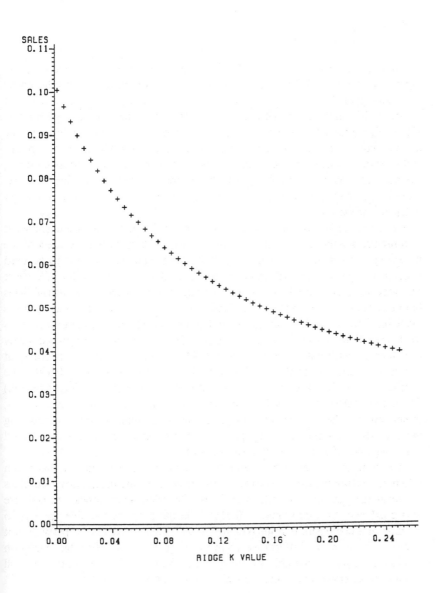

Figure 1.   Ridge Trace of Sales: Nonindustrial Firms

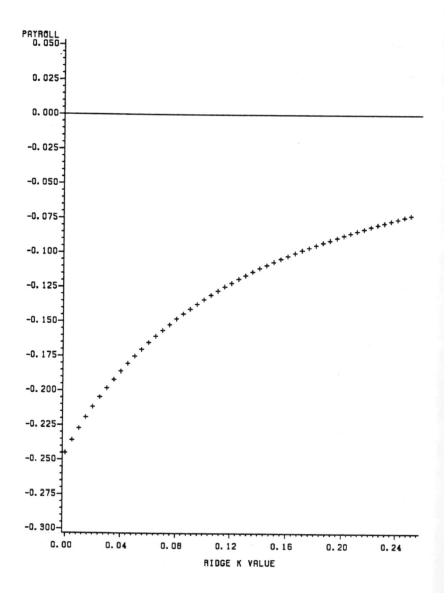

Figure 2.   Ridge Trace of Payroll: Nonindustrial Firms

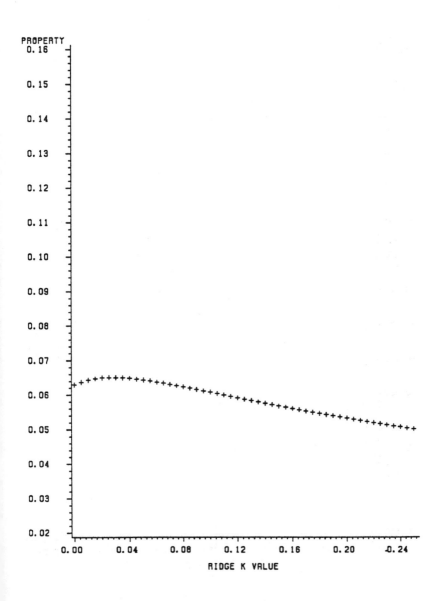

Figure 3. Ridge Trace of Property: Nonindustrial Firms

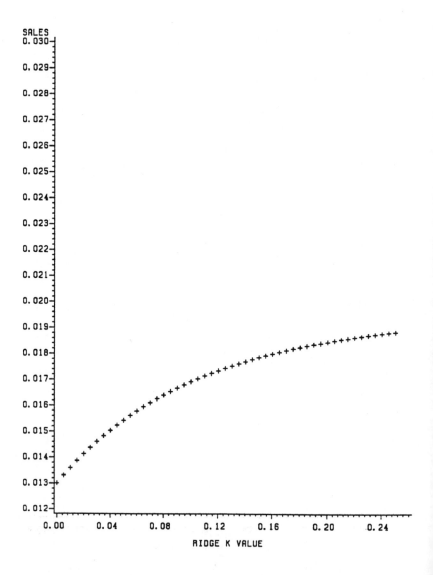

Figure 4.   Ridge Trace of Sales: Industrial Firms

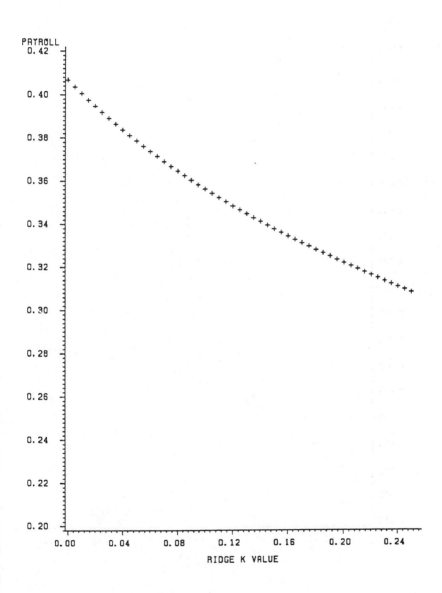

Figure 5. Ridge Trace of Payroll: Industrial Firm

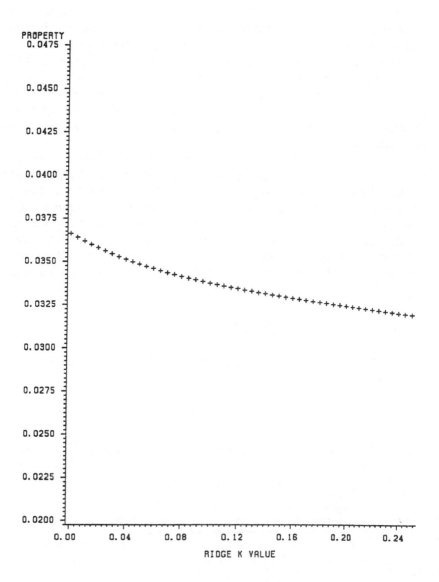

Figure 6.   Ridge Trace of Property: Industrial Firms

CONCLUSIONS

The results of this study can be summarized as follows. First, the pooling of data over time in statistical tests of the three-factor formula appears to be valid. However, pooling of data between industrial and nonindustrial firms does not appear to be appropriate. Second, the payroll factor for nonindustrial firms, in this study, as in the previous studies, has a negative coefficient, and it retains that negative sign even when ridge regression is used to eliminate multicollinearity in the data. Thus, perhaps states should not include a payroll factor in their apportionment formulas for nonindustrial firms, as payroll has a negative effect on accounting income when included in a multifactor formula. However, the positive sign of the payroll factor for industrial firms indicates that perhaps states should include that variable in a multifactor formula for apportioning income of industrial firms.

Third, the results of the ridge regression for nonindustrial firms indicate that the sales factor and the property factor are of almost equal weight. This result, combined with the negative sign of the payroll factor, may indicate that a more appropriate formula than the equally-weighted three-factor formula is an equally-weighted two-factor (sales and property) formula for apportionment of accounting income of nonindustrial firms. However, for industrial firms, the factors for sales, property, and payroll are positive and of unequal weight. Thus, an unequally-weighted three-factor apportionment formula may be appropriate for industrial firms.

ACKNOWLEDGMENT

The author would like to acknowledge the assistance of Professor William A. Raabe, University of Wisconsin—Milwaukee.

REFERENCES

Brown, W.G. and B.R. Beattie, "Improving Estimates of Economic Parameters by Use of Ridge Regression with Production Function Applications," *American Journal of Agricultural Economics* (1975) pp. 21-32.

Container Corporation of America v. Franchise Tax Board, [103 S. CT 2933, 1983].

Dillon, W.R. and M. Goldstein, *Multivariate Analysis: Methods and Application* (Wiley, 1984).

Draper, N.R. and H. Smith, *Applied Regression Analysis,* 2nd ed. (Wiley, 1981).

Exxon Corp. v. Wisconsin Department of Revenue, [447 U.S. 207, 1980].

Farrar, D.E. and R.R. Glauber, "Multicollinearity in Regression Analysis: The Problem Revisited," *Review of Economics and Statistics* (1967) pp. 92-107.

Green, P.E., *Analyzing Multivariate Data* (Dreyden Press, 1978).

Hoerl, A.E. and R.W. Kennard, "Ridge Regression: Biased Estimation of Nonorthogonal Problems," *Technometrics* (1970a), pp. 55-67.

_____"Ridge Regression: Application to Nonorthogonal Problems," *Techonometrics* (1970b), pp. 69-82.

Hreha, K.S. and P.A. Silhan "An Empirical Analysis of Unitary Apportionment," *The Journal of American Taxation Association* (Fall 1986), pp. 7-18.

Judge, G.G., W.E. Griffiths, R.C. Hill, H. Lutkepohl, and Tsoung-Chao Lee, *The Theory and Practice of Econometrics,* 2nd ed. (Wiley, 1985).

Kelejian, H.H. and W.E. Oates, *Introduction to Econometrics* (Harper & Row, 1981).

Kmenta, J. *Elements of Econometrics,* 2nd ed. (McMillian, 1971).

Lin, K. and J. Kmenta, "Ridge Regression Under Alternative Loss Criteria," *Review of Economics and Statistics* (1982), pp. 488-494.

Marquardt, D.W. and R.D. Snee, "Ridge Regression in Practice," *American Statistician* (1975), pp. 3-20.

McLure, C.E. Jr., *Economic Perspectives on State Taxation of Multijurisdictional Corportions* (Tax Analysts, 1986).

Miller Bros. v. Maryland, [347 U.S. 340, 1953].

National Tax Association, "Report of the Committee of the National Tax Association on Allocation of Income," *National Tax Association Proceedings* (1939), pp. 190-228.

Raabe, W., ed., *Multistate Corporate Tax Almanac,* 1987 ed. (Panel Publishers, 1986).

Schmidt, D.R., "Apportionment of Multijurisdictional Corporate Income," *The Journal of the American Taxation Association* (Fall 1986), pp. 19-34.

SUGI Supplemental Library Users' Guide Version 5 (SAS Institute, 1986).

Thiel, H., *Principles of Econometrics* (Wiley, 1971).

Vinod, H.D. and A. Ullah, *Recent Advances in Regression Methods* (Marcel Dekker, Inc., 1981).

Wonnacott, R.J. and T.H. Wonnacott, *Econometrics,* 2nd ed. (Wiley, 1979).

POLICY JUDGMENTS OF TAXPAYERS:

AN ANALYSIS OF CRITERIA EMPLOYED

Valerie C. Milliron, Paul R. Watkins, and
Stewart S. Karlinsky

ABSTRACT

Taxpayers' policy preferences are often thought to mirror their financial self-interest. An emerging body of public and business policy literature, however, suggests that fairness plays an important role in policy choice. Although there is long tradition of normative literature regarding what criteria should be used, little is known about what criteria taxpayers actually do use. In this study, multidimensional scaling is employed to analyze the criteria 56 individuals employ in distinguishing 12 tax policies. The results indicate that three significant constructs account for over one-half of the variance in subjects' judgments. The fairness/equity construct appears twice as salient as the other two constructs: simplicity and self-interest. These results have important implications for understanding taxpayer support of the tax law and for modeling individuals' tax policy preferences.

The popularity of Russell Long's quip, "Don't tax you, don't tax me; tax that fella behind the tree" suggests that economic self-interest may dominate

Advances in Taxation, Volume 2, pages 201-221.
Copyright © 1989 by JAI Press Inc.
All rights of reproduction in any form reserved.
ISBN: 0-89232-783-9

taxpayers' policy preferences. However, studies of other political policy issues indicate that an individual's ideology, rather than an expectation of economic advantage, dominates policy choice [Tyler, 1986]. The purpose of this study is to test the relative salience of alternative perspectives in developing a theory of individuals' tax policy preferences.

Investigating which criteria predict the tax policy option of a person prefers is an essential step in understanding "taxpayer support" of our tax laws. The objective of this line of research is to build a descriptive theory of taxpayer support rich enough to be useful in predicting individuals' policy preferences. The ultimate value of such a theory is to foster greater confidence and commitment by taxpayers through improvement in the design of the tax system. Examining motivation is of particular importance because currently accepted public choice models (e.g., see Mueller [1979]) and taxpayer compliance models (e.g., see Schmidt and Witte [1984]) assume that maximizing economic utility alone adequately explains taxpayer behavior. Measuring the influence of financial motivation will help assess the sufficiency of these models and may aid in developing richer models.

The ratings of 56 individuals awaiting jury duty on 12 tax treatments provide the data necessary in a multidimensional scaling (MDS) analysis to generate information on the constructs taxpayers use to judge tax policies. Correlations between the constructs generated and subjects' ratings of the tax policies on diverse criteria provide objective support for interpreting the MDS results. This support constitutes empirical evidence on both the absolute and relative importance of a specific criterion. Thus, the importance of criteria related to taxpayers' self-interest can be contrasted with commonly suggested criteria such as fairness, simplicity, and economic growth.

This study is the first comprehensive attempt to investigate empirically the criteria taxpayers use to judge the acceptability of alternative income tax treatments. Most other research involving tax policy criteria either investigate what criteria "should" be used (i.e., is normative) or investigate specific provisions by reference to one established criterion. None of these studies addresses the impact of self-interest on taxpayers' judgment.

The following study is organized into five sections. First, the relevant literature is reviewed. Second, the method of inquiry is discussed. Third, the research methods are described. The results are presented in the fourth section, and the policy implications are in section five.

LITERATURE REVIEW

Tax Criteria

Developing standards for evaluating alternative tax provisions has been an evolutionary process. Early political theorists such as Thomas Hobbes [1651],

Adam Smith [1776], and John Stuart Mill [1848] heightened awareness of policy evaluation issues by advocating that tax systems be designed according to reasoned standards. They were concerned with both the equitable distribution of the tax burden among individuals and also the simplicity of the system (generally expressed in terms of maximizing convenience to the taxpayer and minimizing administrative costs). Later political economists led by Seligman [1894], Edgeworth [1925], and Pigou [1928] promoted the use of income taxation as an economic tool. Acceptance of designing the tax system to facilitate macro economic objectives was furthered by the work of Keynes [1936] and Galbraith [1952]. Thus, framing the current reform debate in terms of fairness, simplicity, and economic growth [U.S. Department of the Treasury, 1984; President Reagan, 1985] reflects a long tradition of normative research regarding the criteria upon which the tax law should be predicated.

Descriptive research is of more recent vintage. In the past few years, there have been a few descriptive data-base studies dealing with equity and simplicity and extensive data-base research on the economic efficiency criterion. Madeo and Madeo [1981, 1984] and Anderson [1985] examined the equity of alternative tax policies. An implicit measure of simplicity, the compliance cost of the tax system, has been estimated empirically by Slemrod and Sorum [1984]. Lastly, in regard to the economic efficiency criterion, scores of econometric studies have attempted to estimate the influence of the income tax laws on economic growth (see Chirinko [1986] for a review of this literature).

Although several data-base studies have used specific tax criteria as measures in their design, there is a paucity of descriptive work investigating tax criteria in terms of taxpayers' perceptions or preferences. Porcano [1984a], in an experimental design based on the concept of distributive justice, examined the concept of equity in relationship to individuals' preferences on the structure of the tax law. Milliron [1985] studied tax complexity, focusing on the meaning of this criterion and its influence on tax reporting. In reference to the growth criterion, O'Neil [1982], Porcano [1984b], and Rose and O'Neil [1985] have investigated the perceived influence of different tax incentives on economic growth.

Policy Studies

Although most policy studies have not dealt specifically with the issue of federal income taxation, a number of these studies are relevant. Kramer [1971], Riker and Ordeshook [1973], and Tufte [1978] posit that there exists a strong relationship between economic self-interest and political preferences. Eisenstein [1961, p. 4], a tax theorist, concurs with this view, maintaining that "Our taxes reflect a continuing struggle among contending interests for the privilege of paying the least." However, recent empirical research casts doubt on the validity of this perspective. Sears, Lau, Tyler, and Allen [1980], Feldman [1982], and

Sears and Lau [1983] conclude that fairness plays an important role and there is little or no relationship between financial issues and political preferences. In a study involving property taxes, however, Citrin and Green [1985] found both self-interest and general political orientations (including notions of fairness) to be important determinants of support.

The role of fairness in motivating business decisions has also been recently examined. On the basis of a series of experiments, Kahneman, Knetsch, and Thaler [1986] come to three general conclusions. First, people care about being treated fairly and treating others fairly. Second, they are willing to resist unfair firms even at a cost to themselves. Third, individuals have systematic implicit rules that specify which actions of firms are considered unfair. Kahneman et al. [1986, p. 299] emphasize that "... fairness rules are not describable by the standard economic model ... Instead, judgments of fairness are influenced by framing and other factors considered irrelevant in most economic treatments. By incorporating these traits into an enriched model of customers, tenants, and employees, better predictions about the behavior of the firms with which they deal may be obtained." Similarly, information on the criteria used by taxpayers to judge the tax law could lead to an enriched model of taxpayer behavior and improved predictions of which alternatives are likely to garner long-term support.

METHOD OF INQUIRY

As the preceding review of the literature indicates, there is no theory specific enough to predict or explain the criteria taxpayers use to judge tax policies. Even though the suggested criteria are adequate to provide the initial bases for our research, they are so general that they cannot provide appropriate bases for the a priori development of testable hypotheses. Given this lack of theory, one can proceed by either (a) following the traditional approach found in the accounting literature, that is, borrowing hypotheses from another discipline and testing them in fairly simplified task setting, or (b) beginning the difficult task of gathering data about how taxpayers perceive notions of relevant criteria in a research task, and inducing theory from the results. After theory has been induced, hypotheses can then be developed and tested in the traditional way.

While both of these approaches are reasonable ways to proceed in developing scientific knowledge, the former seems well accepted by accountants while the latter, judging by its absence in the literature, does not seem to be well accepted. Biggs, Mock, and Watkins [1987] argue: "If accounting is in a preparadigm [Kuhn, 1970] or pre-theoretical [Lachman et al., 1979] stage of scientific development, then research aimed at hypothesis generation should be an important part of the work of researchers."[1] We concur with this argument and have consequently choosen a dialectic approach as the basic method of inquiry. With a dialectic approach, alternative views are subject to an empirical process designed to evaluate critically and synthesize differing perspectives [Mitroff and Mason, 1982; Churchman, 1971].

Three distinct perspectives emerge in the literature. One perspective explicitly recognizes the importance of fairness as a criterion in the decision process [Williams, 1987; Kahneman et al., 1986; Porcano, 1984a]. In contrast, the self-interest perspective regards taxes as "a changing product of earnest efforts to have others pay" [Eisenstein, 1961, p. 11]. Finally, the standard promulgated by the U.S. Treasury Department [1977, 1984] recognizes three relevant criteria (fairness, simplicity, and growth), of which only fairness is shared with another perspective.

Reflecting the philosophy that many points of view are required to produce objectivity [Churchman, 1971], we attempt to cover all three perspectives in the list of criteria presented to subjects for rating tax policies. An advantage of the MDS technique, however, is that constructs are generated on the basis of subjects' judgments of the policies regardless of whether all the appropriate tax criteria have been previously identified [Shiffman, Reynolds, and Young, 1981; Shockley and Holt, 1983]. Another advantage is that the regression of each tax criteria on the MDS configuration is independent. This means that terms that are used interchangeably in the literature like equity and fairness (e.g., see the Treasury Department [1977, 1984] and Eisenstein [1961]) may both be employed in the research design to test empirically whether these criteria correlate with a common construct.

Priors

Although there is scant analytical or empirical basis for hypothesizing which criteria are important to taxpayers in making tax policy judgments, a few observations are appropriate. Justice (alternatively defined as fairness, equality, rights, and deservingness) is a pervasive theme in social behavior [Perelman, 1967; Lerner, 1975], so some type of equity related construct may also be relevant to tax policy judgments. The complexity of the income tax reporting process is a documented nuisance [Hall and Rabushka, 1983; Slemrod and Sorum, 1984]; thus, simplicity may be a concern. Further speculation, however, becomes more problematic. Even the U.S. Department of the Treasury [1977, 1984] seems to have vacilated on the importance of using the tax system to achieve social and economic goals such as encouraging economic growth, benefiting disadvantaged taxpayers, and promoting socially desirable activities. Lastly, the results of studies involving self-interest (detailed previously) have been mixed.

Research Questions

Consistent with the literature review that indicates that the criteria taxpayers use are an unsettled issue and consistent with the dialectic method of inquiry, the following research questions are posed:

1. Are the criteria suggested by the U.S. Department of the Treasury [1984] and President Reagan [1985] (fairness, simplicity and growth) in fact the criteria used by taxpayers to distinguish tax policies?

2. Extending Porcano's [1984a]distributive justice study, what is the relative importance of equity related concepts when additional criteria are considered?

3. How does economic self-interest relate to individuals' tax policy preferences?

Test Instrument

Based on a review of the literature, nine criteria were selected for inclusion in the test instrument. Two of the nine criteria, "Taxes those best able to pay" and "Helps equalize the taxes of those in similar economic situations" describe the traditional standards of vertical and horizontal equity, respectively. "Benefits economically disadvantaged taxpayers" refers to an equity criterion predicated on taxpayer need that was found to be relevant in assessing different tax structures [Porcano, 1984a]. Three of the criteria, "Simplifies the law," "Promotes growth in the economy," and "Promotes fairness," reflect the standards promulgated by the Treasury Department [1977, 1984] and President Reagan [1985]. "Encourages socially desirable activities" describes a noneconomic growth criterion. And lastly, two of the nine criteria ("If this is future law, my taxes will probably be lower" and "If this had been past law, I would have paid less tax") are designed to measure the degree of correspondence between each policy and the respondents' financial interests.

Four general topics (charitable contributions, interest expense, IRA contributions, and capital gains) were selected from review of IRS data [Department of the Treasury, 1986]. The topics chosen involve relatively well-publicized and controversial areas of the law. For each topic, it was possible to construct three plausible treatments that might appeal to different interest groups. Although neither the four topics nor the 12 treatments are of inherent interest, they do provide a diverse set of policy alternatives to which the nine criteria could be applied.

A four-part test instrument was designed to gather the data needed to generate a MDS analysis and interpret the results.[2] The first part was used in the multidimensional scaling (MDS) analysis. The next three parts involved alternate methods of obtaining information for describing the dimensions generated by the MDS analysis.

The MDS portion of the test instrument solicited the degree of support for the 12 income tax policies. Respondents were asked whether they favored, were neutral to, or opposed each tax policy (see Appendix A). The tax treatment ratings were used to generate a multidimensional solution where each construct in the solution represents common criteria used by the respondents when making tax policy judgments.

The second part consisted of the open-ended question: What things are important to you in deciding which tax treatments are preferable? Although it is easier for subjects to judge stimuli than articulate the reasoning employed in distinguishing items [Schiffman, Reynolds, and Young, 1981], statements by the respondents may help identify the dimensions underlying the MDS configuration and test whether the criteria employed in the next section covered all relevant tax policy criteria.

In part three of the test instrument, subjects were asked to evaluate each of the 12 tax treatments in terms of the nine criteria suggested by the literature review. Specifically, subjects could agree, disagree, or be neutral as to whether the treatment was consistent with each policy criterion. (See Appendix B for a reproduction of one of the 12 pages from this section of the test instrument.) The correlations between these nine descriptors and the constructs generated from the MDS analysis provide objective measures to help label the constructs.

In the fourth part, respondents were asked to "Please indicate the importance of each of the criteria listed below in deciding your degree of support for a tax provision." An undifferentiated line scale with line end-points labeled "Of No Importance" and "Absolutely Essential" was provided for each of the nine tax criteria. The research objective in this part of the instrument is to furnish evidence on differences in the perceived desirability of the criteria. Relatively low ratings on the financial self-interest descriptors, for instance, may indicate a reluctance on the part of respondents to admit that their tax policy choices are influenced by anticipated personal economic benefit.

Administration

Prospective jurors were used as subjects in this study. This was deemed an appropriate subject pool because court officials take care to randomly select prospective jurors from a population derived from country-wide driver license and voter registration lists. Further, exemption from jury service is difficult to obtain. In addition to accessing a cross-section of individuals, an added advantage of this subject pool is that those called to jury duty are confined for about an hour in the morning before assignments are given. (See Milliron [1985] for a detailed description of the court procedures.)

The test instrument was administered to 63 individuals awaiting jury duty. Respondents took from 20-40 minutes to complete the instrument, with most allocating about one-half hour to the task. Because of missing information, seven responses were discarded, resulting in a final sample of 56 subjects.[3] This is a relatively large sample for a MDS analysis [Schiffman, Reynolds, and Young, 1981].

RESEARCH METHODS

In order to meet the research objectives of the prior section and to induce theory concerning the criteria taxpayers employ to distinguish tax policies, two complementary statistical analyses were implemented to: (1) assess the nature of the underlying conceptual structure of the taxpayer judgments, and (2) relate a priori structural concepts (tax criteria) suggested from the literature to actual structural concepts derived from the data in step (1). This latter analysis helps interpret the underlying conceptual structure in the taxpayer judgment data.

Assessment of Underlying Structure

Multidimensional scaling (MDS) is often used to determine the nature of the underlying structure of a set of judgments consisting of explicit or implicit evaluation of concepts or other items (stimuli) based on some notion of similarity [Shepard, 1974; Watkins, 1984]. A variety of MDS measures and techniques are available and selection of a particular technique is often dependent on the type and measurement scale of the data to be evaluated (for a review see Carroll and Arabie [1980]; Schiffman, Reynolds, and Young [1981]; Takane [1981a]). The MDSORT model [Takane, 1981b] is a maximum likelihood model specifically designed for evaluation of categorical judgments such as those obtained in the present study [Takane, 1980, 1983].

MDSORT is useful where the major interest of the study is the underlying nature of the overall subjects' conceptual structure and where the only interest in individual differences is in the sensitivity of each subject to the task, that is, in this case, individual differences in categorizing the various tax policies. MDSORT allows for the explicit statistical assessment of the appropriate number of constructs to extract from the subjects' judgments based on a version of Bartlett's chi-square test and provides percentages of overall variance explained for each construct extracted.

Relationship of A Priori Concepts to Derived Structure

Once a given set of data have been fit to the MDSORT model, it is necessary to give some interpretation to the underlying constructs derived from the data. One approach for interpreting the constructs is to subjectively attempt to provide some meaning to the implicit structure derived from the analysis. A more objective approach, advocated by Kruskal and Wish [1978] is to regress the set of nine tax criteria shown in Table 2, on the coordinates of the MDS extracted constructs using a special regression procedure, PROFIT [Chang and Carroll, 1968] designed for this purpose.

This procedure provides the well-known measures of goodness of fit between each tax criterion and the set of constructs extracted from the data, and standardized regression coefficients for evaluating the contribution of each construct to the particular tax criterion being evaluated. Using these measures, the tax criteria that have the highest R^2 with the set of derived constructs indicate the tax criteria that best relate to the underlying structure of the data [Kruskal and Wish, 1978]. Further, the standardized regression coefficients indicate the relative importance of each construct to the tax criterion of interest. Thus, both the R^2 and the standardized regression coefficients must be jointly assessed for appropriate interpretation of the constructs. This does not imply that researcher subjectivity is eliminated, but rather that the PROFIT procedure provides a means for augmenting and refining the researcher judgment involved in interpreting the derived constructs.

Task Effects and Subjects' Attention to the Task

To assess the manner in which subjects dealt with the task, the MDSORT routine provides measures and plots of cluster centroids that indicate the way in which subjects evaluate the stimuli. If subjects are consistent in dealing with the task and are attentive to the task, then consistency should be present in the cluster centroids with respect to tradeoffs between various cluster categories and derived construct weights. Individual differences in the manner in which subjects approach the task can also be identified.[4]

RESULTS

Both cluster centroid measures and plots were evaluated by the researchers for consistency and task involvement by the subjects. The evidence indicates that the subjects were interested, consistent, and attentive in carrying out the task. Further support for this conclusion was obtained in ad hoc debriefing conversations by the research assistant and several of the subjects. Individual differences were noticed from the cluster centroid analysis across subjects in performing the task and these differences appear attributable to different underlying perceptual/preference structures.

The results of the MDSORT scaling are shown in Table 1. The eigenvalues and chi-squares were used to determine the statistically appropriate number of constructs to evaluate. The appropriate form of the chi-square statistic [Nishisato, 1980] is:

$$X^2 = - [Nn - 1 - \left(\frac{n + d \, N_k - N \Big|_{k=1}^{N}}{2} \right)] \ln (1 - \text{lambda}_j{}^2)$$

where lambda$_j$ is the jth largest eigenvalue, N is the total number of subjects, n is the number of stimuli, k is the index for classifying the set of n stimuli into N$_k$ groups. This statistic approximately follows the chi-square distribution with:

$$n + d \sum_{k=1}^{N} N_k - N - 2_j \quad \text{degrees of freedom under the hypothesis that } j^{th}$$

largest population eigenvalue is equal to zero. A significant departure of lambda$_j$ from zero can be tested by comparing the observed values of the chi-square statistic in Table 1 against the appropriate critical values of the chi-square distribution.

Three eigenvalues were significant at the .001 level using a chi-square test with the degrees of freedom shown in Table 1. Thus, three constructs were selected as the most appropriate configuration for further analysis and interpretation.

As noted in Table 1, the first three constructs account for 51% of the variance. Construct one explains 26% of the total variance, constructs two and three explain 13% and 12% of the total variance, respectively. The overall variance explained is reasonable for this type of study and task [Kruskal and Wish, 1978]. Takane [1980] points out that in typical MDS studies, "the observed data are typically subject to a sizable amount of measurement error," and goes on to argue that the key for dealing with measurement error is to develop appropriate assumptions about the underlying error process and explicitly incorporate these assumptions in the MDS algorithm. Thus, the MDSORT routine is designed specifically for the kind of data gathered in this study and explicitly incorporates assumptions about the error process into the scaling model (for details see Takane [1980]). Obviously, if all 12 possible constructs had been identified for use and interpretation, 100% of the variance could have been explained by the constructs but the preceeding chi-square test indicates that only the first three constructs were statistically significant (given a model based on maximum likelihood estimation with built-in assumptions about the nature of the error process). Stated another way, these three constructs are statistically significant in explaining the manner in which taxpayers express their preferences for various tax policies. Although the other constructs contribute to the overall variance, their relative contribution is not significant enough to warrant inclusion in the final analysis.

After studying the resulting coordinates and scaling configurations from the MDSORT analysis, tentative interpretations of the underlying constructs were determined. As stated earlier, in order to provide a more objective interpretation of the constructs, each of the nine tax criteria of Table 2 was

Table 1. Statistical Results for Group MDS

Eigenvalues	% of Variance Explained	Chi-Square	Corresponding D.F.
.47	.26	390.26**	110
.24	.13	164.40**	108
.22	.12	150.07**	106
.17	.09	114.88	104
.14	.08	94.46	102
.12	.07	81.67	100
.12	.07	79.35	98
.10	.06	65.87	96
.09	.05	55.79	94
.07	.04	45.39	92
.05	.03	29.72	90
.00	.00	.00	88

Note: ** Significant at the .001 level.

regressed on the set of three MDS derived constructs. Thus nine regressions were performed. Table 2 provides the R-squared values indicating goodness of fit or variance explained between each tax criteria and the three derived constructs. Also in Table 2 are the standardized regression weights that indicate the relative importance of a given construct to a particular tax criteria. We looked for relatively high R-square values and high standardized regression weights to identify which tax criteria best correspond to a given construct.

Reviewing the R-square values in Table 2 reveals that the criterion descriptor based on past financial self-interest ("If this had been the past law, I would have paid less tax") is relatively low. Of the nine criterion measures, this is the least related to the subjects' tax policy judgments (as described by the three constructs). Since this tax criteria measure explains less than half of the variation in subjects' judgments, it is disregarded in the following interpretation of the constructs.

A perusal of Table 2 reveals that all the equity related descriptors show a positive and moderate to high correspondence with construct one. This includes measures of vertical and horizontal equity (a .76 and .59 beta, respectively), the needs of disadvantaged taxpayers (.82), and fairness (.66). The only nonequity related descriptor showing a moderately strong correlation with construct one is that of "Promoting growth in the economy" (.74). It is not possible to specify causal relationships with correlational data, but the correspondance of the economic growth criterion may be evidence of public acceptance of the "fair tax" argument. For instance, Bradley [1984], an initiator of the "fair tax" proposal in Congress, asserts that inequitable tax practices

Table 2. Regression Results of Adjective Descriptors and MDS Dimension Coordinates for Dimensional Interpretation

Tax Criteria	Standardized Regression Weights			R-Squared Value
	*Con 1	*Con 2	*Con 3	
Best Able to Pay	.76	-.07	.65	.63
Horizontal Equity	.59	-.09	.80	.83
Benefits Disadvantaged	.82	-.53	.22	.61
Simplifies	-.02	.81	.58	.88
Promotes Growth	.74	-.05	.67	.91
Fairness	.67	.45	.59	.79
Socially Desirable	.18	.52	.84	.77
Lower Personal Taxes (Future)	.27	.42	.87	.71
Lower Personal Taxes (Past)	.77	-.55	.31	.48

Note: *Con = Construct

are hindering growth in the economy. On the basis of the direction cosines in Table 2, it appears that construct one is best described as an "equity" construct, although it might be alternatively viewed as an "equity/growth" construct.

"Simplifies the law" (.81) stands out as the best descriptor of construct two. None of the other tax criteria corresponds highly with construct two, and all show higher loadings on one of the other constructs. Thus, the term "simplicity" seems to characterize this construct aptly.

Projected financial self-interest as measured by the tax criterion "If this is future law, my taxes will probably be lower" (a .87 beta) shows the highest standardized regression weight on construct three. But this construct is also associated with a number of other positive attributes. "Encourages socially desirable activities" (.84) and "Helps equalize the taxes of those in similar economic situations" (.80) show a high correspondence with construct three. "Best able to pay" (.65), "fairness" (.59), and "simplifies" (.58) show a moderate correspondence with this construct. If Tyler's [1986] conclusion that people have a tendency to view personally favorable outcomes in socially positive terms is accepted, then it appears that subjects' projected financial interest is the dominant criterion in construct three. Tyler's [1986] conclusion, which is based on a review of the political behavior literature, recognizes that individuals tend to describe policies in their financial self-interest as beneficial and just.

The financial self-interest interpretation is corroborated by subjects' responses to the open ended question "What things are important to you in deciding which tax treatments are preferable?" Ten of the 32 subjects responding to this question indicated that anticipated self-interest was an important consideration. The salience of future financial interest was also apparent in the self-ratings collected on the nine criteria.

In subjects' reported importance ratings in part four of the test instrument, eight of the nine criteria received positive importance ratings (i.e., the mean ratings were to the right of the midpoint on undifferentiated lines). The one exception was the tax criterion describing past financial self-interest. Consistent with these results, past financial self-interest was the only criterion omitted from the interpretation of the MDS configuration because of a low R-square value. It appears that subjects, however, will admit that they are influenced by expected future financial benefit.[5] This descriptor, for instance, received a higher importance rating than "Encourages socially desirable activities," even though the latter criterion undoubtedly has a more positive connotation.

IMPLICATIONS, LIMITATIONS, AND EXTENSIONS

Three research questions were posed earlier. First, are the Department of Treasury [1984] criteria used by taxpayers? Second, how important are equity concepts when other criteria are considered? Third, what is the role of financial self-interest?

Based on the results of this study, several observations are relevant. The results generally affirm the governmental position of judging policy alternatives on the basis of fairness, simplicity, and economic growth. The major distinction is that economic growth and fairness do not emerge as separate criteria, but both load with equity concepts on construct one. Governmental authorities and academics may view economic growth and equity as separate issues (e.g., for an academic perspective see Fromm [1971] or Aaron and Pechman [1981]). However, these subjects seem to intertwine the concepts to produce a blur similar to that sometimes evident in the popular tax policy literature (e.g., see Hall and Rabushka [1983] or Bradley [1984]).

The second research question involves the relative importance of the equity criteria. Recall that all the equity related concepts loaded highly on construct one. In addition, this construct accounted for twice as much variance as the next most important construct. This result supports the value of academic endeavors to investigate the role of equity (e.g., Porcano's [1984] study on distributive justice).[6] This finding also adds to the growing body of literature documenting the importance of noneconomic considerations in decision making (e.g., see Hogarth and Reder [1987]).

In reference to the third research question, our results indicate that self-interest is a relevant, but not overwhelming, concern. Self-interest appears less important than equity and on a par with the regard for simplicity. These findings conflict with the common assertion that financial self-interest propels the tax reform movement (e.g., see Hume [1985]). However, the findings are in keeping with recent research on political popularity which concludes that "justice is actually a more important influence than is the level of outcomes received ... citizens act as naive moral philosophers in evaluating government, judging its actions against abstract criteria of fairness" [Tyler, Rasinski, and McGraw, 1985, p. 717].

The findings also raise other issues. For one thing, these results suggest that current efforts to measure public support for alternate tax provisions would be more productive if equity, simplicity, and self-interest perceptions were specifically addressed. The global questions currently asked in government commissioned surveys appear too general to analyze issues adequately when support is predicated on multidimensional criteria (e.g., see the Advisory Commission on Intergovernmental Relations [1986] annual poll and the IRS commissioned study by Yankelovich, Skelly, and White [1984]).

Another implication relates to the debate over the link between tax fairness and tax compliance (see Jackson and Milliron [1986] for a review of this literature). The apparent importance of equity in taxpayers' judgment processes adds credence to concerns expressed by those who assert that perceptions of fairness are linked to tax compliance (e.g., see Porcano [1984a], Spicer [1986], and Etzioni [1986]). It appears that taxpayers are cognizant of equity considerations in judging their support for tax rules, and it is thus plausible that these considerations also affect taxpaying behavior. Part of the noncompliance problem may be, in the words of Wright [1981, p. 52], "the price paid by democratic regimes for pursuing policies that run counter to the policy preferences of its citizens."

A final observation is that the importance of equity is cause for both optimism and concern regarding tax policy formation. It is cause for optimism to the extent it suggests the opportunity to fashion rational tax policy even when changes are contrary to the financial interests of broad constituencies. But this is also cause for concern because, as Tyler [1986] notes, in a democratic process these ideals may be manipulated by special interest groups seeking economic advantage.

The scope limitations of this study suggest several potential research extensions. First, and most importantly, this study establishes a foundation for testing hypotheses and experimentally examining the effect of these criteria on taxpayers' judgments. For example, based on the results of this study, high and low levels of fairness, simplicity, and self-interest can be manipulated in a factorial design to test the effect of these factors on policy preferences and reporting behavior (e.g., see Milliron [1985] for a design based on theory induction followed by hypotheses testing). Second, because fairness was found to be an important construct, an indepth examination of different aspects of equity appears a viable avenue of research (e.g., see recent work by Folger [1984], Messick and Cook [1983], and Greenberg and Cohen [1982]). A third area of investigation involves an examination of the relationship between individuals' background characteristics and their preferences for alternative tax rules. Such an investigation could provide evidence to support or refute Eisenstein's [1965, p. 453] assertion that taxation is a continuing "fiscal warfare" between classes of taxpayers.

The last two extensions identified relate specifically to limitations associated with the language employed in the test instrument. We explicitly instructed subjects to consider a revenue neutral situation (see the directions in Appendix A). It is possible that different levels of taxation may result in different criteria or different weights on the criteria (for a commentary on the influence of the level of perceived well-being, see Alwin [1987]). Lastly, our coverage was limited to federal income tax rules. Expansion to include other types of taxes may alter the criteria. For example, comparing income taxes, property taxes and a hypothesized national sales tax (or value-added tax) may highlight the importance of other criteria such as the ease of payment or the visability of the tax [Hansen, 1983].

CONCLUSION

Contrasting the fairness, self-interest, and Department of the Treasury perspectives, we find that each of these views appears to characterize an aspect of taxpayers' judgment processes. The most striking conclusion is that the first two of the three significant constructs involve nonfinancial criteria. Moreover, although both simplicity and self-interest are also significant, equity appears to be a relatively more important criteria. Thus, each perspective is partially supported, but with the important caveat that the other views are also relevant.

These results add credence to the efforts of those seeking to expand current economic models to incorporate nonfinancial dimensions. Better understanding of taxpayers' policy judgments should facilitate better modeling. The ultimate objective is to enhance the democratic process by improving information regarding the policy options most likely to sustain long-run support. A system fashioned to reflect taxpayer values is more likely to have the confidence and commitment of taxpayers. Perhaps policymakers will be more alert than the British were before the Boston Tea Party.

ACKNOWLEDGMENT

We are grateful to Richard Helleloid, Mark Dirsmith, Fran Ayres, Frank Collins, Tim Fogarty, Frank Selto, Betty Jackson, Julie Collins, Charles Enis, Peggy Hite and Jacci Speelman for their helpful suggestions, and to Glen Freid, Natalie Marvi, and Karin Raub for their assistance. We also appreciate the useful comments from workshop participants at the University of Oklahoma, Texas Tech University, and the University of Colorado—Boulder. Any remaining errors are, of course, the responsibility of the authors. This research was funded by faculty research grants from The Pennsylvania State University, the University of Southern California, and the Peat Marwick Foundation.

NOTES

1.   There is little reason to treat theory that is induced from data as being valueless. In fact, Ericsson and Simon [1984, p. 280] use a Bayesian framework to refute the traditional view that theory and hypotheses must be stated prior to the gathering of data. While recognizing that prior statement of hypotheses has merit, they argue that theories and hypotheses generated after gathering of data have considerable scientific value and they conclude: "The common view that hypotheses must be formulated before experiments are run in order for the data to have value as evidence is simply false."

2.   Twelve versions of the test instrument were prepared. This permitted reordering of questions within subsections to mitigate against a possible presentation bias. In addition, a page was attached to the end of the test instrument that sought demographic information on the respondents to determine if they are representative of taxpayers in the area. (Information was solicited on gender, age, marital status, professional classification, race, education, and income levels.) The test instrument was pilot tested for clarity with undergraduate and graduate students and a convenience sample of nonstudent adults.

3.   The main courthouse in Los Angeles County was the test site for this study. Background data from the 56 subjects was analyzed to determine the characteristics of this sample. The distribution of variables appeared representative of the national population when compared with U.S. Bureau of the Census [1985]data.

4.   These measures and plots are not reported here due to the voluminous nature of the results but are available on request from the researchers.

5.   In the past, social scientists have contended that citizens try to disguise their self-interested behavior with the claim that they are really supporting the public interest (e.g., see Lasswell [1930]). However, the general acceptance of economic notions, of rationality seem to have reversed this situation. Sears and Lau [1983, p. 247] even go so far as to assert that people "claim to be self-interested to avoid admitting to nonselfish causes of their behavior."

6.   Based on these results, political efforts to center tax reform debates on equity issues (e.g., see Murray [1985] and Birnbaum [1985]) appear well-directed. However, the near abandonment of simplicity in the latest tax code revision [Merry and Blustein, 1985] appears to run counter to the values of the subjects tested (since simplicity emerged as a significant construct in the analysis).

7.   This, of course, implies that the current economic models that are delineated in terms of financial interests are underspecified (see commentaries by Coleman [1986] and Gould [1986]). The challenge is to integrate this understanding into models of choice that are capable of providing better input into the policy setting process [Lynn, 1986].

REFERENCES

Aaron, H. and J. Pechman, eds., *How Taxes Affect Economic Behavior* (Brookings Institution, 1981).

Advisory Commission on Intergovernmental Relations, *Changing Public Attitude on Government and Taxes* (Washington DC, 1986).

Alwin, D., "Distributive Justice and Satisfaction with Material Well-Being," *American Sociological Review* 52 (February 1987), pp. 83-95.

Anderson, K., "A Horizontal Equity Analysis of the Minimum Tax Provisions: An Empirical Study," *The Accounting Review* (July 1985), pp. 357-371.

Biggs, S., T. Mock and P. Watkins, *Analytical Review Procedures and Processing in Auditing*, Research Monograph of the Canadian Certified General Accountants Foundation (Fall 1987).

Birnbaum, J., "Tax-Revision Plan Must Convince Public that System is Fair, Rostenkowski Says," *The Wall Street Journal* (March 27, 1985), p. 6.

Bradley, B., *The Fair Tax* (Pocket Books, 1984).

Carroll, J. and P. Arabie, "Multidimensional Scaling," *Annual Review of Psychology* (1980), pp. 607-649.

Chang, J. and J. Carroll, "How to Use PROFIT: A Computer Program for Property Fitting by Optimizing Nonlinear or Linear Correlation," Bell Laboratories manuscript (1968).

Chirinko, P., "Business Investment and Tax Policy: A Perspective on Existing Models and Empirical Results," *National Tax Journal* 39, (June 1986), pp. 137-156.

Churchman, C., *The Design of Inquiring Systems* (Basic Books, 1971).

Citrin, J. and D. Green, "Policy and Opinion in California After Proposition 13," *National Tax Journal* 38, (March 1985), pp. 15-36.

Coleman, J., "Psychological Structure and Social Structure in Economic Models," *The Journal of Business* (October 1986), pp. 365-369.

Edgeworth, F., *Papers Relating to Political Economy* (MacMillian and Company, 1925), pp. 106-117.

Eisenstein, L., The Ideologies of Taxation (Ronald Press, 1961).

_____"Some Second Thoughts on Tax Ideologies," *Tax Law Review,* 20, (1965), pp. 453-477.

Ericsson, K. and H. Simon, *Protocal Analysis: Verbal Reports as Data* (M.I.T. Press, 1984).

Etzioni, A., "Tax Evasion and Perception of Tax Fairness: A Research Note," *The Journal of Applied Behavioral Science* 22, (1986), pp. 177-185.

Feldman, S., "Economic Self-Interest and Political Behavior," *American Journal of Political Science* 26, (August 1982), pp. 446-466.

Folger, R., *The Sense of Injustice: Social Psychological Perspectives* (Plenum, 1984).

Fromm, G., ed., *Tax Incentives and Capital Spending* (Brookings Institution, 1971).

Galbraith, J. K., *American Capitalism: The Concept of Countervailing Power* (Houghton Mifflin Company, 1952)

Gould, J., "Is the Rational Expectations Hypothesis Enough?," *The Journal of Business* (October 1986), pp. 370-377.

Greenberg, J. and R. Cohen, *Equity and Justice in Social Behavior* (Academic Press, 1983).

Hall, R. and A. Rabushka, *Low Tax, Simple Tax, Fair Tax* (McGraw-Hill, 1983).

Hansen, S., *The Politics of Taxation: Revenue Without Representation* (Praeger, 1983).

Hobbes, T., Leviathan (1651) (George Rutledge & Sons, 3rd. ed., 1887), p. 158.

Hogarth, R. and M. Reder, *Rational Choice: The Contrast Between Psychology and Economics* (University of Chicago Press, 1987).

Hume, E., "Polls Indicate that Public Support for Tax Overhaul Is Up for Grabs," *The Wall Street Journal* (May 30, 1985), p. 20.

Jackson, B. and V. Milliron, "Tax Compliance Research, Findings, Problems and Prospects," *Journal of Accounting Literature* 5 (1986), pp. 125-166.

Kahneman, D., J. Knetsch and R. Thaler, "Fairness and the Assumptions of Economics," *The Journal of Business* (October 1986), pp. 285-300.

Keynes, J. M., *The General Theory of Employment, Interest and Money* (Harcourt, Brace and Co., 1936), pp. 372-374.

Kramer, G., "Short-Term Fluctuations in U.S. Voting Behavior, 1896-1964," *American Political Science Review* 65 (March 1971), pp. 131-143.

Kruskal, J. and M. Wish, *Multidimensional Scaling* (Sage, 1978).

Kuhn, T., "Logic of Discovery or Psychology of Reason," in N. Lakatos and A. Musgrave (eds.), *Criticism and the Growth of Knowledge* (Cambridge University Press, 1970).

Lachman, R., J. Lachman and E. Butterfield, *Cognitive Psychology and Information Processing: An Introduction* (Erlbaum, 1979).

Lasswell, H., *Psychopathology and Politics* (Viking Press, 1930).

Lerner, M., "The Justice Motive in Social Behavior: Introduction," *Journal of Social Issues*, 31, (Fall 1975), pp. 1-19.

Lynn, L., "The Behavioral Foundations of Public Policy-Making," *The Journal of Business* (October 1986), pp. 379-384.

Madeo, S. and L. Madeo, "Some Evidence on the Equity Effects of the Minimum Tax on Individual Taxpayers," *National Tax Journal* (December 1981), pp. 457-465.

_____, "The Equity and Motivating Effects of the Maximum Tax," *The Journal of the American Taxation Association* (Spring 1984), pp. 40-49.

Merry, R. and P. Blustein, "Framers Strived for Fairness and Growth, Dropping Original Emphasis on Simplicity," *The Wall Street Journal* (May 30, 1985), p. 20.

Messick, D. and K. Cook, *Equity Theory: Psychological and Sociological Perspectives* (Praeger, 1983).

Mill, J. S., *Principles of Political Economy* (1848) (Longmans, Green and Co., 1923), book 5, chapter 2, section 2.

Milliron, V., "A Behavioral Study of the Meaning and Influence of Tax Complexity," *Journal of Accounting Research* (Autumn 1985), pp. 794-816.

Mitroff, I. and R. Mason, "Business Policy and Metaphysics: Some Philosophical Considerations," *The Academy of Management Review* 7, (July 1982), pp. 361-371.

Mueller, D., *Public Choice* (Cambridge University Press, 1979).

Murray, A., "To Revamp IRS Code Reagan Will Tap Belief That System is Unfair: Inequity Irks People More than Complexity or Rate They Pay, Treasury Says," *The Wall Street Journal* (April 15, 1985), p. 1.

Nishisato, S., *Analysis of Categorical Data: Dual Scaling and Its Applications* (University of Toronto Press, 1980).

O'Neil, C., "The Targeted Jobs Credit: An Evaluation of Its Impact on the Employment Decision Process," *The Journal of the American Taxation Association* (Winter 1982), pp. 15-22.

Perelman, C., *Justice* (Random House, 1967).

Pigou, A., *Study in Public Finance* (MacMillian, 1928), pp. 60-76.

Porcano, T., "Distributive Justice and Tax Policy," *Accounting Review* (October 1984a), pp. 619-636.

_____, "The Perceived Effects of Tax Policy on Corporate Investment Intentions," *The Journal of the American Taxation Association* (Fall 1984b), pp. 7-19.

Reagan, R., "Tax Proposals to the Congress for Fairness, Growth and Simplicity," (The Bureau of National Affairs, Inc., released May 29, 1985).

Riker, W. and P. Ordeshook, *An Introduction to Positive Political Theory* (Prentice-Hall, 1973).

Rose, C. and C. O'Neil, "The Viewed Importance of Investment Tax Incentives by Virginia Decision Makers," *The Journal of the American Taxation Association* (Fall 1985), pp. 34-43.

Schiffman, S., M. Reynolds, and F. Young, Handbook for Multidimensional Scaling (Academic Press, 1981).

Schmidt, P. and A. Witte, *An Economic Analysis of Crime and Justice: Theory, Methods and Applications* (Academic Press, Inc., 1984).

Sears, D. and R. Lau, "Inducing Apparently Self-Interested Political Preferences," *American Journal of Political Science* 27, (2) (1983), pp. 221-252.

Sears, D., R. Lau, T. Tyler, and H. Allen, "Self-Interest vs. Symbolic Politics in Policy Attitudes and Presidential Voting," *The American Political Science Review* 74 (1980), pp. 670-684.

Seligman, E., *Progressive Taxation in Theory and Practice*(American Economic Association, monograph Vol. 9, No. 1-2, 1894), pp. 192-194.

Shepard, R., "Representation of Structure in Similarity Data: Problems and Prospects," *Psychometrika* (December 1974), pp. 373-417.

Shockley, R. and R. Holt, "A Behavioral Investigation of Supplier Differentiation in the Market for Audit Services," *Journal of Accounting Research* (Autumn 1983), pp. 545-564.

Slemrod, J. and N. Sorum, "The Compliance Cost of the U. S. Individual Income Tax System," *National Tax Journal* 37, (December 1984), pp. 461-474.

Smith, A., *An Inquiry into the Nature and Causes of the Wealth of Nations,* (1776) (Dutton, 1910), book 5, chapter 2, part 2.

Spicer, M., "Civilization at a Discount: The Problem of Tax Evasion," *National Tax Journal* 39, (March 1986), pp. 13-20.

Takane, Y., "Analysis of Categorizing Behavior by a Quantification Method," *Behaviormetrika,* (8) (1980), pp. 75-86.

————, "Multidimensional Successive Category Scaling: A Maximum Likelihood Method," *Psychometrika* 46, (March 1981a), pp. 9-28.

————, "MDSORT: A Special Purpose Multidimensional Scaling Program for Sorting Data," *Behavior, Research Methods and Instrumentation* 13, (5) (1981b), p. 698.

————, "Item Response Models for Multidimensional Analysis of Categorial Data," Proceedings of the Behaviormetric Society Meetings, 1983.

Tufte, E., *Political Control of the Economy* (Princeton University Press, 1978).

Tyler, T., "Justice and Leadership Endorsement," in R. Lau and D. Sears (eds.), *Political Cognition* (Erlbaum, 1986), pp. 257-278.

Tyler, T, K. Rasinski, and K. McGraw, "The Influence of Perceived Injustice on the Endorsement of Political Leaders," *Journal of Applied Social Psychology* 15, (8) (1985), pp. 700-725.

U.S. Bureau of the Census, *Statistical Abstract of the United States: 1986* 106th Edition, (U.S. Bureau of the Census, 1985).

U.S. Department of the Treasury, *Blueprints for Basic Tax Reform* (U.S. Government Printing Office, 1977).

————, *Tax Reform for Fairness, Simplicity and Economic Growth* vo.1-3 (Prentice-Hall, 1984).

————, *Statistics of Income Bulletin* vol. 6, No. 1, (Summer 1986).

Watkins, P., "Multidimensional Sealing Measuring and Accounting Research," *Journal of Accounting Research* 22, (Spring 1984), pp. 406-411.

Williams, P., "The Legitimate Concern with Fairness," *Accounting, Organizations and Society* 12, (2) (1987), pp. 169-189.

Wright, J., "Political Disaffection," in S. Long (ed.), *Handbook of Political Behavior* (Plenum, 1981).

Yankelovich, Skelly, and White, Inc., *Survey of Taxpayer Attitudes*, Prepared for the Internal Revenue Service, (December 1984).

APPENDIX A

MDS Task
(Part one of test instrument)

DIRECTIONS

Listed below are 12 possible income tax treatments. Please indicate your degree of support by circling one of the following choices after each item: favor, neutral, or oppose.

Remember there are cost trade-offs when making your judgements. By cost trade-offs we mean the trade-off between allowing deductions or special tax rates and an overall reduction in income tax rates. This trade-off is illustrated in the two following examples.

Example 1:   If a sales tax deduction were not allowed, then tax rates could be lowered.

Example 2:   If interest and dividend income were taxed at lower rates, then other income would have to be taxed at higher rates to raise the same amount of revenue.

Allow all taxpayers (even if they don't itemize) a deduction for the charitable contributions they make.	FAVOR	NEUTRAL	OPPOSE
Allow a deduction for home mortgage interest expense.	FAVOR	NEUTRAL	OPPOSE
Allow all taxpayers to deduct IRA contributions.	FAVOR	NEUTRAL	OPPOSE
Tax profits from the sale of securities at lower rates than other income.	FAVOR	NEUTRAL	OPPOSE
Allow a charitable contributions deduction only for taxpayres that itemize.	FAVOR	NEUTRAL	OPPOSE
Allow a deduction for consumer interest expense.	FAVOR	NEUTRAL	OPPOSE
Disallow IRA deductions for taxpayers who are in a pension plan.	FAVOR	NEUTRAL	OPPOSE
Tax real estate profits at lower rates than other income.	FAVOR	NEUTRAL	OPPOSE
Disallow all deductions for charitable contributions.	FAVOR	NEUTRAL	OPPOSE
Disallow all nonbusiness interest expense deductions.	FAVOR	NEUTRAL	OPPOSE
Disallow all IRA deductions.	FAVOR	NEUTRAL	OPPOSE
Treat all types of income equally.	FAVOR	NEUTRAL	OPPOSE

APPENDIX B

Criteria Ratings to Aid in Labeling MDS Dimensions
(Part 3 of instrument, 12 pages total, one page per rule)

DIRECTIONS

Rate the tax treatment below by circling your response.
(Remember the trade-off between allowing deductions and lower tax rates.)

DISALLOW IRA DEDUCTIONS FOR TAXPAYERS WHO ARE IN A PENSION PLAN

Taxes those best able to pay.	DISAGREE	NEUTRAL	AGREE
Helps equalize the taxes of those in similar economic situations.	DISAGREE	NEUTRAL	AGREE
Benefits economically disadvantaged taxpayers.	DISAGREE	NEUTRAL	AGREE
Simplifies the law.	DISAGREE	NEUTRAL	AGREE
Promotes growth in the economy.	DISAGREE	NEUTRAL	AGREE
Promotes fairness.	DISAGREE	NEUTRAL	AGREE
Encourages socially desirable activities.	DISAGREE	NEUTRAL	AGREE
If this is future law, my taxes will probably be lower.	DISAGREE	NEUTRAL	AGREE
If this had been the past law, I would have paid less tax.	DISAGREE	NEUTRAL	AGREE

ECONOMIC ANALYSIS OF BROAD-BASED INCOME AND CONSUMPTION TAXES

Herbert G. Hunt, III and Charles R. Enis

ABSTRACT

Income and consumption taxes are two general classes of comprehensive tax reforms that exhibit conflict among the policy goals of low tax rates, equity and efficiency. This paper algebraically and graphically analyzes these alternatives to assess their relative impact on one dimension of economic neutrality, the savings/consumption choice. The analysis is performed under both an equal tax-rate assumption and a revenue neutral assumption, and is then expanded to allow for both exogenous and endogenous interest rates and lending and borrowing. The results of the analyses indicate that the consumption tax is neutral with respect to the consumption/savings choice because it avoids the inherent substitution effect of the income tax. However, the consumption tax may be viewed negatively since it tends to favor high income taxpayers over low income taxpayers. The paper also examines efficiency and equity issues, and discusses some policy issues surrounding certain consumption tax features of the current U.S. tax system.

Advances in Taxation, Volume 2, pages 223-245.
Copyright © 1989 by JAI Press Inc.
All rights of reproduction in any form reserved.
ISBN: 0-89232-783-9

INTRODUCTION

The need for significant tax reform in the United States is currently at a point where it may lead to major restructuring of existing tax systems. Break [1984, p. 1]) states that "the economic losses and inefficiencies imposed by existing taxes may be not only large but a great deal larger than was formerly thought possible." In addition, a recent General Accounting Office study [1986] suggests that huge federal budget deficits have renewed the search for significant new sources of tax revenue. These, and other, realizations have resulted in tax reform remaining at the forefront of political and economic debate in recent years (e.g., see Pechman [1984]; Aaron and Galper [1985]).

Most of the specific reform proposals fall into one of two categories: a comprehensive income tax or a comprehensive consumption tax (Bosworth, 1984, p. 198). Although a broad-based income tax and a broad-based consumption tax would each contribute toward achieving the Treasury's goal of low tax rates, they differ in other respects that may affect their relative desirability as models for tax reform [Robinson, 1984]. This paper examines these two general types of tax systems, using simple algebraic and graphical analyses, to assess their relative impact on the consumption/savings choice. Our goal is not to break ground in economic theory. Indeed, many of the concepts that we examine are already well-known and established in the economics literature. Rather, the purpose of this paper is to illuminate the theoretical impact of simple income and consumption taxes on the important consumption/savings choice, and by so doing, provide a frame of reference for analyzing tax reform alternatives for those with a policy-making orientation.

This paper does extend the basic analysis to include both before-tax and after-tax definitions of income, both exogenous and endogenous interest rates, borrowing and lending, liquidity factors, and differing patterns of consumer preferences towards current and future consumption. In addition to the economic analysis, we discuss its implications with respect to efficiency and equity issues and examine components of the current income tax system that resemble features of a consumption tax.

The paper is structured as follows. The next section provides a brief overview of broad-based taxes and discusses the motivation to move from an income-based to a consumption-based tax system. The third section algebraically analyzes the demand for consumption and savings under both a broad-based, flat-rate income tax and under a broad-based, flat-rate consumption tax. The analysis is first performed assuming equal tax rates and then under a revenue neutral assumption. Opportunities for borrowing and lending are then introduced. Section four analyzes the two taxes graphically and discusses the implications of the analysis with respect to the policy goals of efficiency and equity. The last section includes a summary and concluding comments on the consumption-based features of the current tax system.

BACKGROUND

Two major categories of broad-based taxes are income and consumption taxes. These taxes are similar to the extent that the tax base includes all national income as would be the case in the absence of exclusions, exemptions, and deductions [Browning and Browning, 1979, pp. 286-288].[1] Whereas income taxes are direct taxes, consumption taxes can be either direct or indirect.[2] An example of a direct consumption tax is the consumed income tax (CIT) or expenditure tax (ET). Examples of broad-based indirect consumption taxes are the general sales tax (GST) and the value-added tax (VAT).

The two indirect consumption taxes mentioned above would have the same economic impact as an ET if they are fully shifted forward from sellers to buyers [Due and Friedlaender, 1981, pp. 375-381]. The actual shifting of these taxes and the extent to which they mirror an ET is a complex function of many interrelated variables. However, the intended purpose of indirect consumption taxes is the same as that of an ET; that is, to shift resources from consumption to investment. Therefore, we make the assumption that the three consumption taxes have similar economic effects, at least with respect to the issues examined in this paper. The analyses that follow focus on the ET as representative of consumption taxes. Broad-based versions of an ET and an income tax are examined with respect to neutrality and efficiency issues surrounding the consumption versus savings behavior of individuals.

We focus on consumption versus savings behavior for two reasons. First, as Musgrave and Musgrave [1986, p. 210] point out, one of the major requirements of a "good" tax system is minimal interference with "economic decisions in otherwise efficient markets." They suggest that the bias toward present rather than future consumption exemplifies the type of interference to which they refer. Similarly, a recent U.S. Treasury Study [1984, p. 13] specifies economic neutrality as a goal of fundamental tax reform, and states that the ideal tax system would not unduly favor consumption over saving and investment.

Second, those who propose shifting the tax structure from income to consumption allege that taxing income rather than consumption has adverse effects on the rate of capital formation, productivity, and growth in real per capita income [Shoven and Taubman, 1980]. Indeed, capital formation in the United States has been low relative to other Western industrialized economies [U.S. Department of Labor, 1980]. A factor contributing to the capital shortage is purported to be low savings relative to income. All taxes have an adverse affect on savings to the extent they reduce the disposable income that is available for savings in the private sector. However, as we show in the next section, in addition to this "income effect," income taxes have a "substitution effect" which, ceteris paribus, motivates an otherwise indifferent individual to choose consumption over savings.

The theoretical apparatus underlying the present study is the application of the classical theory of consumer behavior to the demand for savings. The consumption versus savings behavior is modeled as essentially the choice between two products, current consumption and future consumption (savings).[3] The former is the income that is consumed currently, while the latter is the present value of the amount saved, plus the interest accumulated until it is consumed in the future.

ALGEBRAIC ANALYSIS

We first perform the analysis in a no-tax environment which involves an individual who earns Y_0 income during period P_0 which is deposited in a noninterest-bearing checking account. At the end of P_0, an amount C_0 is withdrawn and immediately consumed. The amount S_0 remaining in this account at the end of P_0 is saved by a transfer to an account that pays r rate of interest. At the end of n periods, $S_0(1 + r)^n$ is withdrawn and immediately consumed. Using the basic relationship $Y_0 = C_0 + S_0$, we compare two extreme cases. In the first case, all income earned during P_0 is currently consumed ($C_0 = Y_0$); that is, the P_0 average propensity to consume (APC_0) is 1. In the second case, all income is saved ($S_0 = Y_0$); that is, $APC_0 = 0$. In the absence of taxation, comparing these cases is the same as comparing Y_0 and $Y_0(1 + r)^n$; however, the latter amount cannot be consumed until the end of P_n. Using the present value technique to measure future consumption in terms of current consumption, the choice between consuming all of Y_0 and saving all of Y_0 is the choice between Y_0 and $Y_0(1 + r)^n/(1 + i)^n$, where i is an appropriate discount rate. To simplify the analysis, unless otherwise stated, it is assumed that i = r, which would be the case if the opportunity cost of consumption were used as the discount rate. This would result in a dollar of savings being equivalent to a dollar of current consumption. The only other assumption that applies throughout the analysis is that both current and future consumption are normal goods.[5]

In an environment with taxes, income (Y_0) earned in P_0 is comprised of three components: taxes (T_0), after-tax consumption (C_0) and after-tax savings (S_0). The total consumption and total savings cases are compared under (1) a broad-based proportional consumption tax, and (2) a broad-based proportional income tax.[6] Although consumption and income taxes can have progressive rate structures, we restrict the initial analysis to one flat-rate (t) for both taxes for purposes of simplicity.

Equivalent Tax Rate Assumption

Consumption Tax

Under a consumption tax, the relationship among initial period income (Y_o), consumption (C_o), and taxes paid (T_o) is as follows:

$$C_o = a_o (Y_o - T_o) \tag{1}$$

where a_o = the average propensity to consume with respect to after-tax income earned in P_o.

The amount of taxes paid on consumption for P_o is computed as follows:

$$T_o = t_c(C_o + T_o) \tag{2}$$

where t_c = consumption tax rate.

A rearranging of terms in Eq. (2) produces Eq. (3).

$$T_o = \frac{t_c C_o}{1 - t_c} \tag{3}$$

Substituting the relationship in Eq. (3) for T_o in Eq. (1) and solving for C_o results in the following:

$$C_o = \frac{a_o Y_o}{1 + \left(\dfrac{t_c}{1 - t_c} \right) a_o} \tag{4}$$

Finally, savings for P_o is determined by

$$S_o = Y_o - C_o - T_o \tag{5}$$

Given that S_o plus compounded interest is consumed at the end of P_n, the present value of consumption (PV[C]) and tax payments (PV[T]) over n periods are shown by Eqs. (6) and (7), respectively.

$$\text{PV[C]} = C_o + S_o (1 - t_c) (1 + r)^n / (1 + i)^n \tag{6}$$

$$\text{PV[T]} = T_o + t_c S_o (1 + r)^n / (1 + i)^n \tag{7}$$

Equation (6) will equal $Y_o (1 - t_c)$ if the average propensity to consume income in P_o (a_o) is set equal to one. If a_o is set equal to zero, Eq. (6) reduces to $Y_o (1 - t_c)$ given the equivalency of the interest rate (r) and discount rate (i). Thus, PV[C] is the same under both extremes and the returns to the consumer are equivalent whether the entire amount of disposable income is consumed or saved. Therefore, the dollar for dollar equivalence between savings and consumption is unaltered by the imposition of the consumption tax and the tax is neutral regarding the present value of future dollars that must be sacrificed for a given number of dollars of current consumption.

Income Tax

Under a flat rate (t_y) income tax, C_o, T_o, and S_o are determined as follows:

$$C_o = a_o Y_o (1 - t_y) \tag{8}$$

$$T_o = Y_o t_y \tag{9}$$

$$S_o = Y_o - C_o - T_o \tag{10}$$

The present values of consumption and tax payments over n periods are computed using Eqs. (11) and (12), respectively.

$$PV[C] = C_o + S_o(1 + r - rt_y)^n / (1 + i)^n \tag{11}$$

$$PV[T] = T_o + \sum_{j=i}^{n} S_o rt_y (1 + r - rt_y)^{j-1} / (1 + i)^j \tag{12}$$

When a_o is set equal to one, Eq. (11) will equal $Y_o (1 - t_y)$, and the income tax is equivalent to the consumption tax in the all-consumption case (assuming $t_y = t_c$). Alternatively, in the all-savings case $(a_o = 0)$, Eq. (11) reduces to the value $Y_o (1 - t_y)(1 + r - rt_y)^n / (1 + i)^n$, which is less than the amount obtained in the all-consumption case. Therefore, the present value of consumption is lower in the all-saving case $(a_o = 0)$ than in the all-consumption case $(a_o = 1)$ and consequently, a dollar saved is worth less than a dollar consumed under the income tax. Because the relative trade-off between C_o and S_o is disturbed, neutrality is violated, and ceteris paribus, the individual would be motivated to substitute consumption for savings.

Tax Regime Indifference Rates

The relative consequences of consumption and income taxes (assuming $i = r$ and $n = 1$) are illustrated in Eqs. (13) through (16).
Consumption Tax:

$$PV[C] = Y_o (1 - t_c) \tag{13}$$

$$PV[T] = Y_o t_c \tag{14}$$

Income Tax:

$$PV[C] = Y_o (1 - t_y) [1 + \frac{rt_y (a_o - 1)}{1 + r}]$$ (15)

$$PV[T] = Y_o t_y + \frac{rY_o t_y [a_o (t_y - 1) + 1 - t_y]}{1 + r}$$ (16)

Under a consumption tax the respective returns to the private and public sectors (PV[C] and PV[T], respectively) are driven by two variables, pre-tax income and the tax rate. In order to illustrate that the relationship between PV[C] and PV[T] is independent of the consumption-savings decision, Eqs. (13) and (14) can be used to show that the relationship depends only on the tax rate (t_c). By eliminating the Y_o term through substitution, and solving for t_c, we find that $t_c = PV[T]/(PV[C] + PV[T])$ (which reduces to $PV[T]/PV[Y] = t_c$). This relationship holds regardless of the average propensity to consume (a_o), income (Y), the interest rate (r), the tax rate (t_c) or the number of periods (n).[7] In other words, the return to the government in taxes, relative to the return to taxpayers realized in consumption of private goods, is directly proportional to the consumption tax rate t_c.[8] The independence of the relationship between PV[C] and PV[T] with respect to the consumption-savings decision illustrates that the consumption tax is neutral in this regard.

Under an income tax two additional variables are needed to determine PV[C] and PV[T]: the average propensity to consume (a_o) and the interest rate (r). For PV[C] and PV[T] to be identical under both tax systems when $t_y = t_c$, r in Eqs. (15) and (16) would have to be zero regardless of the value of a_o. However, for any given a_o and t_c, Eq. (17) can be used to compute a set of values for t_y and r that would result in identical values for PV[C] and PV[T] under the respective consumption and income tax systems when $n = 1$.

$$\frac{t_y r (a_o - 1)}{1 + r} = \frac{1 - t_c}{1 - t_y} - 1$$ (17)

For example, let $a_o = 0$, $t_c = .1$ and $r = .09$ in Eq. (17). If we assume exogenous interest rates (i.e., $r = i = .09$, regardless of an income or consumption tax regime), a value of .09303 for t_y would satisfy Eq. (17) and PV[C] and PV[T] would be identical under both systems.

Alternatively, if interest rates are allowed to adjust to tax rates (in the same way interest rates differ between taxable and tax-exempt bonds of equal risk), r would be higher under the income tax. The lower return on savings under a consumption tax can be viewed as an "implicit tax" imposed on the tax-free interest build-up on savings until withdrawn for consumption.[9] Given

$a_o = 0$, Eq. (17) can be used to show that in the case of endogenously determined interest rates, r under an income tax system will adjust in tandem with the tax rate (t_y) to produce an income tax regime where $r = .09917$ and $t_y = .09243$.[10] This regime will have the same PV[C] and PV[T] as a consumption tax regime where $r = .09$ and $t_c = .1$.

The preceding discussion indicates that an income tax that is neutral relative to a consumption tax can be designed whether or not interest rates are assumed to be exogenous. To simplify the remaining analyses, interest rates are assumed to be insensitive to the tax system employed (i.e., $r = i = .09$). The important observations to this point are that when the average propensity to consume (a_o) is equal to one (all income is consumed currently), equal tax rates under the two tax systems (i.e., $t_c = t_y$) will lead to identical values of PV[C] and PV[T]. When a_o is less than one, PV[C] and PV[T] will be equivalent under the two tax systems only when the consumption tax rate (t_c) is greater than the income tax rate (t_y).[11]

Because a_o varies across individuals and is usually a function of income and expenditure patterns, any consumption-income tax indifference point will hold only for a unique combination of a_o and r values associated with the given t_c and t_y values. Therefore, an income tax would have to impose different tax rates on individuals as a function of a_o for such a tax to be truly equivalent to a consumption tax. Of course, such a system of individualized tax rates would be impractical.

An income tax system with the tax rate (t_y) based upon average values for a_o and n estimated for the society as a whole may approximate a consumption tax if values for these variables were randomly or uniformly distributed across all segments of the society. However, because the average propensity to consume (a_o) is usually inversely related to income, an income tax with ty based upon the average a_o would favor low income consumers. For example, if half of the total income in the present analysis (holding $n = 1$) was earned by a few wealthy people, each with $a_o = 0$, and the remaining income was earned by many poor individuals, each with $a_o = 1$, an income tax with $t_y = .0964$ would result in the same PV[C] and PV[T] as a consumption tax with $t_c = .10$ for the society as a whole. This is illustrated in Table 1 for hypothetical taxpayers with total income (Y_o) equal to $20,000. As Table 1 shows, an income tax is more favorable to the poor whereas the consumption tax is more favorable to the wealthy. This observation is a reflection of the inherently regressive nature of consumption taxes in general.

Borrowing for Consumption and/or Investment

The present analysis is now extended to allow consumers to borrow and lend (i.e., invest) at the same interest rate $(r = i)$. Based on historical income tax provisions and the probable form of a consumption tax, interest expense

Table 1. The Impact of Consumption and Income Taxes on Income Classes (in US $)

	$PV[C]^a$	$PV[T]^a$	Row Totals
Consumption Tax ($t_c = .10$)			
Wealthy ($a_o = 0$)	$ 9,000	$1,000	$10,000
Poor ($a_o = 1$)	9,000	1,000	10,000
Total	$18,000	$2,000	$20,000
Income tax ($t_y = .0964$)			
Wealthy ($a_o = 0$)	$ 8,964	$1,036	$10,000
Poor ($a_o = 1$)	9,036	964	10,000
Total	$18,000	$2,000	$20,000

Note: ^{a}PV[C] and PV[T] were computed using Eqs. (13) - (14) for the consumption tax and (15) - (16) for the income tax where $r = i = .09$, and $Y_o = $20,000$.

is assumed to be deductible under an income tax but not under a consumption tax. If interest rates adjust endogenously, the relationship between interest rates under a consumption tax (r_c) and those under an income tax (r_y) is shown in Eq. (18).

$$r_y = \frac{r_c}{1 - \dfrac{t_y (r_c - i_c)}{r_c}} \tag{18}$$

Under the assumption that $r = i$, Eq. (18) reduces to $r_y = r_c$. Hence, the present analysis will use identical interest rates under both systems.

Individuals will borrow an amount for consumption (B_c) when $a_o > 1$. The borrowed amount will equal the difference between the total current consumption (C_o) plus current taxes (T_o) and current income (Y_o). In addition to earning Y_o in the current period (P_o), individuals will also earn Y_n in period n (P_n) in an amount sufficient to extinguish all debt and pay taxes, with any remaining Y_n being consumed. Individuals can also borrow any amount to invest (B_I); therefore, the total amount borrowed (B) equals $B_c + B_I$. All borrowings take place in Po and all debt is repaid in P_n.

To allow for borrowing and lending, consumption tax Eqs. (6) and (7) are restated as follows:

$$PV[C] = C_o + \frac{S_o (1 - t_c) (1 + r)^n + Y_n (1 - t_c)}{(1 + i)^n} \tag{19}$$

$$PV[T] = T_o + \frac{t_c \left[Y_n + S_o \left(1 + r\right)^n\right]}{\left(1 + i\right)^n} \qquad (20)$$

Because individuals can borrow and lend at the same rate, amounts borrowed for investment purposes wash out under the consumption tax. Amounts borrowed for consumption are treated as negative savings (-S_o) in Eqs. (19) and (20). Thus, the basic relationship $PV[T]/PV[Y] = t_c$ still holds, and the consumption tax is neutral with respect to borrowing and lending behavior.

Equations (21) and (22) apply to the income tax, given the opportunity to borrow for consumption and investment.

$$PV[C] = C_o + \frac{I \left(1 + r - rt_y\right)^n + Y_n - t_y \left[Y_n - B \left(1+r\right)^n + B\right] - B \left(1+r\right)^n}{\left(1 - i\right)^n} \qquad (21)$$

$$PV[T] = T_o + \left[\sum_{j=1}^{n} \frac{Irt_y \left(1+r-rt_y\right)^{j-1}}{\left(1 + i\right)^j}\right] + \frac{t_y \left[Y_n - B \left(1+r\right)^n + B\right]}{\left(1 + i\right)^n} \qquad (22)$$

where: I = amount invested (i.e., lent) at r rate of interest. If the amount saved (S_o) is greater than or equal to zero, then I will equal the sum of S_o and the amount borrowed to invest (B_I); otherwise $I = B_I$.

B = amount borrowed at r rate of interest; $B = B_I + B_c$ (amount borrowed for consumption). If S_o is less than zero, then $B_c = -1(S_o)$; otherwise $B_c = 0$.

An inspection of Eqs. (21) and (22) reveals that the income tax is non-neutral regarding consuming, borrowing, and investing. For example, under the consumption tax an individual would be indifferent towards borrowing and investing at the same rate as a means of providing for intertemporal utility for money.[12] However, similar borrowing and lending would make the individual worse off under the income tax modeled in Eqs. (21) and (22). Although interest income and interest expense are equal in terms of absolute dollars, the income is taxed as it accrues under the constructive-receipt doctrine, while the expense does not shelter income until it is actually paid in cash (in P_n).

Table 2 provides a numerical example of the influence of the income tax relative to the consumption tax on borrowing and investing behavior. The analysis compares two individuals with equal incomes in P_o and P_n ($Y_o = \$20,000$ and $Y_n = \$40,000$), and an identical opportunity set ($r = i = .09$) and time horizon ($n = 2$). Each individual is assumed to have an a_o equal to 1 and to actually consume $18,000 in P_o. (As pointed out earlier, only in the $a_o = 1$ case

Table 2. A Comparison of Borrowing and Investment Alternatives Under Initially Neutral Consumption and Income Tax Scenarios

(1) Alternatives	(2) a_o^a	(3) C_o	(4) T_o	(5) B	(6) I	(7) $PV[C]^b$	(8) $PV[T]^b$	(9) Implicit Tax (Subsidy)^c
Consumption Tax								
(0) Initial Position	1.0000	18,000	2,000	0	0	48,300	5,367	—
(1) Borrow and Consume^d	1.6579	28,000	3,111	11,111	0	48,300	5,367	0
(2) Borrow and Invest	1.0000	18,000	2,000	10,000	10,000	48,300	5,367	0
(3) Forego Consumption and Invest	.4186	8,000	889	0	11,111	48,300	5,367	0
Income Tax								
(0) Initial Position	1.0000	18,000	2,000	0	0	48,300	5,367	—
(1) Borrow and Consume	1.5556	28,000	2,000	10,000	0	48,459	5,208	(159)
(2) Borrow and Invest	1.0000	18,000	2,000	10,000	10,000	48,294	5,373	6
(3) Forego Consumption and Invest	.4444	8,000	2,000	0	10,000	48,136	5,531	164

Notes: ^{a} a_o is adjusted to provide the same C_o under both taxes with respect to each alternative (see Note 13).

^{b} $PV[C]$ and $PV[T]$ were computed using Eqs. (19) and (20), respectively, for the consumption tax, and (21) and (22) for the income tax, where $r = i = .09$, $Y_o = \$20,000$, $Y_n = \$40,000$, $t_c = t_y = .10$, and $n = 2$. $PV[Y] = PV[C] = PV[C] + PV[T] = \$53,667$ for all alternatives under both taxes.

^{c} The difference in $PV[T]$ under the given and initial alternatives.

^{d} Under the consumption tax an additional \$1,111 must be borrowed to pay the tax to net \$10,000 of the loan proceeds for consumption. On the other hand, if \$10,000 is diverted from consumption to investment, \$1,111 will be saved in consumption taxes which will result in \$1,111 of additional investment.

233

can neutral consumption and income taxes have the same flat tax rate and the same C_o.)[13] Both individuals are given three alternatives: (1) borrow and consume $10,000, (2) borrow and invest $10,000, and (3) invest $10,000 saved by foregoing $10,000 in consumption.

Column (9) of Table 2 shows that the consumption tax is neutral regarding all three alternatives. On the other hand, the income tax provides a subsidy for the borrowing for consumption alternative, a small implicit tax for the borrowing and investing alternative, and a considerably larger implicit tax under the savings and investing choice. The results of this analysis support the notion that income taxes relative to consumption taxes favor consumption and borrowing over saving and investing.[14]

While a switch from an income to a consumption tax may offer incentives for individuals to divert income from consumption to savings, there may be socially undesirable effects of doing so such as a reduction of the vertical equity of the tax structure. A more general comparison between consumption and income taxes with respect to neutrality and other issues can be made using a graphical analysis. A graphical analysis also recognizes that consumer preferences may differ even when present value computations are the same.

GRAPHICAL ANALYSIS

Consumption Tax

The impact of a consumption tax on consumption versus savings behavior is shown in Figure 1. Line DD' shows the marginal cost of substitution (MCS) of consumption for savings (and vice versa) in the absence of taxation. In this example, it is assumed that the interest rate is independent of savings (i.e., $\angle$ DD'0 = 45°), and that a dollar of current consumption is equivalent to the present value of a dollar of savings (i.e., $r = i$).[15] Although all combinations of consumption and savings on line DD' have the same dollar equivalence, each combination may offer a different level of satisfaction for a given consumer. Consumer preferences are captured in indifference maps which show the relative combinations of current consumption and future consumption (savings) that yield the same satisfaction for an individual.

Figure 1 shows the indifference maps for two individuals each having different preferences for current and future consumption for given levels of income. For example, the point of tangency (m_{11}) of DD' to indifference curve I_{11} indicates that individual 'one' would demand OC_1 of current consumption and OS_1 of future consumption in the absence of taxation. Individual 'two' would demand OC_2 and OS_2 of current and future consumption, respectively, in a no tax environment as suggested by the tangency (m_{12}) of I_{12} to DD'. Thus, individual 'one' has greater preference for current consumption at DD' level of income.

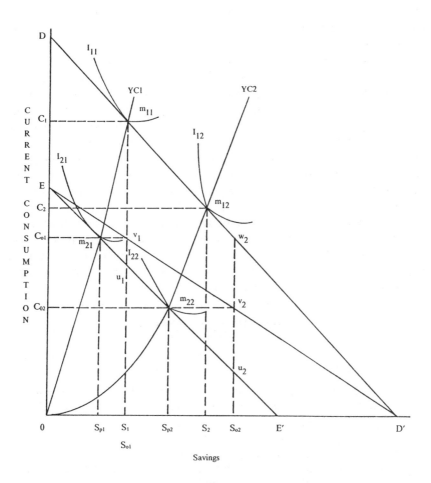

Figure 1. Consumption Versus Savings Under a Broad-Based Proportional Consumption Tax

Given a constant MCS between current and future consumption, lines parallel to DD′ represent greater levels of income the farther they are to the right of the origin. Both individuals have an indifference curve tangent to each possible income level. The locus of these tangency points form the income-consumption lines YC1 and YC2 for individuals 'one' and 'two', respectively. YC1 is a linear function whereas YC2 is an exponential function. Linear or homothetic expansion-paths such as YC1 have several noteworthy properties; (1) The average and marginal propensities to consume (MPC) are constant and identical for all income levels; (2) The slope equals MPC/(1 - MPC); and (3) The change in future consumption relative to a change in current consumption is the reciprocal of the slope. Thus, changes in future relative to current consumption in response to changes in the consumption tax rate will be proportional for individual 'one' but not for individual 'two.'

The MPC for individual 'two' increases at an increasing rate with income. In short, individual 'one' saves the same percentage of each increment in income while individual 'two' saves increasingly smaller portions of each increment in income. However, on the average, individual 'two' is more of a saver over the possible income ranges shown in Figure 1 because YC2 is closer to the x-axis than YC1. Many possible income-consumption functions could have been displayed in Figure 1 each reflecting different patterns of preferences towards current and future consumption. The present analysis is robust regarding any such income-consumption path chosen for demonstration as long as current and future consumption are normal goods.

Next, if we assume that a broad-based proportional consumption tax is imposed, the before-tax MCS line DD' would shift to the after-tax MCS line EE'. Since the price paid for a dollar of future consumption is still a dollar of current consumption, EE' is parallel to DD' and the consumption tax is neutral regarding the relative prices of consumption and savings.

The reductions in current and future consumption resulting from the tax lower consumer satisfaction to indifference curves I_{21} and I_{22} for individuals 'one' and 'two', respectively. Tangency point m_{21} shows that individual 'one' would choose OC_{o1} of current consumption, and $OS_{P}1$ would be the present value of future consumption discounted back to P_o; hence, $OC_{o1} + OS_{P}1 = PV[C] = OE'$. The remaining distance from 0 to D', that is, E'D', represents PV[T]. For individual 'two', m_{22} indicates that OC_{o2} is current consumption and OS_{p2} is the present value of future consumption; hence, $OC_{o2} + OS_{p2}$ (which equals OE') is the present value of consumption (PV[C]) and E'D' is the present value of tax payments (PV[T]). Thus, PV[C] and PV[T] are the same for both individuals, and differences in individual preferences regarding current and future consumption do not affect the relationship

$$\frac{PV[T]}{PV[C] + PV[T]} = t_c$$

under a consumption tax whether the income-consumption expansion path is linear or nonlinear. Under a consumption tax, EE' is parallel to DD' and its position between 0 and DD' is determined by t_c. As pointed out above, OE'= PV[C] and E'D' = PV[T] regardless of the functional forms of the income-consumption expansion paths.

Line ED' represents after-tax income that is available for consumption and/ or savings in P_o (hereinafter the disposable income line). The distance between ED' and DD' represents T_o while the distance between ED' and EE' represents the present value of taxes paid on consumption in the future; hence, the distance

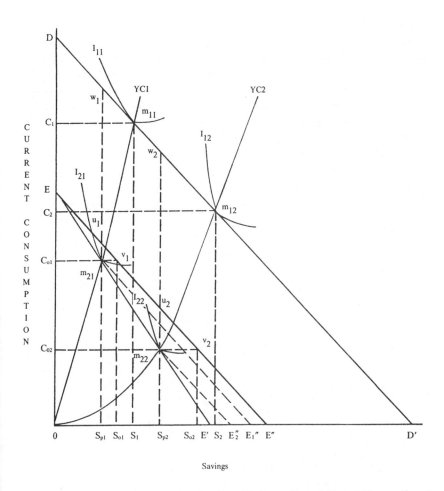

Figure 2. Consumption Versus Savings Under a Broad-Based Proportional Income Tax

between EE' and DD' represents PV[T]. Points v_1 and v_2 are horizontal projections to ED' from m_{21} and m_{22}, respectively. Vertical projections from v_1 and v_2 to the x-axis indicate the amount of Y_o that must be saved to yield the desired future consumption. The disposable income line ED' incorporates the liquidity factor into the consumption-savings decision. For example, individual 'two' must save OS_{o2} of Y_o in P_o for the present value of future consumption after-taxes to be OS_{p2}. Here, $T_o = v_2 w_2$, and $u_2 v_2$ is the present value of future taxes paid.

Income Tax

The imposition of a broad-based income tax with the same proportional tax rate used in the consumption tax analysis is graphed in Figure 2. The dimensions, income-consumption expansion paths, and income levels of Figure 2 are the same as those in Figure 1. Thus, the no-tax situation in Figures 1 and 2 are identical. The income tax causes the before-tax MCS line DD' to shift to the after-tax MCS line EE', and consumers 'one' and 'two' drop to indifference curves I_{21} and I_{22} on their respective income-consumption lines.

The taxation of interest income each period as it accrues, plus the fact that savings come from after-tax dollars, results in a relatively higher cost of future consumption relative to current consumption. Therefore, both individuals are induced to substitute the latter for the former. Because future consumption is more expensive relative to current consumption, EE' in Figure 2 intersects the X-axis at a point closer to the origin than EE' in Figure 1 (i.e., in Figure 2, $\angle$ EE'0 $\angle$ DD'0 = 45°). The periodic taxation of accrued interest results in r being less than i, after taxes. Therefore, ignoring indifference maps and utility functions, the individual's rational choice would be to save nothing.[16] However, individuals would still choose to save since they obtain utility in knowing that some income in the future will be available for consumption. Further, the principle of diminishing marginal utility explains why individuals would still choose not to consume all income even when faced with a relatively higher opportunity cost to save.

Current and future consumption are determined by tangency points m_{21} and m_{22} for individuals 'one' and 'two,' respectively. The former individual will have OC_{o1} in current consumption and OS_{p1} as the present value of future consumption while the latter will have OC_{o2} and OS_{p2} as the current and future consumption, respectively. The savings in P_o necessary to yield the desired levels of future consumption are determined by projecting horizontal lines from the tangency points to the disposable income line (EE'' in Figure 2) and then projecting vertical lines to the x-axis. For example, individual 'one' would have to save OS_{o1} in P_o to yield OS_{p1} as the present value of future consumption after-taxes.

Under an income tax, the disposable income line EE'' is parallel to DD' because consumption and savings in P_o are made from the same after-tax Y_o (disposable income). Thus, T_o is constant across all combinations of C_o and S_o for a given level of Y_o, and is the vertical distance between EE'' and DD'. The vertical distance between EE' and EE'' represents the present value of income taxes paid periodically in the future as interest income accrues on S_o. Tax burdens are determined by projecting vertical lines from the tangency points to DD'. For example, individual 'one' would pay an amount equal to $u_1 w_1$ in taxes in period 0, and the segment $m_{21} u_1$ represents the present value of taxes paid in the future. Thus, for individual 'one', $PV[T] = m_{21} u_1 + u_1 w_1$. Individual 'two' would pay the same amount of current taxes (T_o) as individual 'one' since $u_2 w_2 = u_1 w_1$.

However, individual 'two' would have a greater amount of future tax burden since $m_{22} u_2 > m_{21} u_1$. Thus, PV[T] for individual 'two' is greater than that for individual 'one'. This observation contrasts with the findings in Figure 1 where PV[T] was the same for both individuals. Because the absolute value of the slope of EE' is greater than that of EE", the distance between these lines (i.e., the present value of future taxes) for consumer j increases as C_{oj} decreases and S_{pj} increases. Hence, C_{oj} (current consumption) is more attractive relative to S_{pj} (savings), and the former will tend to be substituted for the latter (i.e., the "substitution effect").

In both Figures 1 and 2, current income (OD') is the same and equals the sum of the present value of consumption (PV[C]) and the present value of taxes (PV[T]). Therefore, if PV[T] differs between the two individuals so will PV[C]. In Figure 1, OD' is broken into two components at point E', where OE' represents PV[C] and E'D' represents PV[T]. In Figure 2, the breakdown of OD' into its PV[C] and PV[T] components is determined by the tangency point of an indifference curve to EE'. Thus, there can be no one common break point. A specific break point is found by projecting a line parallel to EE" from a given tangency point to the x-axis. For individual 'one', the present value of consumption (PV[C]) equals $OE_1"$ and the present value of taxes (PV[T]) equals $E_1" D'$. For individual 'two,' PV[C] equals $OE_2"$ and PV[T] equals $E_2"D'$.[17] These observations indicate that the relative portions of PV[C] and PV[T] are a function of consumer preferences toward current and future consumption under an income tax. The closer the income-consumption line for consumer j is to the x- axis (i.e., the greater the preference for savings), the greater the distance between E" and $E_j"$, and the lesser the distance between 0 and $E_j"$ (i.e., PV[C]); the saver is relatively less well-off under the income tax. To conclude, the consumption tax is neutral regarding the choice between current and future consumption, while the income tax favors current over future consumption.

Revenue Neutrality

In both Figures 1 and 2, the income effect is determined by the average distance between the before- and after-tax MCS lines; DD' and EE', respectively. The substitution effect is determined by the difference between angles DD'0 and EE'0. The decline in savings resulting from the income tax is greater than that resulting from the consumption tax for two reasons. First, the consumption tax, unlike the income tax, has no substitution effect; that is, $\angle EE'0 = \angle DD'0$ in Figure 1, and $\angle EE'0 > \angle DD'0$ in Figure 2. Secondly, because both taxes have the same flat rate (under the assumption used here), they cannot be revenue neutral. The income tax would raise more tax revenue and therefore have a greater income effect.

It follows from the above that the construction of revenue neutral income and consumption taxes requires designing the former with a lower proportional rate. Figure 3 compares the relative influence of consumption and income taxes on

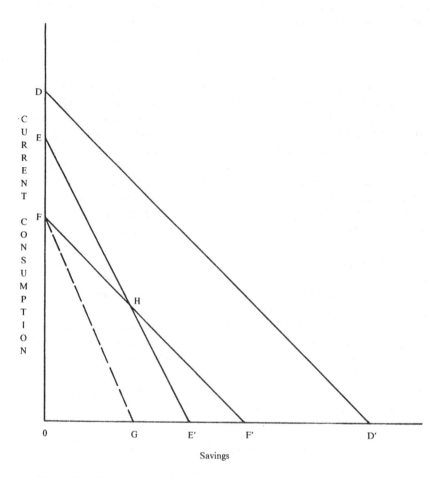

Figure 3. Consumption Versus Income Taxation on an Aggregate Level

aggregate consumption and savings behavior.[18] The MCS line is DD' given no taxation, FF' given a proportional rate consumption tax, and FG given an income tax with the same flat rate as the consumption tax. The area FF'G represents the greater income effect of the income tax relative to the consumption tax when both have equal rates.

The income tax would be revenue neutral with respect to the consumption tax if the flat-rate of the former was reduced to the extent that FG shifted to EE' where areas EHF and HF'E' are equal. The lower tax rate implied by EE' would increase disposable income which would increase the demand for all normal goods including savings. For the purposes of illustration, it would not be unreasonable to assume a scenario where aggregate savings associated with

EE' would equal that associated with FF'. As shown in the algebraic analysis, interest rates and the flat income tax rate would adjust in tandem (see Note 10).

Efficiency and Equity

Even if the consumption tax and the income tax produced the same amount of aggregate tax revenues and savings, they would differ substantially on two important policy goals—efficiency and equity. The efficiency of a tax system hinges on neutrality. A tax system is neutral regarding a given trade-off if the MCS between the two commodities is the same before and after the imposition of the tax. Returning to Figure 3, $\angle$ EE'0 $>$ $\angle$ DD'0 $=$ $\angle$ FF'0, thus indicating that the consumption tax is neutral while the income tax is not.

An inspection of Figure 3 shows that to the left of point H, the income tax line EE' lies above the consumption tax line FF', while the reverse is true to the right of point H. Individuals with income-consumption lines to the left of point H have higher average propensities to consume and thus are likely to have lower incomes than those individuals with income-consumption paths to the right of point H.[19] As we showed earlier, in a revenue neutral situation, the consumption tax rate will be higher than the income tax rate. Therefore, lower income taxpayers will achieve higher levels of satisfaction under an income tax (since most or all of their income is spent currently) while upper income taxpayers will be better off under a consumption tax (since a smaller portion of their income is spent currently) (see Table 1). This tendency for the consumption tax to favor the rich over the poor is contrary to the commonly accepted equity principle (vertical equity) that taxes should be imposed in accordance with ability to pay [Sommerfeld, Anderson, and Brock 1984, pp. 28-29].[20]

CONCLUSIONS

There is agreement that a comprehensive tax base with low tax rates is a desirable feature of a reformed tax system. Most specific tax reform proposals fall into one of two categories: a comprehensive income tax or a comprehensive consumption tax. In this paper, we algebraically and graphically analyze these two taxes in order to assess their relative impact on the choice between present and future consumption.

The analysis indicates that a consumption tax is neutral with respect to the consumption and savings behavior of individuals because it avoids the inherent substitution effect of an income tax, a source of excess burden in the tax system. On the other hand, a consumption tax would be regarded negatively in a political climate that embraces vertical equity since it favors those with higher incomes over those with lower incomes. This conflict between efficiency and equity is a classic example of the type of trade-off often inherent in tax policy objectives.

Indeed, seldom do all tax policy goals lead to a clear choice of one tax system over another; it is often necessary to strike a balance among several competing objectives [U.S. Treasury 1984, p. 18].

In a comparison of various types of consumption taxes, Carlson and McLure [1984, p. 147] observed that

> In recent years there has been a remarkable shift of opinion from income toward consumption as the preferred means of raising federal revenues. This shift has been exemplified by increased interest in the consumed income or personal expenditure tax, by *structural shifts* in the income tax that move its base *from income* to *consumption*, and by revived interest in some form of federal sales tax (emphasis added)

If, in fact, a structural shift has begun from an income to a consumption tax base, the United States may be closer to a consumption tax than is generally acknowledged. Evidence of such a shift is not hard to find, especially in the area of tax-deferred retirement savings. Individual retirement accounts (IRAs), retirement plans for self-employed individuals (Keogh plans), and the so-called 401(k) plans and 403(b) plans all allow tax deductible contributions and tax-deferred accumulation of investment returns.[21] While some of these retirement arrangements have been available for several years, recent tax law changes have liberalized eligibility requirements to a point where virtually all employed taxpayers qualify for at least one such retirement plan. Contributions to and earnings from these plans are not taxed until withdrawn and consumed.

The issue raised is whether policymakers should continue to move in the direction of a consumption tax base, move back to an income tax base, or maintain the current combination of the two. The Tax Reform Act of 1986 [U.S. Congress 1986] restricts the tax-favored treatment of the retirement accounts discussed above for many taxpayers. For example, deductions for contributions to IRAs have been cut back for many middle-income taxpayers and entirely eliminated for high-income taxpayers. Further, the ceilings for contributions to the other types of plans have been significantly lowered.

On the other hand, the new tax law contains other provisions that implicitly favor savings over consumption. For example, the legislation eliminates the deduction for consumer interest and sales taxes. Thus, on balance, the most recent actions of tax policymakers do not allow a clearcut conclusion with respect to the future direction of tax policy in the United States. Whatever direction Congress decides to take, with respect to tax reform, there are certain to be social, political, and economic trade-offs similar to the ones outlined in this paper.

ACKNOWLEDGMENTS

The comments and suggestions of Sally Jones, Sandy Morton, and anonymous reviewers have strengthened this paper and are gratefully acknowledged by the authors. An earlier version was presented at the 1988 Northeast Regional American Accounting Association meeting.

NOTES

1. National income is a loosely-used term that refers to the dollar measure of the aggregate flow of goods and services in the economy. As such, it is more comprehesive than the concept of gross income contained in the Internal Revenue Code since many items are excluded from the definition of gross income.

2. The terms "direct" and "indirect" refer to the manner in which the taxes are collected. "... most writers define direct taxes as those which are imposed initially on the individual or household that is meant to bear the burden. Indirect taxes are taxes which are imposed at some other point in the system but are meant to be shifted to whomever is supposed to be the final bearer of the burden" [Musgrave and Musgrave 1986, p. 227-228].

3. It is assumed that income can be allocated between consumption and savings in a mutuallly exclusive and collectively exhaustive manner. Actually, the distinction may not be as clear-cut, especially regarding expenditures on education, owner-occupied housing, certain collectibles, and so on.

4. This basic relationship in an evironment with taxes would be $Y_o = C_o + S_o + T_o$; where T_o is the dollar amount of taxes paid in P_o regardless of whether a consumption tax or an income tax is in place. Thus, Y_o is berfore-tax income, and C_o and S_o are after-tax consumption and savings, respectively. The average propensity to consume (APC_o) is based upon disposable income and is equal to $C_o/(Y_o - T_o)$. APC_o in the present study applies to Y_o earned in P_o. All of the amount withdrawn at the end of P_o is expended on either consumption or taxes.

5. Normal goods are those for which demand increases as income increases. We make the assumption that current and future consumption are normal goods to avoid a backward-bending income consumption line (e.g., lines YC1 and YC2 in Figure 1).

6. Secondary effects such as, for example, the impact these taxes may have on consumption and savings as a result of their effects on employment, interest rates, and so on, are ignored.

7. This relationship holds for all levels of a_o for a given Y_o. However, levels of a_o may vary with income if consumption is a nonlinear function of income.

8. The benefits to consumers from the public goods financed with the tax revenues are assumed to be the same under both types of taxes as long as the taxes are revenue neutral.

9. An implicit tax is the differential in investment returns that is attributable to market adjustments that compensate for one investment alternative being taxed differently than some frame-of-reference alternative.

10: These figures were derived in tandem by using Eq. (17) where $a_o = 0$, $t_c = t_y = .1$, and r = the interest rate under an income tax regime. The computations involved a two step iterative process. In step 1, r is set equal to $.09/(1 - t_y)$ to reflect the upward adjustment of interest rates in response to the less favorable tax treatment of interest income under an income tax. In step 2, the r computed in step 1 is inserted in Eq. (17) which is solved for a new t_y figure. This computation reflects a lowering of the income tax rate in response to the increase in the interest rate to preserve the revenue neutrality between the two tax regimes. The new t_y figure is used in step 1 to compute a new r figure and so forth. The iterative process continues until r and t_y in Eq. (17) converge in equilibrium.

11. These observations hold in situations where $n > 1$. The greater the value of n, the larger the difference between t_c and t_y. For example, it can be shown using Eqs. (6), (7), (11), and (12) that if $n = 4$ and $a_o = 0$; $t_y = .0768$ given that interest rates are exogenous, and $t_y = .0755$ given an endogenously-determined interest rate of .0973. As shown earlier, $t_c = .10$ for all values of n and a_o.

12.   Risk, transactions cost, and other market frictions are ignored here.

13.   Given a consumption and an income tax having the same PV[C] and PV[T] values, if a_o < 1, then C_o will be greater under the consumption tax and t_c will exceed t_y. On the other hand, if a_o > 1 (i.e., borrowing for consumption), C_o will be greater under the income tax and t_y will exceed t_c. If one wishes to analyze the two tax systems under the condition that C_o be the same for both, a_o under the consumption tax (a_c) can be converted to an a_o under the income tax (a_y) that will satisfy this condition by using the following formula: $a_y = C_{oc}/Y_o(1 - t_y)$, where C_{oc} is the consumption for P_o under the consumption tax computed using a_c and Eq.(4). Deriving both tax systems with the same PV[C], PV[T], and C_o involves solving for a_y and t_y simultaneously in an iterative process that converges on the appropriate values.

14.   Note that we have not addressed the question of what would happen if the income tax system allowed no deduction for interest expense. Although another model could be developed to analyze such a scenario, we chose not to do so in this paper for two reasons. First, our objective here is to examine the income tax and the consumption tax from a traditional perspective. The denial of interest expense under the income tax would constitute a basic reform of the traditional system. Second, although consumer interest deductions are being phased out under the tax reform act of 1986, taxpayers are still relatively free to arrange their finances in such a way (e.g., repackaging debt in the form of a home-equity loan) as to allow for the deduction of interest expense.

15.   If the analysis were conducted under the assumption that r > i, then ∠ DD'O would be less than 45°, and D' would be farther from the origin.

16.   By the same token, in the absence of indifference maps, the rational choice would be to consume nothing at the end of P_o if r were greater than i after taxes.

17.   Also, in Figure 2, $OC_{o1} + OS_{p1} = OE_1'' = PV[C]_1$, and $OC_{o2}, + OS_{p2} = OE_2'' = PV[C]_2$, for individuals 'one' and 'two', respectively.

18.   The comparison illustrated in Figure 3 assumes that variations in indifference maps are uniformly distributed throughout society, and the mean a_o lies between 0 and 1.

19.   This observation is simply a reversal of the commonly-held assumption that low income taxpayers of necessity have a higher level of consumption, relative to income, than high income taxpayers.

20.   This assumes that income is an appropriate measure of "ability to pay."

21.   Other examples which might be included here are tax-deferred annuities and insurance contracts under which interest is allowed to accumulate tax-free until the policy is cashed in. However, these types of arrangements are funded with after-tax dollars rather than before-tax dollars.

REFERENCES

Aaron, H. J. and H. Galper, *Assessing Tax Reform* (The Brookings Institution, 1985).

Bosworth, B. P., *Tax Incentives and Economic Growth* (The Brookings Institution, 1984).

Break, G. F., "Avenues to Tax Reform: Perils and Possibilities," *National Tax Journal* (March 1984), pp. 1-8.

Browning, E. K. and J. M. Browning, *Public Finance and the Price System* (Macmillan, 1979).

Carlson, G. N. and C.E. McLure, Jr., "Pros and Cons of Alternative Approaches To The Taxation of Consumption," *Proceedings of the Seventy-seventh Annual Conference of The National Tax Association-Tax Institute of America* (November 1984), pp.147-154.

Due, J. F. and A.F. Friedlaender, *Government Finance: Economics of the Public Sector* (Irwin, 1981).

Musgrave, R. A. and P. B. Musgrave, *Public Finance in Theory and Practice* (McGraw-Hill, 1986).

Pechman, J. A., ed., *Options for Tax Reform* (The Brookings Institution, 1984).

Robinson, J. R., "Tax Reform: Analyzing a Comprehensive Income Tax," *Journal of Accounting and Public Policy* (Spring 1984), pp. 29-38.

Shoven, J. B. and P. Taubman, "Savings, Capital Income and Taxation," In H. J. Aaron and M. J. Boskin, eds., *The Economics of Taxation*. (The Brookings Institution, 1980), pp. 202-222.

Sommerfeld, R. M., H. M. Anderson, and H. R. Brock, *An Introduction to Taxation* (Harcourt Brace Jovanovich, 1984).

U.S. Congress, *Tax Reform Act of 1986*, Public Law 99-514, 99th Congress, 2nd Session (October 22, 1986).

U.S. Department of Labor, Bureau of Labor Statistics, *Special Summary, Stimulating Technological Programs* (U.S. Government Printing Office, 1980).

U.S. Department of the Treasury, *Tax Reform for Fairness, Simplicity, and Economic Growth: The Treasury Report to the President,* vol. 1 (U.S. Government Printing Office, 1984).

U.S. General Accounting Office, *Tax Policy: Choosing Among Consumption Taxes* (U.S. Government Printing Office, 1986).